THE GARDENER'S GUIDE TO SOUTH AFRICAN PLANTS

NATIONAL
BOTANICAL
INSTITUTE

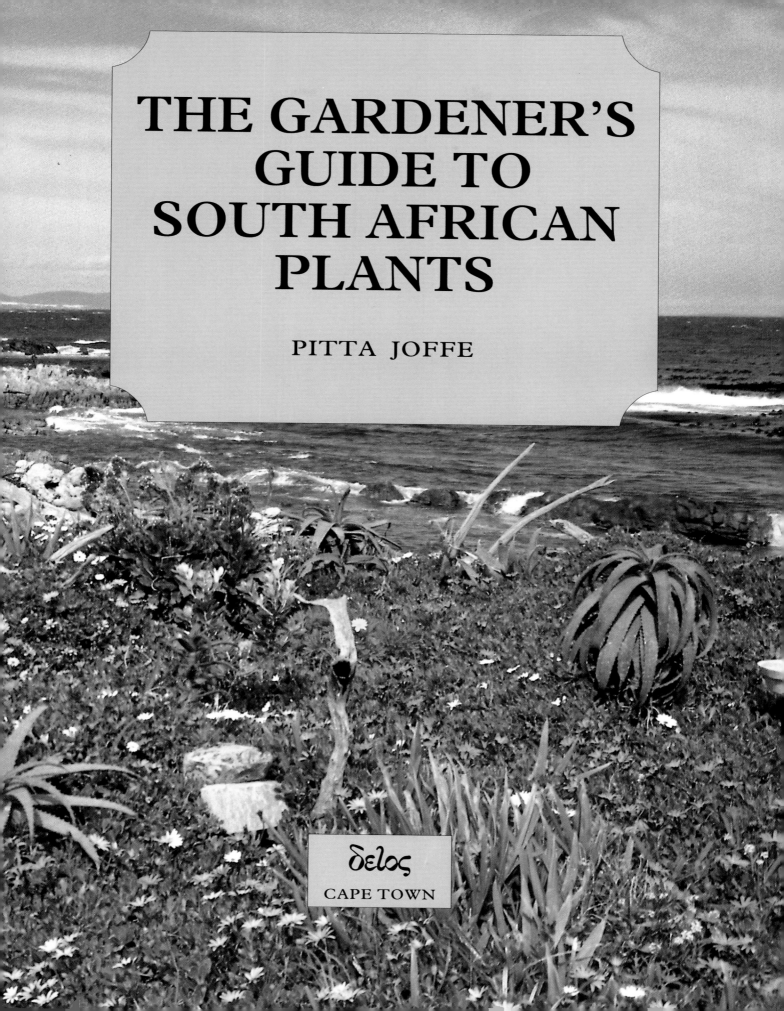

THE GARDENER'S GUIDE TO SOUTH AFRICAN PLANTS

PITTA JOFFE

δελος

CAPE TOWN

My darling wife, the author,
on finishing the task
looked me over coyly
and said: 'I'd like to ask

if you could do a favour,
I'm really tuckered out.
Write an introduction
on what the book's about.'

I stopped to think it over;
well, what's the book about?
About years of dedication,
about years of driving out

to towns and lakes and regions
where plants were known to grow
to take the perfect photo
and choose the one to show.

About nights of pencil writing
and reams of written script,
and reading proofs of typing,
until alarms had tripped.

About waiting as the clock ticked
into the late wee hours,
about helping wade through data
of trees and shrubs and flowers.

About mugs and mugs of coffee
and cups and cups of tea.
I therefore dedicate this
lovely book to me!

(And since I guess the author
would surely not concur,
I also dedicate this
lovely book to her!)

Leon Joffe (*husband*)

© 1993 Tafelberg Publishers Limited
28 Wale Street, Cape Town

Also available in Afrikaans as *Die Tuinier se Gids tot Suid-Afrikaanse Plante*

Text © Pitta Joffe
Photographs © the various individuals and institutions
credited on pp. 366-367
Typography and cover design by Etienne van Duyker
Typeset in 10 on 11 pt Plantin
Typesetting and reproduction by Martingraphix, Cape Town
Printed and bound by Toppan Printing Company (H.K.) Ltd, Hong Kong

First impression 1993

ISBN 1-86826-282-0

FOREWORD

South Africa possesses a truly rich and remarkable flora. With over 22 000 species of flowering plants and ferns, it is unmatched in terms of its diversity by any equal sized area on earth. More than this, our plants are of unusual beauty and horticultural potential – qualities little appreciated by most South Africans but long recognised overseas.

For more than a century, Italian goldsmiths and Belgian diamond-cutters have turned our raw gold and diamonds into exquisite jewellery, earning greater rewards for their labour than do our miners. So too have Dutch and German plant breeders created a multi-billion dollar horticultural industry through the improvement of our native species. The magnificent cultivars of *Gladiolus*, *Pelargonium*, *Gerbera*, *Streptocarpus*, *Gazania*, etc., which generate more foreign exchange for their producer nations than does gold for South Africa, represent the rewards of over 200 years of careful selection and improvement of our genetic resources. Yet only a trivial percentage of our plant species has been introduced into horticulture. The challenge to South African botanists and plant breeders is to identify and exploit the economic opportunities that await discovery in our vast untapped floristic resources.

While we have neglected the financial potential of our indigenous plants, so too have we, as a nation of home-proud gardeners, failed to fully develop the use of our native plants. Our strong Eurocentric gardening traditions, and the availability of a multitude of proven cultivars of exotic species, has resulted in a reluctance to test our gardening skills with native species. The situation is rapidly changing, however, as the experience and expertise developed over the past 80 years in our National Botanical Gardens have become more accessible. More and more commercial nurserymen are producing wide ranges of native plants, and 'growing indigenous' is becoming a popular and rewarding theme.

The advantages of using indigenous species in South African gardens are numerous. Not only does one have an enormous diversity of species from which to choose, but they are genetically and physiologically more tolerant of our often harsh climate, resistant to pests and disease and better adapted to our varied soil conditions.

Given the widely ranging ecological conditions experienced in different parts of South Africa it is not easy to choose the right mix of native plants for a given situation. Pitta Joffe has succeeded in providing a source book which represents answers to the question of what to grow where and when in a succinct and user-friendly format. The book builds on many decades of experience gained in the use of indigenous plants and represents another contribution from the National Botanical Institute towards encouraging the use and enjoyment of our flora by all South Africans.

B. J. Huntley
Chief Director, National Botanical Institute
Harold Pearson Professor of Botany,
University of Cape Town

ACKNOWLEDGEMENTS

My sincere thanks go to Dr Otto Leistner of the National Botanical Institute in Pretoria and his staff for their valuable assistance in the preparation of the manuscript, and especially to Joan Mulvenna for her prompt and excellent word processing. Special thanks as well to Emsie du Plessis for the Afrikaans translation, help with proofreading and for supplying me with words on occasion! Words, though, are not enough to thank Trudé Botma for her dedication as editor and the tremendous amount of work she put in around the clock during the production of this book.

I greatly appreciate the assistance of the staff of the National Herbarium. Gerrit Germishuizen, Hugh Glen, Paul Herman, Elizabeth Retief, Clare Reid, Mariana van Wyk, Lyn Fish and Mienkie Welman always willingly identified my plants, even when only transparencies were available.

Thanks to Kathy Clarke of the NBI in Pretoria and Karen Behr of the Witwatersrand National Botanical Garden for helping to locate various plants for me to photograph. I am most grateful to Nick Klapwijk (NBI, Pretoria) for checking the chapters on tree and shrub planting and for providing valuable practical advice.

My sincere appreciation to Professor Brian Huntley, Chief Director of the NBI, for his strong encouragement.

A big thank you to the most patient impatient person I know – my husband, Leon, who always (well, almost!) stopped the car immediately I yelled, 'Stop! I need a picture of that.' His support made the completion of this book possible. Thanks are also due to my friend and fellow enthusiast, Fay Silverman (Cape Town), for housing me at times, providing encouragement and for dragging me up Table Mountain to photograph *Oxalis* and *Lobostemon*. Many thanks also to Marianne Alexander for putting in an extra special effort to photograph some of the Cape plants in Kirstenbosch Gardens and to Cathy Knox of the NBI in Cape Town for her hard work in promoting this book amidst all her numerous other commitments.

Finally, my thanks go to Mike Wells of the NBI in Pretoria, for his support since I started at the Institute, and for forcing me to learn photography in the first place.

CONTENTS

INTRODUCTION

Being a botanist, I am often asked for advice by friends and acquaintances. I started making notes of the solutions to their specific garden problems and in this way accumulated a bank of information which gradually became more useful as I arranged it according to important features such as the shape and size of the plants and flower colour. This practical experience prompted me to compile a book where I have deliberately departed from the more traditional A-Z presentation in order to make the information as accessible as possible to the reader and to simplify the task of finding a suitable plant for a specific purpose. As I have a bias towards our own beautiful, versatile and often hardy plants I have made them the subject of this book. I have, however, included a few plants from further north in Africa, for example species of *Pentas*, *Ruttya* and *Khaya*, because they do well in South African gardens.

Plants have been identified according to their botanical names (genus and species) followed by the family name and the common name. As plants are frequently being reclassified, the botanical names do change and where this has occurred fairly recently the previous botanical name has been given in brackets below the present one. The botanical names used in this book were correct at the time the manuscript was submitted for publication. The common names of plants are a grey area as they frequently differ from one region to another, causing considerable confusion. There is a national tree list which records the official common names of trees, but unfortunately this is not the case with other plants. In this book the common name or names current in the region of origin have been used. Although duplication has been avoided where possible, there remain cases where widely differing plants are known by identical common names. English common names have been used as far as possible, but where these do not exist the Afrikaans name has been given.

It is well known that South Africa possesses one of the richest floral kingdoms in the world. Many of our indigenous plants have been popularised locally and abroad and species like gazanias, vygies, agapanthus, irises, ixias, watsonias, gladioli and lobelias – to name but a few – are common in South African gardens. Yet many of our most attractive plants remain relatively unknown.

It is argued that gardeners do not use these plants because they are not readily available commercially and nurserymen maintain that it is not worthwhile to cultivate the lesser-known species for which there is no demand. The Kirstenbosch National Botanical Garden and the seven regional botanical gardens in various parts of the country are doing much to help remedy this situation. They are promoting the use of many of our lesser-known species by cultivating and selling them to the public through their nurseries.

The Botanical Society of South Africa produces a seed catalogue and, depending on the type of membership (individual or family), even supplies a certain number of seed packets to its members free of charge. It also publishes a quarterly magazine *Veld & Flora* to keep its members informed of the latest developments in the field of indigenous flora.

As our native plants have become better known popular demand for them has increased, which has prompted nurseries and garden centres to stock them more widely so that many beautiful, previously unknown species are now available. A directory of nurseries which sell indigenous plants appears on p. 368.

I hope this book will stimulate an even wider interest in our native South African plants and provide much pleasure to those involved in that most rewarding pastime, gardening.

Pitta Joffe, Pretoria

HOW TO USE THIS BOOK

Study the gaps in your garden carefully and ask yourself the following questions:

- What shape of plant would I like in that gap?
- How big should the plant be when it is fully grown?
- What kind of plant would be most suitable, e.g. a tree or shrub?
- Do I want an evergreen?
- Must the plant be frost hardy?
- Will the plant be in the sun or shade?
- What colour flowers do I want?
- When should they bloom?

This book will make it easy for you to find a suitable plant for your purpose. If you decide that you would, for instance, like to find a small shrub, turn to that section of the book and use the symbols to help you make your selection.

HOW THE SECTIONS ARE DIVIDED

- Trees (small, medium and large): grouped according to size and then according to shape.
- Shrubs (small, medium and large): grouped according to size.
- Herbaceous perennials, ground covers and bulbs: arranged ac-cording to flower colour.
- Annuals: arranged alphabetically according to their botanical names.
- Climbers: arranged alphabetically according to their botanical names.

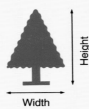

SIZE

10 m is the height, which is always given first. Always allow enough room for a plant to spread – its natural shape will be spoilt if it is crowded.

Speed of growth, height and spread are based on my experience in the Pretoria area. These figures are approximate and will vary according to climate, soil conditions and the care the plant receives.

KEY TO SYMBOLS

CROWN SHAPE (TREES)

 Rounded, dense

 Bare stem, small rounded crown of leaves and branches

 Rectangular, dense

 Weeping

Rounded – sparse, open texture

Long narrow – sparse, open texture

 Contorted

 Flat to umbrella-shaped

 Conical

 Low-branching, round-ed, dense

SHAPE (ALL OTHER PLANTS)

 Rounded

 Clump of strap-shaped leaves

 Clump of stiff, leathery or succulent leaves

 Tree fern

 Bulb or corm

 Oval crown, base bare and untidy

 Ground cover

 Palm or banana-like

 Climber

 Aquatic or water-loving

GROWTH REQUIREMENTS

 Requires little water

 Requires moderate water

 Requires lots of water

 Requires full sun

 Requires semi-shade

 Requires full shade

 Frost hardy

 Half-hardy; young plants require protection*

 Frost tender

CHARACTERISTICS

 Deciduous (loses leaves)

 Attractive flowers

 Succulent (cactus-like)

 Wind resistant

 Attracts birds

 Attracts insects (Not all insects are harmful, e.g. butterflies and bees; many also attract birds to the garden.)

* A mature plant indicated as half-hardy may be burnt by frost during an average Pretoria winter, but will recover in spring. A younger plant of the same species could, however, be killed by the same frost, and would therefore require some protection.

HOW THE INFORMATION ABOUT EACH PLANT IS PRESENTED

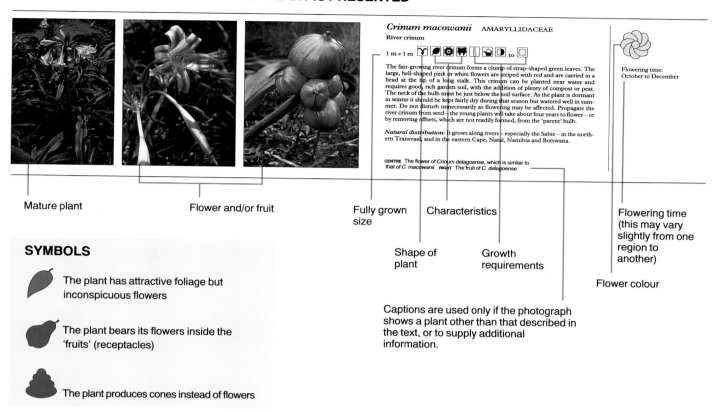

Crinum macowanii AMARYLLIDACEAE
River crinum

1 m × 1 m to

The fast-growing river crinum forms a clump of strap-shaped green leaves. The large, bell-shaped pink or white flowers are striped with red and are carried in a head at the tip of a long stalk. This crinum can be planted near water and requires good, rich garden soil, with the addition of plenty of compost or peat. The neck of the bulb must be just below the soil surface. As the plant is dormant in winter it should be kept fairly dry during that season but watered well in summer. Do not disturb unnecessarily as flowering may be affected. Propagate the river crinum from seed – the young plants will take about four years to flower – or by removing offsets, which are not readily formed, from the 'parent' bulb.

Natural distribution: It grows along rivers – especially the Sabie – in the northern Transvaal, and in the eastern Cape, Natal, Namibia and Botswana.

CENTRE The flower of *Crinum delagoense*, which is similar to that of *C. macowanii*. RIGHT The fruit of *C. delagoense*.

Flowering time:
October to December

Mature plant

Flower and/or fruit

Fully grown size

Characteristics

Flowering time (this may vary slightly from one region to another)

Shape of plant

Growth requirements

Flower colour

Captions are used only if the photograph shows a plant other than that described in the text, or to supply additional information.

SYMBOLS

The plant has attractive foliage but inconspicuous flowers

The plant bears its flowers inside the 'fruits' (receptacles)

The plant produces cones instead of flowers

Every garden has a number of microclimates, allowing the gardener to grow a wide variety of plants. For example, some of the more frost-tender ones may thrive against a north-facing wall warmed by the winter sun and offering protection from cold winds. Similarly, trees provide shelter for more delicate, shade-loving plants planted beneath them.

The map gives a rough indication of the frost areas in South Africa. But like a garden, a town also has different microclimates, so when starting a new garden or moving to a new area, consult your neighbours or local nursery.

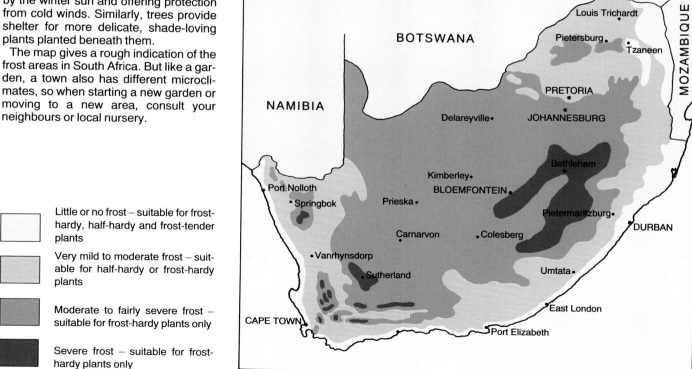

A GUIDE TO THE FROST AREAS OF SOUTH AFRICA

ZIMBABWE

BOTSWANA

MOZAMBIQUE

Louis Trichardt

Pietersburg

Tzaneen

PRETORIA

NAMIBIA

Delareyville

JOHANNESBURG

Bethlehem

Kimberley

BLOEMFONTEIN

Port Nolloth

Springbok

Prieska

Pietermaritzburg

DURBAN

Carnarvon

Colesberg

Vanrhynsdorp

Sutherland

Umtata

East London

CAPE TOWN

Port Elizabeth

Little or no frost – suitable for frost-hardy, half-hardy and frost-tender plants

Very mild to moderate frost – suitable for half-hardy or frost-hardy plants

Moderate to fairly severe frost – suitable for frost-hardy plants only

Severe frost – suitable for frost-hardy plants only

1 TREES

As trees are the most permanent plants in a garden and therefore represent a long-term investment, they should be chosen and positioned with great care. A tree should be selected according to the contribution it will make to the garden throughout the year – flower colour is only an added seasonal bonus. Bear in mind that many trees develop with age and that the shape of the tree may change as it grows older. Many of the smaller trees can at first be grown as large background shrubs and later shaped into a tree.

As the ultimate size of a tree is usually the main determining factor in its selection, the trees in this book have been grouped according to their size – small, medium and large. Within these categories the trees have been grouped according to their shape. The natural distribution of the tree serves as an important practical guide to whether a tree will be suitable for a particular climatic region. Bear in mind that a tree growing in a garden where it receives adequate water, fertiliser and plenty of compost will probably grow faster than in its natural habitat. Trees that are frost-tender can often be grown in a protected position in a garden in an area to which they are not necessarily suited. This applies particularly to the broad-leaved evergreen forest trees. If grown in a favourable climate where the winters are mild, i.e. not too long, cold and dry, some normally deciduous trees may become semideciduous or even evergreen. This has been indicated in the text where applicable.

Propagating a tree from seed is a very specialised and slow process and the average gardener will find it more convenient to purchase a young tree from a nursery. It should then be planted with care to minimise transplantation shock and ensure that its roots become established as soon as possible. Dig a hole twice the diameter of the nursery bag, keeping the topsoil separate from the subsoil. Loosen the soil at the bottom of the hole and water well. Add the following to the topsoil: compost (equivalent to about half the amount of topsoil removed), 280 g (one cup) of superphosphate and 150 g (one cup) of slow-release 3:2:1 fertiliser. Mix thoroughly. Place approximately one third of this mixture into the hole. Remove the tree from its container, taking care not to damage the roots. Only if the root-ball has become very compacted should it be loosened. Hold the tree upright in the hole and add the remaining topsoil mix. Tamp soil firmly around the root-ball. If necessary, add compost to the remaining subsoil and use to fill the hole. The soil below and around the root-ball should be firm enough not to settle excessively after watering. Ensure that the top of the soil around the root-ball aligns with the surrounding soil once the tree has settled.

Make a generous basin around the trunk, at least as wide as the tree's aerial spread and 15 cm deep. Mulch with a 10 cm thick layer of organic material. Water thoroughly directly after planting and carefully for the next four to six months, especially in dry weather. Good, deep watering (at least 10-20 litres at a time) is essential. Shallow watering (wetting only the top 5-10 cm of soil) encourages roots to remain near the surface of the soil instead of growing down deeply to find the moisture below. A tree with a deep, well-developed root system tends to have some drought resistance.

If necessary, stake the tree, using a metal fence pole or wooden stake about 30 cm higher than the planted tree. Knock the stake at least 50 cm into the ground *before* planting the tree to ensure that it does not penetrate the root-ball and damage the roots. Attach the tree to the stake with either approved tree ties, strips of tyre tube or a nylon stocking. Tie loosely enough to prevent damage to the bark and check the ties regularly to ensure that they have not begun to chafe. For a very tall or top-heavy tree, use two or three stakes. Remove the stakes once the tree has become established.

Acacia erubescens   FABACEAE
Blue thorn

6 m × 6 m

This graceful spreading tree, which is often multistemmed, is slow growing. It has a very attractive, corky, yellow bark which peels off in thin flakes. The stems are grey and the thorns short, paired, hooked and very sharp. The pale yellow flowers are tinged pink and sweetly scented. The nutritious pods are flat, thin and oblong and are browsed by cattle and game. Prune lower branches to keep the tree neat and propagate from seed. To improve germination, pour boiling water over seed, and allow to soak overnight before sowing. Young plants may need protection from frost.

Natural distribution: It occurs in dry woodland and thornveld in the eastern, northern and central Transvaal, across Botswana and into Namibia.

National tree number 164

Flowering time:
September to October

Baphia racemosa   FABACEAE
Violet pea, Natal camwood

5 m × 3 m to

This plant, which will grow moderately fast given good soil and water, may form a shrub or a small tree (lower branches could be pruned away to encourage a tree-like shape). The bark becomes brown and rough with age. The plant has evergreen, glossy foliage and attractive, sweetly scented, pea-shaped white flowers, in short sprays. The fruit is a flat, pointed pod. Propagate the violet pea from seed and protect young plants from frost.

Natural distribution: It grows in thick bush and riverine forest along the coast of Natal and Zululand.

National tree number 224

Flowering time:
November to December

Bequaertiodendron magalismontanum
SAPOTACEAE

Stamvrug

4 m × 3 m

This slow-growing tree will reach a height of more than 4 m in warmer areas. The scaly bark, which cracks with age, is light brown or grey. The dense, dark green foliage is slightly glossy and young leaves are golden brown. The strongly scented, small cream flowers are borne in clusters on the older stems. Pleasant tasting and rich in vitamin C, the edible, fleshy, oval fruits are red when ripe, and are eaten by many different birds. Propagate this tree from seed, which must be very fresh, or from truncheons.

Natural distribution: It almost always grows on rocky ridges and hillsides (usually quartzite and granite), and occurs in the central Transvaal, Zululand, northern Natal, Swaziland and Botswana.

National tree number 581

Flowering time:
June to December

Calpurnia aurea subsp. *aurea*   FABACEAE
Natal laburnum

4 m × 3 m

A slender, graceful ornamental suitable for a smaller garden, the Natal laburnum is fast growing in good soil with sufficient water. The trunk is dark brown and the long sprays of golden yellow flowers are produced while the tree is still young. The fruit is a lightweight, thin pod. The tree is easily propagated from seed. Although young plants must be protected from frost, they are drought resistant once established.

Natural distribution: It occurs in evergreen and riverine forest, from the eastern Cape (from about Port Elizabeth northwards) through Natal to the south-eastern Transvaal.

National tree number 219

Flowering time:
December to February

Cassine burkeana   CELASTRACEAE
Transvaal kooboo-berry

6 m × 4 m

The Transvaal kooboo-berry has a moderate growth rate and with its dense crown of leaves is a good hedge or screen plant. Drought resistant, it has rough, dark brown bark and small greenish-yellow flowers. The oval, berry-like fruit, bright orange-red when ripe, has a thick, sweet flesh and is eaten by birds. Prune the tree to keep it neat and propagate from seed.

Natural distribution: It occurs in the dry bush and on the rocky outcrops around Pretoria and Johannesburg, extending all the way to Rustenburg.

National tree number 411

Flowering time:
January

Cordia caffra   BORAGINACEAE
Septee

6 m × 4 m

Fairly fast growing, the septee is an attractive ornamental, with a spreading crown of glossy, slightly drooping foliage. The unusual creamy-white to light brown bark, which sometimes flakes, is blotched with red and grey. The small, sweetly scented, bell-shaped cream flowers are followed by plum-shaped, fleshy, yellow to orange-red (when ripe) fruits, which are eaten by coucals and other birds. Easily propagated from seed, young plants must be protected from frost.

Natural distribution: It occurs in coastal evergreen forest, on forest margins further inland and in wooded kloofs, from the eastern Cape through Natal and Zululand to the eastern and northern Transvaal.

National tree number 652

Flowering time:
September to October

Craibia zimmermannii FABACEAE
Small craibia, Peawood

5 m × 3 m

Flowering time:
September to November

A well-shaped, slow-growing, decorative tree, with glossy, very dark green foliage and large bunches of sweetly scented, pea-shaped white flowers which are produced in sprays and borne in spring. It has slightly flaking, pale grey bark and a flat, woody pod, 6-11 cm long. Easily propagated from seed, young plants must be protected from frost.

Natural distribution: It occurs in forests and on forest margins in northern Zululand and Swaziland.

National tree number 229

Croton gratissimus var. *gratissimus*
EUPHORBIACEAE

Lavender fever berry

6 m × 4 m

Flowering time:
Almost throughout summer

The lavender fever berry is a moderate to slow-growing, graceful drooping tree which may be multistemmed. Old stems are rough and brownish black. The leaves, which are carried on silver-and-red leaf stalks, glint in the sun and are green above and silver, dotted with cinnamon brown, below. When crushed, they smell of lavender. The small creamy-yellow flowers are borne in spikes. Fruits are small, three-lobed capsules which are eaten by crested guineafowl, emeraldspotted wood doves, tambourine doves, terrestrial bulbuls, francolins and probably many others. Propagate this tree from seed.

Natural distribution: It is often found on rocky outcrops, but also occurs in a variety of woodland types, extending from Zululand and Swaziland through the Transvaal to Namibia and the north-western Cape.

National tree number 328

Cussonia paniculata ARALIACEAE
Highveld cabbage tree

5 m × 2 m

Flowering time:
November to May

This lovely, fairly slow-growing, drought-resistant little tree is very distinctive – with its thick, crooked, yet squat trunk and rounded head of large, leathery, blue-green to grey, cabbage-like foliage, it makes an excellent 'form' plant for a garden. Although deciduous, it may be evergreen in a milder climate. The bark is rough, brown, fissured and corky. The small green-cream flowers attract many insects while the small, round, fleshy fruits – purple when ripe – are eaten by a variety of birds. The highveld cabbage tree is easily propagated from fresh seed.

Natural distribution: It is often found growing on mountains and in rocky places, extending from the Karoo and eastern Cape through the Orange Free State, Lesotho, Natal Drakensberg and the Transvaal highveld to Botswana.

National tree number 563

Dais cotinifolia   THYMELAEACEAE
Pompon tree

6 m × 4 m

Very fast growing, the pompon tree flowers while still young and, when in flower, the tree is covered with pinkish-mauve pompon-like inflorescences. Evergreen in a mild climate, it can be planted in the centre of a lawn. It has a rounded crown of slightly glossy, blue-green foliage, and smooth brown bark. The fruit is a very small, reddish-brown nutlet. The tree is easily propagated from seed.

Natural distribution: It usually grows on forest margins and wooded hill slopes in the eastern part of South Africa, from the Buffalo River northwards through the Transkei, Lesotho, Natal and Zululand to the north-eastern Transvaal.

National tree number 521

Flowering time:
November to February

Deinbollia oblongifolia   SAPINDACEAE
Dune soap-berry

4 m × 2 m

This shrub or small tree, of moderate growth rate, would make a good accent plant. It has long, bare, unbranched stems, each with a cluster of large leaves at the top. The flower buds of the smallish white to cream flowers are pale red-brown and furry. The pale yellow, berry-like fruits are eaten by Layard's bulbul, the speckled coly, the Cape glossy starling and the masked weaver. Propagate this tree from seed. Young plants grow slowly and may need protection from frost.

Natural distribution: It grows in open coastal forest and dune scrub, extending from East London northwards through Natal and Zululand to Mozambique.

National tree number 430

Flowering time:
April to May

Dichrostachys cinerea subsp. *africana*   FABACEAE
Sickle bush, Kalahari Christmas tree

4 m × 3 m

This small shrub or multistemmed tree with its intertwined branches is fairly fast growing in good soil but very thorny and not suitable for small gardens. The bark is rough, grey-brown and shallowly grooved, and modified, thorn-like twigs occur in pairs. The flowers are pendent, cylindrical spikes, 4-5 cm long, with the basal part bright pink and the rest pale yellow. The pods are twisted and intertwined in spherical clusters. Easily propagated from seed, young plants must be protected from frost. Prune the tree to keep it neat.

Natural distribution: Very widespread, this tree occurs in wooded grassland, extending from the dry parts of Natal and the Transvaal into Botswana and Namibia.

National tree number 190

Flowering time:
Usually spring but may be
from September to February

Diospyros whyteana   EBENACEAE

Bladder-nut

5 m × 3 m

This fairly fast-growing small tree has very attractive, dense, glossy, dark green foliage, and would make an excellent hedge or screen plant. Its bark is grey to almost black and the sweetly scented, pendulous flowers are creamy yellow. The fruits are roundish berries enclosed in a papery, inflated 'pod'. Easily propagated from seed, young plants must be protected from frost.

Natural distribution: It grows in open forest, on mountain slopes and along riverbanks, from Table Mountain eastwards to the eastern Orange Free State, Natal, Zululand, the Transvaal and Swaziland.

National tree number 611

Flowering time:
August to November

Dodonaea angustifolia   SAPINDACEAE

Cape sand olive

4 m × 3 m

The Cape sand olive – which is fast growing given good soil and water – usually forms a multistemmed shrub although the lower branches may be pruned away to encourage a tree-like shape. It is a good hedge or screen plant and is both wind and drought resistant. It has stringy, dark grey bark and glossy foliage with small yellow-green flowers and decorative, winged greenish-red fruits. This tree is easily propagated from seed.

Natural distribution: It grows in arid, semi-desert areas, on rocky hill slopes and along the margins of subtropical, evergreen forest, extending from Namibia to the south-western Cape, the eastern Cape, Natal, Zululand and the south-eastern Transvaal.

National tree number 437.1

Flowering time:
April to August

Euclea crispa subsp. *crispa*   EBENACEAE

Blue guarri

6 m × 4 m

A neat, well-shaped, drought-resistant tree, suitable for smaller gardens, the blue guarri is fairly fast growing under favourable conditions. The smooth to slightly rough bark is grey as is the foliage. The scented flowers are very small, pendulous and greenish yellow. The fruits are tiny, round, black when ripe and are eaten by both birds and buck. The tree is easily propagated from seed.

Natural distribution: It grows in kloofs, open woodland and on forest margins, extending from the eastern and north-eastern Cape to Natal, Zululand, Swaziland, Lesotho, the Orange Free State and the central, eastern and northern Transvaal.

National tree number 594

Flowering time:
October to February

Euclea divinorum   EBENACEAE
Magic guarri

6 m × 5 m

The magic guarri, which bears its branches close to the base of the tree, is fairly fast growing under favourable conditions. The older stems are grey and rough, and the bark breaks off in small sections. The foliage is grey-green and the tree bears small creamy flowers. Male and female flowers are borne on separate plants. Grey, yellowbilled and redbilled hornbills and many other birds eat the small, fleshy, round berries, which are purple when ripe. Propagate this tree from seed. Young plants are slow growing.

Natural distribution: It usually grows in open woodland, thorn scrub, or sometimes along riverbanks, in hot dry areas extending northwards from Zululand, Swaziland and the eastern and northern Transvaal into Botswana and northern Namibia.

National tree number 595

Flowering time:
August to October

Euphorbia cooperi   EUPHORBIACEAE
Transvaal candelabra tree

7 m × 2 m

The Transvaal candelabra tree, which is drought resistant, grows very slowly and is suitable for a large rock garden in warmer, drier areas, or may be planted in a container against a hot, sunny, north or west wall. It sheds its branches with age, leaving a straight, bare trunk topped with a crown of living branches. Small yellow-green flowers are followed by green fruits with reddish markings. Birds feed on the seed. When cut the plant exudes latex which is poisonous and which causes severe skin irritation. Propagate from cuttings (do not get latex on the skin or in the eyes), which must be kept fairly dry or they will rot.

Natural distribution: It occurs in wooded grassland and on rocky ridges, extending from central Natal through Zululand and Swaziland to the Transvaal (as far north as Messina).

National tree number 346

Flowering time:
May to August

Euphorbia evansii   EUPHORBIACEAE
Lowveld euphorbia

5 m × 3 m

This drought-resistant plant would do well in a rockery in warmer, drier areas, or as a container plant for a hot, sunny, north or west wall. Its growth rate has not been assessed in a garden situation, but is probably slow. It is usually single-stemmed, but may branch and each branch may then be topped by a sparse crown of dark green branches. Thorns occur in pairs on the ridges of the stem. The tree bears small greenish-yellow flowers followed by fruit in the shape of three-lobed capsules. Propagate the lowveld euphorbia from seed or from cuttings, which must be kept fairly dry to prevent rot.

Natural distribution: It occurs in hot, dry woodland, often amongst rocks, from the eastern Transvaal southwards to Muden in Natal.

National tree number 348

Flowering time:
August to September

Ficus abutilifolia   MORACEAE

Large-leaved rockfig

6 m × 6 m

Fruiting time:
Throughout the year

This slow-growing plant is ideal for planting between rocks in a large rock garden – it will even grow in the cracks – or on a rocky hillside. It has a lovely, short, crooked, low-branching yellow-grey to yellow-white trunk, the bark of which peels off in paper-thin flakes. The leaves are large and rounded. The tree bears small flowers inside the fruits, which are 2,5 cm in diameter, pale to dark red when ripe, and eaten by birds and humans alike. Propagate the large-leaved rock fig from seed or from cuttings. Seedlings grow very slowly.

Natural distribution: It is always found growing over rocks, often out of cracks or splits, and extends from Natal (except the extreme south), Zululand and Swaziland to the Transvaal (except the south-western region), Botswana and further north.

National tree number 63

Gardenia volkensii subsp. *volkensii*   RUBIACEAE

(= *G. spatulifolia*)

Transvaal gardenia

6 m × 5 m

Flowering time:
August to December

The Transvaal gardenia, which is fairly fast growing given good soil and water, is an attractive garden shrub or small tree. The smooth, pale grey bark offsets the glossy, dark green leaves and it bears large, attractive, sweetly scented white flowers. These are followed by unusual, oval, ribbed grey-green fruits. Easily propagated from seed, young plants must be protected from frost.

Natural distribution: Fairly widespread, this plant occurs in the Transvaal bushveld, Zululand, Botswana and north-east Namibia.

National tree number 691.2

Heteropyxis natalensis   MYRTACEAE

Lavender tree

6 m × 4 m

Flowering time:
December to March

This lovely, neat, ornamental tree, with a small crown of slightly drooping, glossy green foliage which turns red in autumn, is fairly slow growing. Its beautiful and distinctive pale grey, almost white bark flakes thinly and the crushed twigs and leaves smell of lavender. Small, fragrant cream to yellow flowers are followed by fruits which are tiny, oval, dark brown capsules. Propagate this tree from seed.

Natural distribution: It usually grows on the margins of evergreen forests, in riverine bush and on rocky slopes, and is plentiful in parts of Natal, Zululand, Swaziland and in the central, eastern and northern Transvaal.

National tree number 455

Loxostylis alata ANACARDIACEAE
Tigerwood

6 m × 4 m

This is a compact, well-shaped, drought-resistant tree which has a moderate growth rate. The light grey bark sometimes flakes and the young leaves are yellow, tinged with red. White male flowers and green female flowers – the sexes are on separate trees – appear in dense clusters at the ends of the branches. The bright red sepals that surround the fruit (female tree only) are very decorative and the tree is particularly attractive at this time. Propagate the tigerwood from seed and protect young plants from frost.

Natural distribution: It grows on forest margins, in kloofs and along rivers, from about Uitenhage northwards to Natal and Zululand.

National tree number 365

Flowering time:
September to January

CENTRE The white flowers of the male tree. **RIGHT** The fruit of the female tree surrounded by bright red sepals.

Maytenus undata CELASTRACEAE
Koko tree

6 m × 5 m   to

A hardy, evergreen, ornamental tree or shrub for gardens, the koko tree is slow growing and drought resistant. It has grey-brown stems; the bark on old stems is rough and often peels off in small rectangular blocks. The dentate, glossy, leathery leaves are dark green to grey-green and the flowers are very small and pale yellow to yellow-green. The fruit is a red-brown capsule, which splits open to expose the bright orange seeds, which are eaten by birds. Propagate this tree from seed or cuttings.

Natural distribution: It occurs in forests, along forest margins and on riverbanks in all the provinces of South Africa, and in Swaziland and Botswana.

National tree number 403

Flowering time:
July, August or September

Pittosporum viridiflorum PITTOSPORACEAE
Pittosporum

7 m × 5 m   to

This plant, which is fast growing in good soil with sufficient water, has a very variable habit – it may form a large shrub, or a hardy, neat, well-shaped tree. The bark, which is smooth when young and rough with age, is light or dark grey, often with crosswise seams. It smells like liquorice. The plant bears small, sweetly scented cream-green to yellow flowers. The fruit is a brown capsule which splits to expose the moist orange-red seeds inside. These seeds are sticky, have a pleasant smell and are eaten by redeyed doves and several species of starling. Propagate the pittosporum from seed.

Natural distribution: It grows in forest and scrub, on the edges of streams and on rocky ridges, at the coast and inland from Knysna through the Karoo and eastern Cape to the southern Orange Free State, throughout Natal, Lesotho, Swaziland, the south-eastern Transvaal and Botswana.

National tree number 139

Flowering time:
November to December

Rhus chirindensis   ANACARDIACEAE
Red currant

6 m × 5 m

A neat, ornamental tree for the garden which sometimes forms a shrub, the red currant has a moderate growth rate – faster if the soil and water are good. It has smooth or rough brown bark and young plants may be thorny, although the mature tree is spineless. It bears a dense, rounded crown of glossy, dark green foliage. Young leaves are reddish. Large sprays of minute greenish-yellow flowers are followed by edible fruits which are small, roundish, shiny, slightly fleshy and red when ripe. They are eaten by bulbuls, barbets, white-eyes and parrots. Propagate this tree from seed and protect young plants from frost.

Natural distribution: It grows in open woodland, mountain scrub, forests and along the edges of streams, from Swellendam through the eastern Cape, Natal, Zululand and Swaziland to the eastern and northern Transvaal and Botswana.

National tree number 380

Flowering time:
November to December

Rhus dentata   ANACARDIACEAE
Nana-berry

5 m × 4 m

The nana-berry, known for its attractive autumn foliage, has a moderate growth rate and may form a bushy shrub or a tree. It has greyish-brown bark, soft foliage and small, sweet-smelling yellow-green flowers. Small, shiny fruits – red when ripe – are borne in heavy clusters. Propagate this tree from seed.

Natural distribution: Very widespread, the nana-berry grows in forests, on forest margins, in kloofs, thick bush and on hillsides, from Humansdorp in the south-eastern Cape to the central Transvaal.

National tree number 381.1

Flowering time:
September to November

Rhus undulata   ANACARDIACEAE
Kunibush

5 m × 4 m

The kunibush is a large, bushy evergreen, with a moderate growth rate. It may form a dense shrub or tree and can therefore be used as a hedge or screen plant. Some plants are very thorny, others less so. It has grey to brown bark, leathery, dark green foliage and small, sweetly scented creamy flowers. These are followed by small, roundish, flattened fruits, red when mature, which are eaten by birds. Propagate the kunibush from seed.

Natural distribution: It grows on mountainsides, along rivers, in evergreen forest, and in arid areas, in central and southern Namibia and all the provinces of South Africa.

National tree number 395

Flowering time:
February to April

Sparrmannia africana   TILIACEAE

Cape stock-rose

4 m × 2 m   to

Flowering time:
June to November

This bushy tree/shrub grows well in a slightly sheltered position under larger trees and is fast growing. It has smooth grey-green to light brown bark. The hairs of the large, rounded leaves may produce a skin irritation. The Cape stock-rose bears showy white flowers with a central mass of golden stamens and its fruit takes the form of a spherical capsule covered in bristles. Propagate this tree from seed.

Natural distribution: It is usually found growing in damp places, along rivers and on forest margins in the George, Knysna, Uniondale and Humansdorp areas.

National tree number 457

Phoenix reclinata   ARECACEAE

Wild date palm

5 m × 4 m

Flowering time:
November to December

An attractive, fairly hardy, ornamental palm for the garden, the wild date palm is reasonably fast growing and usually produces suckers to form a multistemmed plant, so that enough room must be allowed for it to spread. Its foliage takes the form of long, glossy, dark green fronds. Small cream flowers are borne in long sprays with male and female flowers on separate plants. The orange-brown fruits (dates) which are edible and reasonably tasty are eaten by many different types of birds. Propagate this palm from seed.

Natural distribution: It usually grows in damp places, along the coastal belt from Port Elizabeth northwards to Natal and Zululand and inland to the eastern Transvaal, Mozambique, Zimbabwe, northern Botswana and northern Namibia.

National tree number 22

Acacia davyi   FABACEAE

Corky thorn

5 m × 4 m

Flowering time:
November to March

This neat, compact acacia, usually smaller than indicated above, is fairly slow growing and ideal for smaller gardens. It has an attractive, corky, pale buff-brown bark and bright yellow flowers. Thin, straight or slightly bent thorns are borne in pairs. The pods are narrow, slightly curved and up to 10 cm long and are borne in clusters. Propagate this tree from seed, which has been immersed in boiling water and then soaked overnight. Young plants may need protection from frost.

Natural distribution: It occurs in the bushveld and grassland of Zululand, Swaziland and the eastern, central and northern Transvaal.

National tree number 163.1

Albizia tanganyicensis subsp. *tanganyicensis*
FABACEAE

Paperbark false-thorn

7 m × 3 m

Flowering time:
September to November

This unusual and striking tree, which is fairly fast growing, has a long, crooked, bare stem with papery orange-yellow bark which peels off revealing a beautiful, smooth creamy-white trunk. Plant it in a rock garden or near a house with dark-ish facebrick walls, where the bark will show up to advantage. It has very sparse, feathery, rich green foliage. The sweetly scented creamy-white flowers form half spherical, fluffy heads which resemble powder puffs. The pods are oblong, smooth and pale brown. Propagate this tree from seed or from truncheons, and protect young plants from frost.

Natural distribution: It occurs on rocky granite or quartzite hillsides, from Warmbaths northwards to the Soutpansberg (Transvaal) and Botswana.

National tree number 157

Bridelia mollis   EUPHORBIACEAE
Velvet sweetberry

5 m × 4 m

Flowering time:
November to February

This plant has a dark grey to black trunk and rough bark. The soft velvety foliage tends to droop and turns an attractive golden yellow in autumn. The flowers are very small and yellow-green and the round fruits, which are the size of a pea, turn black when ripe. These are eaten by birds and humans. Propagate this tree from seed. Young plants are slow growing, and need protection from frost.

Natural distribution: It usually grows on rocky ridges, but sometimes also occurs in dry, open bushveld, from the central and northern Transvaal into Botswana and northern Namibia.

National tree number 325

RIGHT The fruits of *Bridelia cathartica*, which are very similar to those of *B. mollis*.

Cassia abbreviata subsp. *beareana*   FABACEAE
Sjambok pod

6 m × 4 m

Flowering time:
August to October

A beautiful ornamental tree for warmer gardens, this cassia grows fairly slowly. The old stems are rough and dark brown to black. Bunches of sweetly scented, dark yellow flowers are followed by long, cylindrical, rounded pods which are up to 80 cm long. Propagate the sjambok pod from seed and protect young plants from frost.

Natural distribution: It grows in bushveld, open woodland, and sometimes on riverbanks, in the northern and eastern Transvaal and in northern Namibia.

National tree number 212

Commiphora glandulosa   BURSERACEAE

Common corkwood

5 m × 4 m

Flowering time:
September to October

This unusual and interesting tree, which grows fairly fast, could be planted in a large rock garden or in a lawn. The bark peels off in small, paper-thin yellow flakes from the dark grey, yellow-grey or grey-green stem. Short lateral branches are spiny. The small green or yellow flowers, which turn red with age and grow in bunches on the branches, appear before the leaves, which occur in dense groups at the ends of the branches. The rounded to egg-shaped fruits are red or brown when ripe, and are eaten by yellowbilled hornbills. Propagate the common corkwood from seed or from truncheons.

Natural distribution: It usually occurs in dry woodland, from Zululand, Swaziland and the Transvaal to Namibia and Botswana.

National tree number 285.1

Dombeya rotundifolia   STERCULIACEAE

Wild pear

6 m × 3 m

Flowering time:
July to September

The wild pear is fast growing (3 m in five years) given good soil and adequate water and is a neat, well-shaped tree, suitable for smaller gardens. Its bark is rough and dark brown. One of the first trees to flower in spring, it has creamy white (sometimes pink) flowers followed by very small spherical brown fruits. This tree is easily propagated from seed.

Natural distribution: It grows in open woodland and bushveld, often on hills and koppies, from central Natal and Zululand through Swaziland to the northern, central and eastern Transvaal, Botswana and Namibia.

National tree number 471

Grewia hexamita   TILIACEAE

Giant raisin

5 m × 3 m

Flowering time:
September to November

This plant grows slowly and may form a shrub, or fairly tall, spreading tree, with glossy, dark green foliage. Old stems are dark grey and rough and the bark breaks off in sections. It bears star-shaped, bright yellow flowers. The edible fruits are two-lobed and yellowish brown when ripe. The tree is easily propagated from seed.

Natural distribution: It grows in deciduous woodland and river valleys, from Swaziland to the eastern and northern Transvaal, Zimbabwe and Mozambique.

National tree number 460

Greyia sutherlandii GREYIACEAE

Natal bottlebrush

5 m × 3 m

Flowering time:
August to October

This attractive bottlebrush, which has smooth reddish-grey bark, would be suitable for a rock garden in warmer areas. It grows fairly fast given good soil and water, but must be planted in a protected spot. The leaves are large and almost circular. Showy red, bottlebrush flowers produce large quantities of nectar much enjoyed by birds and bees. Propagate the Natal bottlebrush from seed, cuttings or from suckers.

Natural distribution: It grows on the slopes and rocky ridges of the Drakensberg, and in the eastern Cape, eastern Orange Free State, Natal, Swaziland and the eastern Transvaal.

National tree number 446

Heteromorpha trifoliata APIACEAE

(= *H. arborescens*)

Parsnip tree, Parsley tree

5 m × 4 m

Flowering time:
December to January

Suitable for planting in a lawn, the parsnip tree is fairly fast growing. It has attractive, smooth reddish to purplish-brown bark which is somewhat waxy in appearance and peels off in papery flakes. Glossy, light green or grey-green foliage droops gracefully and turns yellow to red in autumn. A dense, round head of small, strong-smelling green or yellow flowers is followed by small, oval, three-winged fruits. Propagate this tree from seed.

Natural distribution: Very widely distributed in many different habitats, it grows from the Cape northwards to the Orange Free State, Natal, the Transvaal, north-eastern Namibia and Botswana.

National tree number 568

Ozoroa paniculosa   ANACARDIACEAE

Common resin tree

7 m × 5 m

This plant, which can form a shrub or tree, is moderately fast growing and, in favourable climates, sometimes evergreen. The bark of young trees is smooth and grey while that of old trees is brown, rough and scaly. Branches are red-brown and inclined to droop and the crown is sparse and poorly spreading. The leaves are smooth and dark green above with hairy, silvery undersides. Long terminal sprays of tiny, strongly scented white to cream flowers are followed by small, shiny, kidney-shaped green fruits, which become black and raisin-like when ripe. Propagate this tree from seed, although germination is usually poor.

Natural distribution: This is a common bushveld species growing in northern Natal, Zululand, Swaziland, through the Transvaal (especially in the Pretoria and Johannesburg areas) to Botswana and Namibia.

National tree number 375

Flowering time:
November to February

LEFT The greyish-green foliage of a mature specimen of *Ozoroa paniculosa* contrasts with the yellow-green foliage of two *Psydrax livida*.

Sesamothamnus lugardii   PEDALIACEAE

Transvaal sesame bush

4 m × 4 m

This curious, unusual, slow-growing and drought-resistant plant would be ideal for a rock garden in a hot, dry area. It has an interesting shape, and makes a good container plant for a sunny north or west wall. The exceptionally thick, fleshy, semisucculent stem always subdivides into several branches near the ground. The bark, which is grey to yellowish and marked with black, peels off into fine paper-thin strips. The crown is sparse with long, thin, upright or drooping branches, which are armed with strong, straight or slightly curved spines, and the leaves are soft and a dull buff-green. The solitary, sweet-smelling flowers (up to 15 cm long) consist of a dark red-brown tube with large white to cream-coloured petals and are followed by woody brown fruit capsules. Propagate the Transvaal sesame bush from seed or from cuttings. Plant in very well-drained soil (at least half the mixture consisting of coarse riversand) and give very little water.

Natural distribution: It is usually found growing in hot, dry areas, often on rocky hillsides, in the northern Transvaal and Botswana.

National tree number 680

Flowering time:
November to February

Ximenia caffra var. *caffra*   OLACACEAE

Large sourplum

5 m × 5 m

Flowering time:
September to October

A slow-growing and drought-resistant plant, the large sourplum has a short, rough black stem and spiny branches. The dark green leaves are smooth and leathery and the small flowers are cream-green. Many different types of birds eat the smooth, glossy, oval fruits. Red when ripe and with a high vitamin C content, they are edible but sour. Propagate the large sourplum from seed.

Natural distribution: It grows on rocky hillsides, and in woodland, from the Magaliesberg northwards to the Soutpansberg (northern Transvaal) and westwards to Botswana and Namibia.

National tree number 103

Zanthoxylum capense   RUTACEAE

Small knobwood

7 m × 3 m

Flowering time:
October to January

This slow-growing, drought-resistant plant often forms a multistemmed shrub, sometimes a small tree. The stems are dark grey and the trunks of larger trees are armed with corky, spine-tipped knobs while younger branches have short, sharp, rounded spines approximately 1 cm long. The leaves are dark green, shiny above and dull below. When crushed, they smell strongly of oranges. Dense clusters of small, sweet-smelling creamy flowers are followed by round orange-red fruits borne in pendent clusters. Inside each fruit is a small, shiny black seed which may be used for propagation.

Natural distribution: It occurs in dry woodland and on rocky hillsides, from Knysna northwards through Natal, Zululand, Swaziland and the central Transvaal to Zimbabwe.

National tree number 253

Faurea speciosa   PROTEACEAE

Broad-leaved beech

6 m × 4 m

Flowering time:
March to September

This slow-growing tree has rough, deeply furrowed, dark grey bark. The leaves are largish, hairy when young, glossy dark green when old and turn red in autumn. Copious nectar is produced by the cream to pink flowers which are borne in spikes. The fruits are small, round brown nuts. This tree is difficult to propagate from seed.

Natural distribution: It grows in mountain grassland, and mixed deciduous woodland, in Zululand, Swaziland, the eastern and north-eastern Transvaal and Zimbabwe.

National tree number 76

Leucosidea sericea   ROSACEAE

Oudehout, Ouhout

7 m × 5 m

This very fast-growing plant may form a dense, much-branched shrub or contorted small tree. It prefers moist conditions and thrives planted next to a dam or stream. The bark is red-brown and flakes off in strips. The upper surfaces of the aromatic, deeply serrated leaves are dark green and the lower ones silky white. Starry yellow-green flowers are produced in spikes at the ends of the branches. Small hard fruits are enclosed in the old flower bases. Propagate this tree from seed.

Natural distribution: It grows along streams and in kloofs, from the eastern Cape to Lesotho, western Natal, Swaziland, the eastern Orange Free State, the western, eastern and northern Transvaal and eastern Zimbabwe.

National tree number 145

Flowering time:
Spring and early summer

Mundulea sericea   FABACEAE

Cork bush

3 m × 2 m

The slow-growing cork bush is an attractive, neat, ornamental tree for a small garden. Its bark, which is light grey, deeply furrowed and corky, is poisonous. The foliage is silver-grey and the tree bears sprays of pea-shaped mauve to purple flowers, followed by small flat pods covered with velvety golden-brown hairs. Propagate the cork bush from seed and plant it in well-drained soil.

Natural distribution: It grows in bushveld, wooded grassland, and on rocky koppies, from Zululand and the central, eastern and northern Transvaal into Zimbabwe, Botswana and Namibia.

National tree number 226

Flowering time:
October to January

Ochna pulchra   OCHNACEAE

Peeling plane

5 m × 3 m

Although slow growing and very difficult to cultivate, the peeling plane is one of our most attractive indigenous trees, with its striking bronze foliage in both spring and autumn and masses of sweetly scented, pale lemon yellow flowers borne in dense sprays. The old stems are smooth and creamy white and are partly covered by curled grey-brown flakes of peeling bark. Decorative fruits – at first shiny green, ripening to black – are borne in pendent clusters and are eaten by birds. Attempts to propagate this tree have mainly been unsuccessful as seed germinates poorly, and the young plants do not transplant well. Possibly very fresh seed planted *in situ* would succeed.

Natural distribution: It grows in open woodland, in sandy soil (northern Kalahari), and on granite or quartzite koppies, from the central Transvaal northwards to Zimbabwe and westwards to Botswana and Namibia.

National tree number 483

Flowering time:
August to October

CENTRE A young tree covered in blossoms in early spring before the leaves appear.

Pappea capensis   SAPINDACEAE

Jacket plum

7 m × 6 m

The jacket plum is a neat, well-shaped tree for the garden. Of moderate growth rate, it may be evergreen in milder climates. It has smooth, pale grey to brownish bark and a dense crown of smooth, leathery, dark green leaves which are fairly glossy above but rough underneath. The small, scented greenish-yellow flowers attract bees. Male and female flowers are borne on separate trees. The fruit is a furry green capsule which splits to reveal an edible, pleasantly flavoured, shiny black seed completely covered in a fleshy, brilliant orange-red jelly. It is eaten by redfaced mousebirds, green pigeons and blackcollared barbets. Propagate this tree from seed.

Natural distribution: Very widespread, the jacket plum occurs in a number of different habitats, in all the provinces of South Africa, as well as in Zimbabwe, Botswana and Namibia.

National tree number 433

Flowering time:
January to May

Rhus pyroides   ANACARDIACEAE

Firethorn, Common wild currant

5 m × 4 m

The drought-resistant firethorn, which may be evergreen in favourable climates, is of moderate growth rate and may form a shrub (useful for hedges) or the lower branches may be pruned away to form a tree. The dark brown bark sometimes bears stout thorns and a scratch from one of these will sting for some time. The plant has velvety foliage and very small yellowish flowers. Small roundish fruits, red when ripe, are borne in large quantities and are eaten by wattled starlings, redeyed bulbuls and other birds. Propagate the firethorn from seed.

Natural distribution: Very widespread, this plant occurs in a number of different habitats, in all the provinces of South Africa, as well as in Zimbabwe, Botswana and Namibia.

National tree number 392

Flowering time:
October to January

Rothmannia capensis   RUBIACEAE

Wild gardenia

6 m × 4 m

This hardy, well-shaped tree of moderate growth rate is suitable for smaller gardens and has attractive, glossy, leathery, dark green foliage. Its bark is dark brown and slightly rough and it bears large, bell-shaped, sweetly scented cream flowers, with maroon markings in the throat. The round fruits are 5-6 cm in diameter. Seeds germinate easily if removed from the pith before planting. Keep seedlings and young plants moist.

Natural distribution: It grows in forests, kloofs, and on rocky ridges, along the eastern Cape coast, and northwards into Natal, Zululand, Swaziland, the southern, eastern and western Transvaal and Botswana.

National tree number 693

Flowering time:
December to February

Tapiphyllum parvifolium   RUBIACEAE
Small wild medlar, Mountain medlar

4 m × 3 m

An interesting, small, contorted tree, with a strongly branched 'zig-zag' pattern, the small wild medlar is drought resistant, slow growing and suitable for a large rockery, or a smaller townhouse garden. It has fairly smooth, light grey bark and leaves which are covered in dense, fine, soft hairs on both surfaces. Small greenish to yellow-green flowers are followed by edible, rounded, fleshy fruits which are brown or reddish when mature and are eaten by different types of birds. Propagate this tree from seed.

Natural distribution: It usually occurs on rocky koppies and hills, in the Transvaal (especially around Pretoria and Johannesburg), northern Natal, Botswana and northern Namibia.

National tree number 703

Flowering time:
October to December

Vangueria infausta   RUBIACEAE
Wild medlar

5 m × 3 m

The slow-growing, drought-resistant wild medlar has a smooth grey trunk and leaves densely covered with short, soft, golden hairs. The greenish-white to yellowish flowers attract insects and are followed by edible, more or less spherical fruits which contain vitamin C. These are yellow to brown when mature and have a pleasant sour-sweet flavour. Propagate the wild medlar from seed.

Natural distribution: It grows in woodland, on stony koppies, and on sand dunes, from the Transkei and northern Orange Free State to eastern Natal, Swaziland, almost the entire Transvaal, north-western Cape, Botswana, Zimbabwe and Namibia.

National tree number 702

Flowering time:
September to October

Rhamnus prinoides   RHAMNACEAE
Dogwood

4 m × 4 m

A fairly fast-growing evergreen, with attractive dense, glossy, dark green foliage, the dogwood may form a bushy shrub or a multistemmed tree. Suitable for a small garden, it may be used as a hedge or screen plant. It has dark brown bark and small greenish flowers which attract insects. Brightly coloured, round, fleshy fruits the size of a pea are purple when ripe, and are eaten by birds. Propagate the dogwood from seed.

Natural distribution: It grows along streams, in riverine forest and on forest margins, from Swellendam through the eastern Cape, Orange Free State and Lesotho to the Transkei, Natal, Swaziland, eastern and north-eastern Transvaal and Zimbabwe.

National tree number 452

Flowering time:
October to December

Freylinia lanceolata   SCROPHULARIACEAE
Honey-bell bush

5 m × 5 m

The honey-bell bush grows fast if watered well and, as it enjoys moist conditions, can be planted at the edge of a pond or stream, or towards the back of an informal border. It has smooth grey bark and willow-like foliage with drooping branches. Honey-scented, golden-yellow flowers are followed by small brown fruit capsules. Prune the honey-bell bush to keep it neat. It is easily propagated from seed.

Natural distribution: It is usually found growing in moist areas, along streams or on the edge of vleis in the Cape Province, from about Uitenhage in the east to Calvinia in the north.

National tree number 670.1

Flowering time:
Sporadically
throughout the year

Olinia emarginata   OLINIACEAE
Transvaal hard pear

5 m × 3 m

The Transvaal hard pear is a fast-growing, neat, ornamental evergreen with a dense crown of glossy, dark green foliage and very decorative fruits. Its trunk is creamy white, mottled or marked with orange, and the small pink flowers are lightly scented. The fruits are small, round and bright red when ripe. This tree is difficult to propagate from seed or from cuttings.

Natural distribution: It occurs in evergreen forest, along rivers and on rocky hillsides, from about Queenstown in the eastern Cape through the Transkei, Natal and the eastern Orange Free State to the Transvaal.

National tree number 514

Flowering time:
October to January

Rhus leptodictya   ANACARDIACEAE
Mountain karee

5 m × 5 m

The mountain karee, which is evergreen under favourable conditions, is fairly drought resistant and has a moderate growth rate. Well-shaped and hardy, it makes an excellent shade tree for the garden or for street planting and will tolerate most soil types. The trunk is rough, deeply furrowed and either dark brown or grey. It has reddish branches and a rounded, drooping crown of light green leaves. Sprays of very small yellowish flowers are followed by small, shiny, flattened fruits which are yellow-brown to brown when ripe and are eaten by doves and other birds. Propagate this tree from seed, cuttings or from truncheons.

Natural distribution: It occurs in open woodland, on forest margins and rocky hillsides, from the central Orange Free State and northern Cape to the western and central Transvaal, Swaziland, Botswana and Zimbabwe.

National tree number 387

Flowering time:
January to April

Cassine papillosa CELASTRACEAE
Common saffron

6 m × 4 m

With its moderate to slow growth rate, the common saffron is a neat ornamental for the garden. It has a smooth grey trunk and very thin bark with a bright orange underbark which shows through in patches. The leaves are dark green, leathery and thick and the flowers are small and whitish or pale green. The oval, berry-like fruit is pale yellow to pink, becoming red when ripe, and is eaten by birds. Propagate this tree from seed.

Natural distribution: It occurs on the margins of evergreen forest, in dune forest, and on wooded hillslopes, from George through the eastern Cape and Transkei to Natal, Zululand, the eastern Transvaal, Swaziland and Zimbabwe.

National tree number 415

Flowering time:
October to November

Halleria lucida SCROPHULARIACEAE
Tree-fuchsia

4 m × 2 m

Fast growing under favourable conditions, this plant forms a shrubby tree. It has rough, grooved, pale grey bark and bright green foliage. Tubular brick red and orange flowers are borne directly on the branches and are rich in nectar which attracts birds and bees. The edible fruits are fleshy, almost spherical and black when ripe. They are eaten by white-eyes, bulbuls, Cape thrushes, Natal robins and fiscal flycatchers. Propagate this tree from seed or cuttings.

Natural distribution: It grows in a variety of habitats – along streams, on mountain slopes, in deep forest and on forest margins, from the southern, central and eastern Cape to Lesotho, Natal, Zululand, Swaziland, the eastern Orange Free State and the north-western and south-eastern Transvaal.

National tree number 670

Flowering time:
May to December

Portulacaria afra PORTULACACEAE
Spekboom

4 m × 3 m

One of our most valuable fodder plants, the spekboom grows fairly fast and is drought resistant. It may be planted to form a hedge or used as a small tree in a rockery. The succulent, glossy red-brown trunk supports a dense crown of succulent leaves and stems. Small, star-shaped pink flowers, filled with nectar, attract bees and are followed by small, papery, three-winged fruits. The tree is easily propagated from cuttings, which must not be overwatered or they will rot.

Natural distribution: The spekboom grows on dry hillsides and in succulent scrub, and is common in the eastern Cape. It also occurs in Natal and the hot, dry river valleys of the eastern Transvaal.

National tree number 104

Flowering time:
October to November

Vepris lanceolata   RUTACEAE

White ironwood

7 m × 5 m

This plant has a moderate growth rate and may form an attractive, bushy shrub, triangular in shape (if planted in the open), or a tree with a neat rounded crown (if planted amongst other bushes). The smooth, grey to purple-grey trunk bears a crown of soft, light green foliage. When crushed, the leaves smell of lemon. Very small yellowish flowers in dense terminal sprays are followed by smooth, fleshy fruits, black when ripe, which are eaten by redwinged starlings and Layard's bulbuls. Propagate the white ironwood from seed and water young plants well.

Natural distribution: It grows in most forests (inland and coastal), on forest margins and sometimes on sand dunes close to the sea, from the eastern Cape through the Transkei, Natal and Zululand to Swaziland, the eastern and central Transvaal, and Mozambique.

National tree number 261

Flowering time:
December to March

Widdringtonia nodiflora   CUPRESSACEAE

(= *W. cupressoides*)

Mountain cypress

5 m × 4 m

This cypress has a moderate growth rate and a neat conical shape when young, but as it ages it spreads to form a more rounded tree. The grey bark peels off lengthwise to reveal red bark below. The blue-green foliage consists of needle- or scale-like leaves. Male and female cones are borne on the same tree. Propagate this cypress from seed.

Natural distribution: It usually grows on rocky mountainsides, from the south-western Cape, east- and northwards through Natal to the Soutpansberg in the northern Transvaal. The *Widdringtonia cedarbergensis* (Clanwilliam cedar), which is very similar to the *W. nodiflora* but grows up to 10 m tall, occurs on rocky mountain tops in the Clanwilliam district in the Cape (national tree number 19).

National tree number 20

LEFT *Widdringtonia schwarzii*, which is very similar to *W. nodiflora*, but taller growing.

Cones borne
throughout the year

Acacia caffra FABACEAE

Common hook-thorn

9 m × 6 m to

Flowering time:
September to October

The fast-growing common hook-thorn is one of the most attractive and least messy acacias for the garden. Its pale to dark grey bark is shallowly grooved lengthwise and it bears hard, brown, hooked thorns in pairs, which do not 'shed' easily. The sweetly scented flowers are cream to pale yellow and the oblong, straight, flat pods are up to 10 cm long. This tree is readily propagated from seed. To improve germination, pour boiling water over the seeds and allow to soak overnight before sowing.

Natural distribution: It grows in woodland and wooded grassland, on mountain slopes and along streams and rivers, from the eastern Cape to Natal, Zululand, Swaziland, all over the Transvaal and into southern Botswana.

National tree number 162

Acacia karroo FABACEAE

Sweet thorn

8 m × 8 m

Flowering time:
October to February (on and off throughout summer)

This fast-growing acacia makes a good shade tree for the garden. It attracts bees and insects and the leaves, pods and flowers provide excellent fodder. The trunk is dark brown to blackish and the plant has long, straight white thorns, in pairs. The flowers appear on short stalks in sweetly scented golden-yellow balls (each of which is composed of many tiny flowers). Sickle-shaped pods up to 12 cm long follow. Prune the tree to keep it neat. It is easily propagated from seed which has been immersed in boiling water and then soaked overnight.

Natural distribution: This is one of the most widespread trees in South Africa, occurring in all the provinces, in a variety of habitats.

National tree number 172

Bolusanthus speciosus FABACEAE

Tree wisteria

7 m × 4 m

Flowering time:
September to October

Fairly fast growing, given good soil and sufficient water, the tree wisteria is a graceful, neat tree with glossy foliage and drooping sprays of beautiful pea-shaped mauve flowers in spring. The rough bark is dark brown to black. The sprays of flowers are up to 15 cm long and are followed by thin, oblong pods up to 8 cm long, also borne in pendent clusters. Propagate the tree wisteria from seed. Young seedlings must be transplanted with care and protected from frost.

Natural distribution: It occurs in the bushveld of the Transvaal, Swaziland, Zululand, Natal, Zimbabwe and Botswana.

National tree number 222

Brachylaena discolor subsp. *discolor*   ASTERACEAE

Coast silver oak

7 m × 10 m

A dense, widespreading tree/shrub which tolerates pruning and makes an excellent hedge or windbreak, the coast silver oak is fast growing and tolerant of coastal conditions. It has fibrous, light brown bark, leaves which are dark green above and greyish white below and creamy white flowers. Propagate this tree from seed.

Natural distribution: It occurs in coastal woodland and bush, and on the margins of evergreen forest, from Port Alfred to Natal, Zululand and the Transvaal.

National tree number 724

Flowering time:
September to October

Cussonia spicata   ARALIACEAE

Common cabbage tree, Lowveld cabbage tree

8 m × 4 m

An unusual and distinctive tree, well suited to modern architecture, the common cabbage tree is fast growing and has thick grey stems and a corky, fissured bark. It has a widely spreading, roundish crown of large, smooth, palmately compound, dark green leaves. The small, densely packed greenish flowers are borne on erect candlestick-like inflorescences. The flowers and the small fleshy fruits, which are soft and purple when ripe, are eaten by blackeyed bulbuls, Knysna louries, speckled mousebirds, redwinged starlings and many others. Propagate this tree from seed but do not plant it too close to paving or pools – the roots may cause damage.

Natural distribution: It occurs on mountain slopes, in the dry lowveld, on rocky outcrops and in forests in all four provinces of South Africa.

National tree number 564

Flowering time:
November to May

Euclea natalensis   EBENACEAE

Natal guarri

10 m × 10 m

A good screen plant although it has a slow to moderate growth rate, the Natal guarri may form a tree or a dense rounded shrub. The bark is grey to dark grey and smooth to rough. It has a dense, spreading, rounded crown of dark green foliage – young leaves are covered with rusty-coloured hairs while mature leaves are hard, leathery, shiny above and paler below. The plant bears sprays of small, heavily scented, bell-shaped cream flowers but carries male and female flowers on separate trees. The round, fleshy fruits are at first green and become orange, then red and finally black when ripe. They are eaten by a variety of birds, especially green pigeons and glossy starlings. Propagate the Natal guarri from seed and protect young plants from frost.

Natural distribution: It grows in coastal dune bush and open grassland, in forests and on forest margins, on riverbanks and rocky outcrops, from the eastern Cape to Natal, Zululand, Swaziland, the eastern, central and northern Transvaal, Botswana and Zimbabwe.

National tree number 597

Flowering time:
May to January

Euphorbia confinalis subsp. *confinalis*
EUPHORBIACEAE

Lebombo euphorbia

8 m × 2 m

The slow-growing, drought-resistant Lebombo euphorbia is a spiny, succulent tree ideally suited to rockeries in warmer, drier parts of South Africa. It will probably also grow well in a container against a hot north or west wall. A sturdy, straight main stem supports a rather small crown of succulent green branches, each approximately 2 m long. The flowers are small and pale yellow. Fruits are smooth, glossy capsules which are red when mature and the seeds of which are eaten by birds. Propagate this tree from seed, or from cuttings which must be kept fairly dry to prevent rot.

Natural distribution: It grows on rocky hillsides near Punda Maria (northern Kruger National Park), and southwards on the Lebombo Mountains.

National tree number 345

Flowering time:
June to August

RIGHT The fruits of *Euphorbia cooperi*, which are very similar to those of *E. confinalis*.

Euphorbia ingens   EUPHORBIACEAE

Common tree euphorbia

10 m × 9 m

The slow-growing, drought-resistant common tree euphorbia – only for use in large gardens in warmer areas – is a spiny, succulent tree which, when cut, exudes poisonous latex which may cause blindness. The short, straight stem is grey, rough and dented and the short spines (sometimes absent in old trees) occur in pairs. The tree bears a large, dense crown of dark green branches and small yellow-green flowers. The smooth, more or less spherical green fruits are eaten by crested guineafowl, purplecrested louries, blackeyed bulbuls, turtle doves, emeraldspotted wood doves and francolins. Propagate this euphorbia from cuttings, which must be kept fairly dry to prevent rot.

Natural distribution: It grows on rocky outcrops and in flat bushveld and coastal forest, from the south coast of Natal northwards to Zululand, Swaziland and the warmer areas of the Transvaal and Zimbabwe.

National tree number 351

Flowering time:
April to June

Ficus ingens   MORACEAE

Red-leaved rock fig

12 m × 12 m

Fruiting time:
July to February

Ideal for a large rock garden, or for planting on rocky outcrops, this drought-resistant plant grows fairly fast and usually occurs as a short dense tree, creeping over rocks. It has a short, dented stem with silver or yellow-grey bark and beautiful coppery-red spring foliage. The pea-sized figs are white, becoming pink or purple as they ripen, and are popular with bulbuls. Propagate this plant from seed or from cuttings. Young seedlings grow slowly.

Natural distribution: It usually occurs on rocky hillsides, but sometimes in thick bush or along riverbanks, and is widely distributed from the Albany district in the eastern Cape to Natal, Zululand, Swaziland, the eastern, western and northern Transvaal and Zimbabwe.

National tree number 55

Harpephyllum caffrum   ANACARDIACEAE

Wild plum

10 m × 8 m

Flowering time:
February

Its glossy, evergreen foliage and compact shape make this slow-growing plant an excellent ornamental for the garden or for street planting. It has rough bark which may crack into segments. The dark green foliage forms a compact or spreading crown. Small whitish flowers are borne in sprays at the ends of the branches with male and female flowers on separate trees. The plum-like fruit is oblong, fleshy, red when ripe and edible but sour. It is eaten by Knysna louries, Cape parrots and blackeyed bulbuls. Propagate this tree from seed or from truncheons.

Natural distribution: It usually grows in riverine forest, extending from the eastern Cape to Natal, and also in some parts of the Transvaal.

National tree number 361

Ilex mitis   AQUIFOLIACEAE
Cape holly

10 m × 5 m

An attractive ornamental with its crown of glossy, dark green foliage, the Cape holly has a medium to fast growth rate and needs to be well watered – in fact it thrives when planted near water. The whitish to pale grey bark is smooth and both young branches and leaves are red. Small, sweetly scented white flowers are produced in bunches with male and female flowers on separate trees. The small round berries are bright red when ripe and are eaten by a variety of birds. Seed germinates easily and seedlings transplant well. Young plants must be protected from frost.

Natural distribution: It is usually found growing in moist situations, along riverbanks and in moist evergreen forest, in all the provinces of South Africa and in Lesotho, Swaziland and Zimbabwe.

National tree number 397

Flowering time:
September to December

RIGHT Young foliage in spring before the leaves mature to a darker green.

Kirkia wilmsii   SIMAROUBACEAE
Mountain seringa

8 m × 8 m

The mountain seringa has a moderate growth rate and prefers well-drained soil in a warm, sheltered position, particularly in cold areas. This multistemmed or low-branching tree, with its smooth, light to dark grey stems at or near the ground, has a rounded crown of delicate, feathery foliage which turns a beautiful yellow to red-brown in autumn. The leaves tend to be clustered at the ends of the branches as are the compact heads of small greenish-white flowers. The fruits are small, four-angled brown capsules. The mountain seringa is easily propagated from seed or from hardwood cuttings taken in summer.

Natural distribution: It is found growing on rocky mountain slopes (usually granite and dolomite) in the central, northern and eastern Transvaal.

National tree number 269

Flowering time:
October to December

Millettia grandis   FABACEAE
Umzimbeet

8 m × 7 m

A well-shaped, decorative tree, this plant is fairly fast growing and usually evergreen. Its trunk is light brown and flaky. The mature foliage is glossy and dark green and the new foliage reddish and velvety. Long spikes of pea-shaped mauve to purple flowers are borne at the ends of the branches followed by woody, flat pods, covered in velvety golden-brown hairs. Propagate the umzimbeet from seed and water young plants well.

Natural distribution: This is a coastal forest species, occurring north-east of the Kei River, in the Transkei, Natal and Zululand.

National tree number 227

Flowering time:
November to January

Mimusops zeyheri　SAPOTACEAE
Transvaal red milkwood

8 m × 8 m　 to

This slow-growing plant forms an attractive, spreading shade tree or screen plant. The bark, which is grey or dark brown to black, is smooth in young trees to rough in old specimens. Young twigs are covered in rusty-brown hairs. It has a very dense, widely spreading crown of glossy, dark green foliage. The young leaves are rust-coloured and have a velvety undersurface. The flowers are small, white and fragrant. The edible, pleasant-tasting fruit is an oval to roundish, shiny, fleshy berry, 2-3 cm long. Yellow to orange when mature, it has a high vitamin C content. Birds love the berries, especially barbets and green and rameron pigeons. Propagate this tree from seed, and plant in a well-drained position.

Natural distribution: It occurs on rocky hillsides, in wooded grassland and on the margins of evergreen forest, in the Transvaal, Swaziland, Botswana and Zimbabwe.

National tree number 585

Flowering time:
October to January

Olea europaea subsp. *africana*　OLEACEAE
Wild olive

8 m × 6 m　 to

The slow-growing, drought-resistant wild olive is a neatly shaped, rounded tree which makes a good shade or screen plant. The trunk is dark grey and rough and the bark sometimes peels off in strips. The tree has a dense, rounded crown of glossy, grey-green leaves which are dark green above and dull below. Sprays of tiny, lightly scented white or greenish flowers are followed by small, spherical, slightly fleshy fruits which are purple-black when ripe and are popular with birds. Propagate the wild olive from seed or from hardwood cuttings.

Natural distribution: It occurs in a variety of habitats, often near water, in all the provinces of South Africa, and in Zimbabwe and Namibia.

National tree number 617

Flowering time:
October to February

Olea woodiana　OLEACEAE
Forest olive

9 m × 6 m　

This handsome evergreen, with its rounded crown of glossy, dark green foliage and its smooth, pale grey bark, makes an excellent ornamental for the garden. The growth rate is moderate to slow. The tree produces loose sprays of small white flowers and its small oval fruits, which are greenish yellow when ripe, are popular with birds, especially rameron pigeons. Propagate this tree from seed.

Natural distribution: It occurs in evergreen forest and coastal bush, from Port Elizabeth northwards through the Transkei to Natal, Zululand and Swaziland.

National tree number 620

Flowering time:
November or December

Olinia ventosa   OLINIACEAE
Hard pear

12 m × 8 m

This fast-growing evergreen – it grows a metre or more per year – makes a decorative, hardy shade tree which is tolerant of poor or stony soil. The thin bark, which is light-coloured to dark with a reddish tinge, is often ragged and scaly. The tree bears a dense, symmetrical crown of glossy, deep green leaves and bunches of very small, sweetly scented whitish or pinky-white flowers. The hard, pea-sized fruit is coral pink to red when ripe and contains several small seeds. It is eaten by bush doves, speckled and redfaced mousebirds and louries. The seed is slow to germinate, but young plants grow exceptionally fast.

Natural distribution: It occurs in coastal scrub and evergreen forest, and on forest margins and rocky hillsides, from the Cape Peninsula to the Kei River mouth.

National tree number 513

Flowering time:
October to March

Ptaeroxylon obliquum   PTAEROXYLACEAE
Sneezewood

10 m × 6 m

A neat, well-shaped tree for the garden with a slow to moderate growth rate and colourful (yellow, rusty red, bronze) autumn foliage, the sneezewood is said to prefer shale or lime soils. Young trees have pale grey bark while that of old trees is dark grey and fibrous. Usually evergreen, it has a fairly sparse, rounded, poorly spreading crown of glossy, dark green foliage (though the crown may occasionally be dense). Small, sweetly scented, pale yellow flowers are borne in dense clusters with male and female flowers on separate trees. The fruit is a small, two-lobed red-brown capsule. Propagate the sneezewood from seed.

Natural distribution: The tree occurs in a variety of habitats from low-altitude woodland and scrub forest (where it is low growing) to evergreen mountain forest (where it grows into a large, handsome tree). It reaches from the eastern Cape to Natal, Zululand, Swaziland, the eastern and northern Transvaal and into Botswana and Namibia.

National tree number 292

Flowering time:
August to December

Pterocarpus angolensis   FABACEAE

Transvaal teak, Kiaat

10 m × 9 m   to

This distinctive, fairly flat-topped tree, with its circular, bristly pods, makes an interesting and attractive garden subject. Slow growing, it is also fairly drought resistant. The bark is rough and dark and cracked into sections. The tree has a fairly dense, widely spreading, flattened crown of graceful, drooping, light green leaves and long sprays of fragrant, pea-shaped golden-yellow flowers. The round pods are 8-10 cm in diameter, with a thick, bristly centre portion surrounded by a light wing. Before planting, the seeds must either be removed from the pods (which is difficult), or the pods must be filed – in both cases germination is not very good. Truncheons planted in October are said to grow easily.

Natural distribution: This tree is usually found growing in woodland and bushveld, in deep, sandy soil, from northern Natal, Swaziland and the eastern and northern Transvaal to Zimbabwe and northern Namibia.

National tree number 236

Flowering time:
September to November

BELOW LEFT The tree covered in flowers in early spring before the leaves appear.

Pterocarpus rotundifolius subsp. *rotundifolius*

FABACEAE

Round-leaved teak

8 m × 8 m

This graceful tree, with its fairly dense, widely spreading crown of glossy, dark green foliage, makes an excellent ornamental shade tree which is extremely beautiful in full flower. It has a moderate growth rate and is often multistemmed. The bark, which is pale grey to light brown, cracks and peels off in irregular, flat strips. Sweetly scented, brilliant yellow, sweetpea-like flowers with crinkled petals are borne in long sprays. The pods, which are oval and flattened, are swollen in the centre where the seed lies, and are brown when ripe. Propagate this tree from seed.

Natural distribution: It grows in bushveld and woodland, from Zululand through Swaziland and the eastern, central and northern Transvaal to Zimbabwe, Botswana and northern Namibia.

National tree number 237

Flowering time:
September to December

Schefflera umbellifera   ARALIACEAE

Forest cabbage tree

7 m × 3 m

Flowering time:
January

The forest cabbage tree is a slow-growing, attractive ornamental for warmer, subtropical gardens. It must be planted in good soil and watered well. It has smooth grey bark and a dense crown of shiny, palmately compound, leathery, dark green leaves. Small cream flowers are borne in umbels, which stand out above the leaves. The small round berries, which are dark red when mature, are eaten by birds. The seed germinates poorly, and the seedlings grow very slowly.

Natural distribution: It grows in moist, warm forests, from the eastern Cape to the Transkei, Natal, Zululand, Swaziland, the eastern and northern Transvaal and Zimbabwe.

National tree number 566

Schotia brachypetala   FABACEAE

Weeping boer-bean

12 m × 8 m   to

Flowering time:
September or October

This fairly drought-resistant plant forms a widespreading, well-shaped shade tree of moderate growth rate – watering well will speed up its growth. In a warm, moist climate it will have only a short deciduous period at the end of winter. The rough, dark grey bark may break into small blocks which then peel off. The tree bears a dense, round to umbrella-shaped crown of leathery, glossy, dark green foliage – the spring foliage is red to copper-coloured. Deep crimson, cup-like flowers appear in clusters and are rich in nectar, which drips from the flowers and attracts a variety of birds (especially sunbirds) and insects. The big, flattened, woody brown pod, which is about 12 cm long, contains approximately six light brown seeds, each with a lime-green aril covering one end. The tree is easily propagated from seed and grows faster in deep, sandy soil. It should not be planted too close to a patio or driveway – it may damage paving and 'weep' on parked vehicles.

Natural distribution: It occurs in deciduous woodland and dry scrub forest, from Natal northwards to Swaziland, the Transvaal and Zimbabwe.

National tree number 202

ABOVE LEFT A young specimen of *Schotia brachypetala* before it has reached its mature shape.

Schrebera alata　OLEACEAE

Wild jasmine

8 m × 7 m　

A graceful, well-shaped tree suitable for smaller gardens, the wild jasmine is fast growing and often forms a multistemmed tree. The stem is grey-brown and the soft, rough bark breaks off in small sections. The reasonably dense, roundish, poorly spreading crown bears slightly glossy foliage. Although the tree loses some of its leaves, it is virtually evergreen. The sweetly scented, white, pink or wine-coloured (depending on their age) flowers occur in bunches. The fruit is a woody, pear-shaped capsule, brown when mature, which splits to release approximately eight seeds, each with a papery wing. Propagate this tree from seed and protect young plants from frost.

Natural distribution: It grows in evergreen forest and coastal bush, from eastern Natal through Swaziland to the south-eastern and north-western Transvaal and Zimbabwe.

National tree number 612

Flowering time:
December to February

Senna petersiana　FABACEAE

(= *Cassia petersiana*)

Monkey pod, Eared cassia

8 m × 6 m　

A graceful tree with a dense, roundish, slightly spreading crown of glossy, dark green foliage, the monkey pod is fairly fast growing and may form a bushy shrub or the lower branches may be pruned away to encourage a tree-like shape. Under favourable conditions it is evergreen. The bark is rough and dark brown and the tree bears large, showy sprays of dark yellow flowers in late summer to autumn. The pendulous pods are eaten by birds, baboons and monkeys. Propagate the monkey pod from seed and protect young plants from frost.

Natural distribution: This tree is usually found growing in riverine bush, but also occurs in the bushveld and on moist hillsides, from Zululand and Swaziland to the eastern and northern Transvaal and Zimbabwe.

National tree number 213

Flowering time:
February to June

Sideroxylon inerme   SAPOTACEAE

White milkwood

8 m × 8 m   to

Flowering time:
January to July

The white milkwood is a large, dense, spreading evergreen, which may be planted as a shade tree or as a windbreak in coastal areas and which is initially slow growing. The bark is brown and varies from smooth in young trees to black and rough in old trees. The tree has a very dense, roundish, spreading crown of tough, leathery leaves which are dark green and smooth above and paler below. Young leaves are covered with rusty red hairs. The small, unpleasantly scented yellow-green flowers are eaten by speckled mousebirds. A variety of birds eat the round, berry-like fruits which are shiny, smooth and black when ripe. Propagate this tree from seed.

Natural distribution: Though the white milkwood is mainly a coastal species, it does occur inland in riverine bush and open woodland, growing from the Cape Peninsula east- and northwards to Zululand, the Transvaal, Mozambique and Zimbabwe.

National tree number 579

Syzygium cordatum   MYRTACEAE

Water berry

9 m × 7 m 

Flowering time:
September to November

A well-shaped, decorative shade tree which is moderate to fast growing and which must be well watered, the water berry usually occurs near permanent water in its natural habitat. The bark is dark brown, rough and fissured and the dense, roundish, spreading crown is of smooth, leathery, blue-green leaves. The young foliage is bright red. The flowers, which are cream to pale pink and scented, resemble small powder puffs. Borne in terminal sprays, they yield an excellent nectar which attracts bees. Edible but sour, the fruit is an oval, fleshy berry, shiny and smooth and almost black when ripe. It is eaten by many different types of birds. Propagate this tree from seed, which must be very fresh.

Natural distribution: It is a water-loving tree which grows along streams and in riverine bush and swamp areas, from the eastern Cape coast northwards to Natal, Zululand, Swaziland and the central and eastern Transvaal. It also occurs in northern Zimbabwe and northern Botswana.

National tree number 555

Trichilia emetica   MELIACEAE

Natal mahogany

10 m × 10 m 

This handsome evergreen has a very dense, round, widely spreading crown of glossy, dark green foliage and makes an excellent shade tree or screening plant of moderate to fast growth rate. The bark varies from dark grey to brown and from smooth to rough. Scarletbreasted sunbirds and spottedbacked weavers are attracted by the nectar of the compact bunches of small cream-green flowers, which smell of orange blossom. The hard, roundish, wrinkled grey-green fruits each contain one or two black, bean-like seeds, partially covered with a red aril – these are eaten by many different types of birds. Propagate the Natal mahogany from seed. Water young plants well.

Natural distribution: It occurs in open woodland, coastal forest and riverine bush, from north-eastern Natal, Zululand and Swaziland to the eastern and northern Transvaal, Botswana and Zimbabwe.

National tree number 301

Flowering time:
August to October

Ziziphus mucronata   RHAMNACEAE

Buffalo-thorn

9 m × 9 m   to

A well-shaped, widely spreading shade tree, the drought-resistant buffalo-thorn is very hardy, tolerates all types of soil and can be pruned to keep it neat. The leaves can provide fodder for stock in times of drought. It has a moderate to slow growth rate. The bark, which is grey to dark grey and fissured, sometimes peels off in strips. The tree has a fairly dense to sparse, spreading crown with drooping branches of glossy, light to dark green foliage. It bears shiny, smooth, hard, very sharp thorns in pairs, one straight and the other curved backwards. Small bunches of yellow-green flowers produce copious nectar which attracts bees. The pea- to cherry-sized berries are round, red-brown to deep red, smooth and shiny with a leathery skin. A thin layer of sweetish, mealy pulp surrounds a single seed – birds love this pulp. The tree is easily propagated from seed.

Natural distribution: It occurs in a wide variety of habitats in all four provinces of South Africa, and in Zimbabwe, Botswana and Namibia.

National tree number 447

Flowering time:
November to February

Antidesma venosum   EUPHORBIACEAE
Tassel berry

7 m × 5 m to

Flowering time:
October to January

This graceful tree, with its moderate growth rate and short, low-branching, crooked stem, may form a tree or shrub which is evergreen under favourable conditions. The bark is either grey or grey-brown and smooth to rough. The crown of glossy, dark green foliage may be rounded and spreading or slender and drooping – the branch ends always droop. Male (dull yellowish) and female (reddish) flowers are carried on separate trees in spikes approximately 8 cm long. A male and female tree are necessary to produce the long tassels of shiny, brightly coloured fruits, and the tree is particularly beautiful at this stage. These fruits are small, round and fleshy and range in colour from green to yellow, pink, red and then black when ripe. They are eaten by a variety of birds. Propagate the tassel berry from seed.

Natural distribution: It occurs in coastal bush, on forest margins, along riverbanks and in grassland, from Port St. Johns to Zululand, Swaziland, the eastern and northern Transvaal, Botswana, Zimbabwe and northern Namibia.

National tree number 318

Brachylaena rotundata   ASTERACEAE
Mountain silver oak

8 m × 3 m

Flowering time:
August to September

This moderate to fast-growing, neat, compact tree – which may be evergreen under favourable conditions – is suitable for smaller gardens or for planting in a lawn. It has a fissured blackish-brown trunk and a graceful, sparsely spreading crown of dense silver-grey foliage. Sprays of butter-yellow flowers are borne at the ends of the branches with male and female flowers on separate trees. The seeds are small, light and tufted with hairs. The tree is easily propagated from seed and the seedlings transplant well.

Natural distribution: It occurs in open woodland, on rocky ridges and in riverine bush, in the central and western Transvaal, Botswana and Zimbabwe.

National tree number 730

Calodendrum capense RUTACEAE
Cape chestnut

10 m × 4 m

This is one of our most beautiful indigenous trees, especially in full flower. It is a good, decorative shade tree suitable for the garden or for street planting and is fairly fast growing. The smooth, grey trunk offsets the glossy, dark green foliage which turns yellow in autumn. Under favourable conditions it may not lose all its leaves in winter. Slightly scented flowers, ranging from white to pale mauve and marked with purple or wine red, are borne in large terminal sprays. The hard, woody, roundish fruits – approximately 4 cm in diameter – are covered with wart-like protuberances and contain smooth black seeds which are eaten by rameron pigeons. The seed germinates easily and seedlings transplant well. Young plants must be watered well. Deep soil with plenty of compost will speed up growth. The tree can also be propagated from cuttings of half-ripe wood.

Natural distribution: It occurs in forest, kloofs, evergreen fringe forest and scrub, from Swellendam eastwards along the coast to Natal and Zululand, and inland to Swaziland, the eastern and northern Transvaal and Zimbabwe.

National tree number 256

Flowering time:
October to December

Celtis africana ULMACEAE
White stinkwood

10 m × 4 m

The drought-resistant white stinkwood is fast growing (1-2 m per year) if planted in good soil and watered well, and forms a neat, well-shaped tree which can be planted in a lawn to provide shade or used as a street tree. The stem is smooth and pale grey. The spring foliage is pale green and in summer the tree has fairly dense, dark green foliage. Small yellowish flowers are followed by small round fruits, yellow when ripe. These are eaten by Cape and blackeyed bulbuls, mousebirds, blackcollared barbets and others. The tree is easily propagated from seed.

Natural distribution: It occurs in a variety of habitats in all four provinces of South Africa and in Zimbabwe.

National tree number 39

Flowering time:
August to October

Combretum molle COMBRETACEAE
Velvet bushwillow

9 m × 4 m

Flowering time:
September to November

Fairly fast growing, the velvet bushwillow – which is evergreen under favourable conditions – is a neat, graceful tree with attractive fruits and is suitable for planting in a lawn. The bark of the grey-black stems breaks up into small blocks which peel off. It has a fairly dense, poorly spreading crown of leaves which are velvety above and slightly rough below. The foliage turns yellow to bronze in autumn. The spikes of tiny, honey-scented yellowish flowers appear before the leaves. The papery, four-winged fruits are red-brown when mature. The tree is easily propagated from seed.

Natural distribution: It occurs in open woodland and on rocky hillsides (often quartzite), from northern Zululand through the Transvaal (very common around Pretoria and Johannesburg) to Zimbabwe and Botswana.

National tree number 537

Combretum zeyheri COMBRETACEAE
Large-fruited bushwillow

9 m × 6 m

Flowering time:
August to September

Slow growing, this is a good spreading shade tree for the garden and is often multistemmed. The bark of young trees is grey and fairly smooth, but it later becomes rough and mottled. The foliage of the spreading crown turns yellow in autumn. The leaves are hairy when young but, once mature, are almost hairless and leathery. Small, fragrant greenish-yellow flowers are borne in cylindrical spikes. The fruits are large (up to 6 cm in diameter) and four-winged, changing from green to yellow-brown when mature. They remain on the tree long after the leaves have dropped. Propagate this tree from seed.

Natural distribution: It occurs in open woodland, on rocky koppies and along streams, from Natal, Zululand and Swaziland through the Transvaal to Zimbabwe, Botswana and northern Namibia.

National tree number 546

Erythrina lysistemon   FABACEAE
Common coral tree

10 m × 6 m

Flowering time:
July to October

This striking tree, with its bright red flowers, is one of the first to flower in spring. Plant it near to *Dombeya rotundifolia*, which has masses of white flowers, for a lovely spring display. Fast growing and drought resistant, it has smooth, dark grey to grey-brown bark. Both branches and foliage are thorny and the tree has a fairly sparse crown. Beautiful clear scarlet flowers in dense heads of about 9 cm long appear on the bare branches, before the foliage. The fruit is a slender, cylindrical black pod which splits to expose the orange and black seeds inside. These are eaten by the brownheaded parrot. The nectar in the flowers attracts olive, scarletchested and grey sunbirds, and also yellow weavers. Propagate this tree from seed or from truncheons.

Natural distribution: It grows in dry woodland, on rocky koppies and in coastal dune bush and grassland, from Natal northwards to Swaziland, the central, northern and eastern Transvaal and Zimbabwe.

National tree number 245

Faurea saligna   PROTEACEAE
Transvaal beech

8 m × 6 m

Flowering time:
August to February

A slender and graceful tree with red autumn foliage, the Transvaal beech would make a good garden ornamental, but is fairly slow growing. The very rough, deeply grooved bark is blackish, with young branches reddish and inclined to droop. The tree bears a fairly sparse, poorly spreading crown of long, narrow, leathery, shiny grey-green leaves. The young foliage is pink. Drooping spikes of small, honey-scented cream to green flowers contain copious nectar which attracts birds. The fruit is a small nutlet which is covered with soft hairs. The Transvaal beech is difficult to propagate.

Natural distribution: It grows in the Transvaal bushveld and lowveld and in Natal, Zululand, Swaziland, Botswana and Zimbabwe.

National tree number 75

Lonchocarpus capassa   FABACEAE
Apple-leaf

9 m × 6 m

Flowering time:
September to November

This slow-growing, well-shaped tree, with its unusual grey-green foliage, is suitable for planting in a lawn and may be semideciduous under favourable conditions. The bark is creamy brown and varies from smooth to cracked and flaking. The sparse to fairly dense, formless crown bears leaves that are hairless and rough on the upper surface and hairy below. The small, sweetly scented, mauve, sweetpea-like flowers are borne in dense, pendent sprays at the ends of the branches. The fruit is a flat grey-green pod containing several seeds. Propagate this tree from seed and water young plants well to speed up growth.

Natural distribution: It grows in woodland, and sometimes along riverbanks, from Swaziland northwards to the eastern and northern Transvaal, Zimbabwe, northern Botswana and north-eastern Namibia.

National tree number 238

Tabernaemontana elegans   APOCYNACEAE

Toad tree

7 m × 7 m

Its glossy foliage, unusual fruits and fragrant flowers make the moderate to fast-growing toad tree an interesting and decorative shade tree for the garden. The brownish-grey bark is cracked lengthwise into deep, corky segments and the tree has a fairly dense, roundish to spreading crown of smooth, glossy, dark green leaves. The trumpet-shaped, waxy white flowers, which are up to 2 cm in diameter, are borne in loose clusters. The large fruit – 7 cm × 5 cm – is dark green and dotted with pale grey warts, resembling a toad. When mature, it splits to expose bright orange pulp containing many brown seeds. This pulp is eaten by hornbills and white-eared barbets. The tree is easily propagated from seed and must be well watered.

Natural distribution: It grows along riverbanks, in coastal scrub forest, and in woodland, from Zululand and Swaziland to the eastern and north-eastern Transvaal and Zimbabwe.

National tree number 644

Flowering time:
October to February

Terminalia sericea   COMBRETACEAE

Silver cluster-leaf, Silver tree

7 m × 5 m   to

Of moderate growth rate, the silver cluster-leaf is an attractive, well-shaped tree, with silver-grey foliage, suitable for planting in a lawn. The trunk is pale to dark grey and deeply fissured lengthwise. As the branches tend to be horizontal with the ends somewhat drooping, the tree appears to grow in layers. It has a fairly sparse, moderately spreading crown. The unpleasantly scented flowers are small and cream to yellow. The decorative, flat, oval fruits are pink to rose-red when mature. The tree is difficult to propagate as seeds germinate sporadically, and the seedlings tend to damp off easily. It prefers deep, sandy soil and moderate water.

Natural distribution: It is a common species of the sandy bushveld and occurs from north-eastern Natal, Zululand, Swaziland and the south-eastern, central and western Transvaal to Zimbabwe, Botswana, the northern Cape and Namibia.

National tree number 551

Flowering time:
September to December

Nuxia congesta   LOGANIACEAE

Brittlewood, Wild elder

8 m × 6 m

Flowering time:
May to July

The shape and size of this plant are very variable and it may develop into an evergreen shrub or, more usually, a tree with a moderate growth rate. It has rough and stringy, dark brown bark. The rounded crown has its leaves arranged in whorls of three. They may be smooth, velvety or sticky. The small, fragrant, tubular white or cream flowers, which sometimes have a purplish tint, are borne in dense bunches at the ends of the branches. The fruit is a small capsule. Propagate the brittlewood from seed. Young plants grow very slowly.

Natural distribution: It occurs in coastal and evergreen forest, and on rocky koppies, from the eastern Cape through eastern Natal, Zululand and Swaziland to the central, western and south-eastern Transvaal and Zimbabwe.

National tree number 633

Combretum erythrophyllum   COMBRETACEAE

River bushwillow

12 m × 10 m

Flowering time:
August to November

The drought-resistant river bushwillow is a large, widely spreading shade tree suitable for parks and larger gardens. It is fast growing (4,6 m in three years) if given good soil and sufficient water. The stems are smooth, crooked and grey-brown with a yellow tinge and the plant usually forms a multistemmed or low-branching tree. The foliage forms a dense, spreading crown and is a soft delicate green in spring, darker and more glossy when mature, and red in autumn. The small greenish-yellow flowers are lightly scented and the fruits are four-winged and green turning light brown. The seed germinates easily and young plants grow fast.

Natural distribution: It usually grows in moist places, especially along river-banks, from the northern and eastern Cape to Natal, Zululand, Swaziland, the Transvaal (widespread), Botswana and Zimbabwe.

National tree number 536

Galpinia transvaalica   LYTHRACEAE

Transvaal privet, Wild pride-of-India

8 m × 8 m

Flowering time:
January to April

A well-shaped, low-branching shade tree with glossy, dark green foliage, this plant is fast growing under good conditions and usually forms a multistemmed tree. It has smooth, pale grey stems. The faintly scented, cream-white flowers are borne in dense, terminal sprays followed by the fruits, which are small, round red-brown capsules. The seed germinates easily and young plants grow fast and must be protected from frost.

Natural distribution: It occurs in woodland from Zululand and Swaziland to the eastern and north-eastern Transvaal.

National tree number 523

Kiggelaria africana   FLACOURTIACEAE
Wild peach

12 m × 11 m

Flowering time:
August to January

This well-shaped, reasonably robust tree could be planted to provide shade or screening or to serve as a windbreak. It is fast growing and has smooth, pale grey bark which becomes rough with age. The leaves are variable, but may resemble those of the peach. It bears small greenish-yellow flowers. The fruit is a hard, round, knobbly greenish-yellow capsule which splits to expose the shiny black seeds, enclosed in an oily red coat. These are eaten by crowned hornbills, olive woodpeckers, Cape thrushes, Cape robins, Cape white-eyes, boubou shrikes and mousebirds. Propagate the wild peach from seed or cuttings. Young plants are fast growing under good conditions.

Natural distribution: It grows in coastal and inland forest, in bushveld and woodland, along streams and on rocky koppies, from the Cape Peninsula eastwards to Natal, Zululand, Swaziland, Lesotho, the south-eastern and north-eastern Transvaal and Zimbabwe.

National tree number 494

Peltophorum africanum   FABACEAE
Weeping wattle

9 m × 8 m

Flowering time:
October to February

An attractive, widely spreading, low-branching shade tree with fine, feathery foliage and large sprays of bright yellow flowers in summer, the weeping wattle is fairly fast growing under good conditions. It has rough, fissured grey-brown bark. The crown is fairly dense and the large, terminal sprays of pea-shaped, bright yellow flowers are followed by flat, oval grey-brown pods. Easily propagated from seed, young plants transplant well and grow fairly fast. They must be protected from frost.

Natural distribution: It occurs in wooded grassland and on the edges of vleis, from Zululand, Natal, Swaziland and the eastern, central and western Transvaal to Zimbabwe, Botswana and Namibia.

National tree number 215

Diplorhynchus condylocarpon   APOCYNACEAE
Horn-pod tree, Wild rubber

8 m × 8 m

Flowering time:
September to December

Of moderate growth rate, the horn-pod tree occurs either as a shrub or as a graceful tree with drooping foliage and interesting fruits. The bark is grey-brown to blackish and flakes in square sections. The fairly sparse, widespreading or poorly spreading crown has drooping branches and fine, somewhat weeping foliage. The leaves are light to dark green, smooth and glossy. Sprays of small, fragrant white to cream flowers are borne terminally. The fruit consists of a pair of halfmoon-shaped pods with pointed tips. These pods are hard and brown and covered with white spots. Propagate this tree from seed or truncheons.

Natural distribution: It is usually found growing on rocky hillsides, and in open woodland, from the central Transvaal northwards to Zimbabwe, eastern and northern Botswana and northern Namibia.

National tree number 643

Nuxia oppositifolia   LOGANIACEAE

Water elder

7 m × 5 m   to

The water elder – which may be evergreen under favourable conditions – is slow growing, likes wet conditions and is an attractive plant for waterside planting. It may form a shrub or, more usually, a slender, multistemmed tree, with glossy, pale green foliage. The stems are grey-brown, the bark peels off in strips and the branches tend to droop. Small tubular white flowers, which eventually become cream, are borne in dense sprays at the ends of the branches. The fruits are small oval brown capsules. Propagate this tree from seed.

Natural distribution: It grows along rivers and streams, from eastern Natal, Zululand and Swaziland to the northern and eastern Transvaal, Zimbabwe and northern Namibia.

National tree number 635

Flowering time:
October to January

Rhus lancea   ANACARDIACEAE

Karee

7 m × 7 m

With its moderate to fast growth rate – it grows faster if watered well – the drought-resistant karee is a well-shaped, hardy evergreen which makes an excellent shade tree. It could also be used as a street tree or by farmers to form a windbreak. The bark is very dark brown and rough and the branches are reddish brown. The tree has a dense crown of drooping, dark green foliage and bears sprays of minute, sweetly scented greenish-yellow flowers. The small, shiny, slightly flattened, roundish fruit is brown and sometimes sticky when ripe, and is eaten by birds. The plant is easily propagated from seed, cuttings or truncheons.

Natural distribution: It occurs in a variety of habitats, and often on riverbanks, from the Cape Province (except the west coast) and the entire Orange Free State to the southern, central, western and northern Transvaal, Zimbabwe and Namibia.

National tree number 386

Flowering time:
July to September

Rhus pendulina   ANACARDIACEAE

(= *R. viminalis*)

White karee

8 m × 7 m

This karee has a willow-like habit, with attractive, fresh, light green leaves, and makes a lovely shade tree for the garden. It could also be planted as a street tree or windbreak. It is drought resistant and has a moderate to fast growth rate. The grey to brown bark is slightly rough. Sprays of minute greenish-yellow flowers are followed by almost spherical fruits, which are reddish when mature and which are eaten by birds. Propagate the white karee from seed or from cuttings and water young plants well.

Natural distribution: It grows on riverbanks and along the edges of streams in the central Cape and northwards into southern Namibia.

National tree number 396

Flowering time:
September to January

Salix mucronata   SALICACEAE

Cape willow, Wild willow

7 m × 7 m

Flowering time:
August to October
(sometimes March to April)

This is an attractive indigenous willow, with a moderate growth rate, that could be planted near a dam or stream. The rough brown bark scales off in narrow flakes. The dense to sparse crown is of drooping, light green, willow-like foliage. Small yellowish flowers are borne in short spikes with male and female flowers on separate trees. The fruits are small capsules, which split to release tufted, woolly seeds. The tree is easily propagated from cuttings or from truncheons.

Natural distribution: It occurs along rivers and streams in the southern Orange Free State, the Cape Province (except the far north and the west coast), and southern Namibia.

National tree number 36.1

Acacia erioloba   FABACEAE

Camel thorn

9 m × 7 m

Flowering time:
July to October

The drought-resistant camel thorn is a handsome, umbrella-shaped tree which grows very slowly. It has deeply furrowed, grey to blackish-brown bark and brown thorns, which are from 1-5 cm long, straight or slightly curved, and often inflated at the base. The crown is dense and widespreading. The sweet-smelling flowers form golden-yellow balls and are followed by thick, hard, halfmoon-shaped pods covered with velvety grey hairs. They are highly nutritious and can be eaten by stock. The seed is difficult to germinate, even after immersing it in boiling water and soaking overnight. Water young plants well.

Natural distribution: It occurs in dry woodland and arid, stony or sandy areas, from the northern Cape eastwards to the western Orange Free State, the western and central Transvaal and northwards into Namibia, Zimbabwe and Botswana.

National tree number 168

Acacia tortilis subsp. *heteracantha*   FABACEAE

Umbrella thorn

9 m × 7 m

Flowering time:
November to January

This extremely thorny, slow-growing and drought-resistant acacia can form an attractive, fairly flat-topped, spreading shade tree if the lower branches are pruned. The fissured bark is grey to dark brown. Two types of thorn appear on the tree – the one is long, straight and white, and the other small, hooked and brown. The foliage is very fine and a blue-grey-green colour. The flowers appear in masses of small, round, fragrant balls, white to pale yellow in colour. The small, narrow pods, which are rich in protein and can be eaten by cattle, are twisted and contorted. The umbrella thorn is easily propagated from seed that has been immersed in boiling water and soaked overnight.

Natural distribution: It grows in drier types of woodland in the northern Cape, north-eastern Natal, the western Orange Free State and the Transvaal (except the extreme south), Swaziland, Botswana, Zimbabwe and Namibia.

National tree number 188

Leucadendron argenteum PROTEACEAE

Silver tree

7 m × 3 m

Flowering time:
August to September

A beautiful ornamental tree with lovely silky silver-grey foliage, the silver tree is conical in shape when young, but becomes more spreading as it ages. It is fast growing and will reach 6-7 m in eight years. The smooth grey bark bears horizontal leaf scars. Male and female flowers are borne on separate trees, the male flowers – apricot in colour with a silver sheen – in short compact heads. The female flowers develop into silvery 'cones', held upright on the tree. They ripen in autumn, to release the small black seeds. The silver tree is easily propagated from seed. It likes acid soil, good drainage and ventilation but no root disturbance. Do not apply artificial fertiliser but do provide a thick mulch of pine needles.

Natural distribution: The silver tree occurs in the Cape Peninsula and is abundant on the eastern slopes of Table Mountain.

National tree number 77

Podocarpus falcatus PODOCARPACEAE

Outeniqua yellowwood

12 m × 4 m

Cones produced:
September to May

This is an attractive evergreen for the garden which is slow growing at first, but which, once established, grows fast. It is conical in shape when young, but spreads as it ages. The bark is greyish brown to dark brown and peels off in rough, curled, circular or rectangular flakes. The small, dark green leaves have a greyish bloom. The male cones are about 10 mm × 3 mm and the seeds are large, fleshy, spherical and deep yellow when ripe, and are eaten by bats and birds. Very fresh seed, sown as soon as possible after collection, germinates the fastest.

Natural distribution: It grows in coastal swamp forest as well as mountain forest, from Swellendam eastwards and northwards to the northern Transvaal and Mozambique.

National tree number 16

Podocarpus henkelii PODOCARPACEAE

Henkel's yellowwood

10 m × 4 m

Cones produced:
September to January

This fairly slow-growing evergreen has dense, drooping, glossy, dark green foliage and makes an attractive ornamental or screen plant. Its yellowish-grey to brown bark peels off in long narrow strips to expose red-brown underbark. The individual leaves are long and narrow. Male cones are about 3 cm × 0,4 cm. In the female cones the stalk remains green. The seeds are large, oval and olive green in colour. The tree is easily propagated from seed and must be well watered.

Natural distribution: It occurs in evergreen mountain forest, and sometimes in coastal forest, in East Griqualand and southern Natal.

National tree number 17

Acacia galpinii   FABACEAE

Monkey thorn

18 m × 16 m

Flowering time:
September to October

The monkey thorn is one of our largest acacias and is suitable for large gardens and parks. It is fast growing and fairly drought resistant. The bark, which is whitish yellow, cork-like and very flaky, becomes darker with age. The paired, shiny brown thorns are short, strong and hooked. It has a fairly dense, rounded crown of feathery, light green foliage. The flowers, in creamy yellow to yellow spikes tinged with red, are honey-scented and attract bees. The fruit is a reddish to purple-brown pod and is about 8-20 cm × 2,5 cm. The monkey thorn is easily propagated from seed that has been immersed in boiling water and soaked overnight. Do not plant it near paving or driveways – its roots will lift and damage them as it grows.

Natural distribution: It occurs in wooded grassland and along streams in the Transvaal bushveld, Zimbabwe and Botswana.

National tree number 166

Albizia versicolor   FABACEAE

Large-leaved false-thorn

12 m × 14 m   to

Flowering time:
October to November

This is a beautiful, sturdy, spreading tree of moderate growth rate suitable for larger gardens. The stem is long and bare and the bark grey, rough and broken into small blocks. There is a fairly dense, spreading, roundish to nearly umbrella-shaped crown of feathery, dark green foliage. The young leaves are red-brown and the tree produces large, half-spherical, fluffy heads of creamy white or yellow flowers – sometimes with a reddish tinge. The large – about 20 cm × 5 cm – flat, oblong pods change colour from green to yellow-green, then wine red and finally pale brown when ripe. These pods are said to be poisonous to cattle. Propagate this tree from seed and protect young plants from frost.

Natural distribution: It occurs in various types of open woodland, from northern Natal to Swaziland, the northern and eastern Transvaal, Zimbabwe, northern Botswana and northern Namibia.

National tree number 158

Croton sylvaticus EUPHORBIACEAE

Forest fever-berry

12 m × 10 m

Flowering time:
October to December

A fast-growing decorative shade tree for warmer gardens, and particularly beautiful when covered with bunches of bright orange fruits, the forest fever-berry can be evergreen under favourable conditions. The bark is smooth and pale grey, becoming darker and rougher with age. The tree has a dense, spreading, rounded crown of dark green foliage. Spikes of cream to pale yellow flowers are followed by rounded, pea-sized capsules, bright orange when ripe and borne in pendent clusters. They are eaten by forest weavers, cinnamon doves, green pigeons, hornbills and redeyed turtle doves. Propagate this tree from seed and protect young plants from frost.

Natural distribution: It grows in coastal and inland forest, often along streams, from Port St Johns through Natal, Zululand, Swaziland and the eastern and northern Transvaal to Zimbabwe.

National tree number 330

Ekebergia capensis MELIACEAE

Cape ash

12 m × 12 m

Flowering time:
September to November

The Cape ash is a beautiful shade tree for parks and larger gardens. It has a moderate to fast growth rate and is usually evergreen. The bark, which is grey to brown and either smooth or rough, sometimes flakes. The stems become fluted and dented when old. There is a dense, widespreading crown of glossy, dark green foliage and the branch ends tend to droop. Sweetly scented, small white flowers are borne in sparse sprays with male and female flowers on separate trees. The round, fleshy, berry-like fruits, about the size of a cherry, are borne in pendent clusters. They are smooth, shiny, bright red when ripe, and are eaten by a variety of birds. Fresh seed germinates well, and the young plants grow reasonably fast given good soil and sufficient water. They must be protected from frost for the first few years.

Natural distribution: It occurs in coastal and inland forest, as well as riverine forest and scrub, from the eastern Cape to Swaziland, the Transvaal, Zimbabwe and northern Botswana.

National tree number 298

Ficus sycomorus   MORACEAE

Sycamore fig

12 m × 14 m

The sycamore fig is a good shade tree for larger, warmer gardens. Slow growing, it may be evergreen under favourable conditions. It has a short, very thick, deeply fluted trunk with a smooth, yellow to creamy brown stem, the outer bark of which may flake off. The crown of light to dark green foliage is very dense and widespreading. The round fruits, which are up to 3 cm in diameter, are carried in branched masses on the trunk and main branches, and are yellowish to reddish when ripe. Edible and reasonably tasty, they are eaten by a variety of birds. Propagate this tree from seed, cuttings or truncheons. Seedlings grow very slowly, whereas cuttings or truncheons produce faster results.

Natural distribution: It grows in mixed woodland and riverine bush, and along riverbanks, from northern Natal, Zululand and Swaziland through the eastern and northern Transvaal to Zimbabwe and northern Namibia.

National tree number 66

Fruiting time:
July to December

Khaya nyasica   MELIACEAE

Red mahogany

15 m × 10 m

A beautiful tree for parks and larger gardens in warmer areas, the red mahogany is fast growing under good conditions. The bark is grey to brown and mainly smooth, but it may flake in characteristic scales. The crown is dense and sometimes widespreading, but is usually more compact and poorly spreading. The leaves are large, glossy and light to dark green. Sprays of sweetly scented white flowers are followed by large, oval creamy-brown capsules which are 3-5 cm in diameter. Propagate the red mahogany from seed.

Natural distribution: It occurs in evergreen forest and riverine fringe forest in Zimbabwe and Mozambique.

Flowering time:
September to December

Xanthocercis zambesiaca   FABACEAE

Nyala tree

15 m × 15 m

A good shade tree for large gardens and parks in warmer areas, the nyala tree is slow growing and usually evergreen under favourable conditions. Old stems are deeply fluted and dented and the bark is rough and brown or light grey tinged with yellow. The branch ends of the very dense, rounded, widespreading crown of glossy, dark green foliage are pendent and bear terminal sprays of small, rose-scented cream-white flowers. The edible fruit is plum-shaped, about 2,5 cm long, and has a smooth brown skin enclosing one shiny black seed in a thin fleshy pulp. Grey and yellowbilled hornbills, green pigeons, brownheaded parrots, francolin and guineafowl all love these fruits. The seed germinates well, but seedlings tend to damp off easily. Protect young plants from frost.

Natural distribution: It usually grows in deep, sandy soil along rivers in the eastern and northern Transvaal and Zimbabwe.

National tree number 241

Flowering time:
September to December

Acacia albida FABACEAE
Ana tree

15 m × 10 m   to

This is one of the largest acacias, and is suitable for medium to large gardens and for parks. Fairly drought resistant, it is also one of the fastest growing indigenous trees and increases its height by about 1,5 m per year. The bark of older trees is rough and dark brown while that of young trees is smooth and greenish grey. The tree has straight pale-coloured thorns in pairs, and these are up to 4 cm long. Young trees are slender but older trees have widespreading crowns with pendent branches. The foliage is soft, feathery and blue-green in colour. Small creamy yellow flowers are borne in spike-like inflorescences. The large pods are red or orange-brown when mature, and are twisted, curled and intertwined. Propagate this tree from seed that has been immersed in boiling water and soaked overnight. Protect young plants from frost.

Natural distribution: It grows in woodland and along riverbanks, in the eastern and northern Transvaal, Mozambique, Zimbabwe, eastern and northern Botswana and north-western Namibia.

National tree number 159

Flowering time:
May to September

Acacia xanthophloea FABACEAE
Fever tree

12 m × 10 m   to

As the most striking features of this graceful and fast-growing acacia are its smooth, powdery, yellow-green trunk and branches, the tree should be planted where these can be seen to advantage. It has a slender to spreading, sparse, usually roundish crown of feathery, light green foliage and long, straight, paired white thorns. The sweetly scented golden-yellow flowers appear as fluffy balls. The fruit is a small, straight, thin, papery, light brown pod. The tree is easily propagated from seed that has been immersed in boiling water and soaked overnight. Protect young plants from frost.

Natural distribution: It always grows near rivers and swamps, from Zululand and Swaziland to the eastern and northern Transvaal, Zimbabwe, Botswana and Mozambique.

National tree number 189

Flowering time:
September to November

Kirkia acuminata   SIMAROUBACEAE
White seringa

12 m × 12 m   to

Flowering time:
October to November

A well-shaped, graceful tree which has striking golden to red autumn foliage, the white seringa is suitable for gardens in warmer areas. It is fairly drought resistant and has a moderate to fast growth rate. The bark is smooth and grey but becomes flaky with age. The crown of feathery, light green foliage is rather sparse, widespreading and fairly flat-topped but can sometimes be rounded. Terminal sprays of small white flowers are followed by woody, four-angled, light brown capsules. Easily propagated from seed or from truncheons, young plants must be protected from frost and planted in sandy soil in a sheltered position.

Natural distribution: It grows in deep sandy soil, or on rocky koppies, in the bushveld and lowveld of the north-eastern Transvaal, Zimbabwe, eastern Botswana, Zimbabwe and north-western Namibia.

National tree number 267

Acacia sieberiana var. *woodii*   FABACEAE
Paperbark thorn

12 m × 14 m

Flowering time:
September to November

This is one of our most striking acacias, and five or six trees planted fairly close together (on a large property) make an impressive group. The tree is fast growing given good soil and water. It has an attractive, corky, yellow-grey stem with bark that peels off in papery strips and long, strong, straight white thorns that occur in pairs. The flat-topped, spreading crown is of feathery, light green foliage. The flowers appear as cream to pale yellowish balls. The creamy brown pods, which are straight, thickened, woody and sometimes covered with velvety hairs, have a heavy, sweet scent. Grey hornbills crack open the pods and eat the seeds. This acacia is easily propagated from seed that has been immersed in boiling water and soaked overnight. Protect young plants from frost.

Natural distribution: It occurs in woodland, wooded grassland and along riverbanks, from Natal (except the extreme north-east), Zululand and Swaziland to the central, south-eastern and northern Transvaal, Zimbabwe, northern and eastern Botswana and north-western Namibia.

National tree number 187

Albizia adianthifolia   FABACEAE
Flat-crown

12 m × 14 m

This well-shaped, spreading, flat-topped shade tree has a moderate growth rate and is suitable for large gardens or parks in warmer areas. The bark is grey to grey-brown, and flakes off in small patches from the long bare stem. The crown of attractive, dark green foliage is dense and flat to umbrella shaped. The spring foliage is pale yellow-green. The tree bears spidery, half-spherical inflorescences of greenish-white flowers which are sweetly scented and contain copious nectar that attracts insects and sunbirds. These are followed by flat, papery, pale brown pods. Easily propagated from seed, young plants must be protected from frost.

Natural distribution: It grows in open forest and on forest margins, along the coast from Port St Johns through Natal, Zululand and Swaziland, and inland to the eastern and northern Transvaal and Zimbabwe.

National tree number 148

Flowering time:
August to November

Widdringtonia schwarzii   CUPRESSACEAE
Willowmore cedar

15 m × 4 m

This slow-growing conifer is a neat and attractive ornamental for the garden. The reddish-grey bark is thin, fibrous and flaking. It bears a dense 'conical' crown of dark green, needle- or scale-like foliage. Young trees are tall and slender with older trees tending to be more spreading. The male cones are very small, while the female cones are woody and about 2 cm long, with four rough, warty valves that open to release flat, dark, winged seeds from which the tree may be propagated.

Natural distribution: It occurs on the rocky southern face of the Baviaanskloof and Kouga mountains in the Willowmore area of the Cape Province.

National tree number 21

Cones at various stages of development can be found on the trees throughout the year

2 SHRUBS

Indigenous shrubs offer such a large variety of shapes, textures and foliage and flower colours that their effective use will contribute greatly to making your garden interesting and attractive. The fruits, seeds and nectar of many of these plants attract a wide variety of birds and this alone makes them well worth growing.

When planning the layout of your garden, always bear in mind the ultimate size of a shrub when fully grown and allow enough room for the plant to spread so that it can reach its full potential without having to be pruned merely to control its size. The approximate height and spread of each shrub have been given in the text to assist you in your planning.

To facilitate your choice the shrubs discussed in this book have been divided into categories of small, medium and large according to their height. As many small trees can also be used as background shrubs before they reach their full height, a few plants included in the section on small trees have been repeated here under large shrubs. If you are looking for a large shrub you might also find a useful plant by consulting pp. 14-55 of the previous chapter.

Most shrubs can be planted in the same way as trees (see p. 13) but usually grow more vigorously if planted into well-prepared flowerbeds (see p. 227) which have been enriched with plenty of compost and organic matter. Feed with slow-release fertiliser (3:2:1 for foliage shrubs and 3:1:5 for flowering shrubs) at two-monthly intervals throughout the growing season. Shrubs that have been planted in a lawn need to be fed and watered particularly well as the grass will compete with the plants for moisture and nutrients. Leave a grass-free circle around the base of the plant to facilitate mulching, watering and feeding.

If proteas, ericas, leucospermums and leucadendrons are to be cultivated successfully, it is important to note that they have special requirements. They should always be planted in a well-ventilated spot and never in a hot corner without any air movement. These plants prefer light and porous acid soil, i.e. with a pH of approximately 5, to which plenty of lime-free compost – made from pine needles or wattle leaves – has been added. If you do not have acid soil, aluminium sulphate can be sprinkled around the base of the shrubs to remedy this. Apply about two handfuls per square metre and water well. Repeat after six weeks. This should be done twice a year to maintain the acidity of the soil. These plants will also under no circumstances tolerate artificial fertiliser or manure. Always mulch with an acidic organic mulch (at least 10 cm thick) and repeat regularly. This type of mulch can consist of pine needles, peat moss, wattle leaves and bark, well-rotted sawdust or oak leaves. Mulching keeps the root area moist and cool and suppresses weed germination. Do not disturb their roots by digging or weeding around these plants.

If shrubs that originate in the winter rainfall region are grown in the summer rainfall area they must be kept well watered during the dry winter months. Gardeners in the winter rainfall areas will, however, water less in winter.

Pruning can be used both to extend a shrub's life span and to ensure the regular formation of better quality flowers. Some shrubs require only occasional trimming to remove dead flowers or branches to keep them neat. It is usually better to prune after flowering. Use good quality, sharp secateurs and make the cut just above a leaf bud. Choose a bud pointing in the same direction as you would like the new branch to grow. When removing an unwanted branch, cut flush against the healthy stem without leaving a stump. First saw upwards from underneath and then downwards from above to meet the bottom cut. This will prevent a strip of bark from being torn off when the branch falls.

Agathosma ovata   RUTACEAE
Oval-leaf buchu

1,75 m × 1 m to

This fairly fast-growing shrub has aromatic, heath-like foliage and tiny, star-shaped white to pink flowers. Plant it in light, well-drained soil, adding plenty of compost and/or peat, and water well in winter but less in summer. At the coast it can tolerate full sun, but inland prefers light shade for part of the day. Propagate the oval-leaf buchu from seed sown in autumn or from cuttings, and protect young plants from frost.

Natural distribution: This plant usually grows on mountain slopes in the south-western and southern Cape, Natal and Lesotho.

Flowering time:
Spring

Aloe striatula var. *caesia*   ASPHODELACEAE
Basuto kraal aloe

1 m × 1 m

This is a fast-growing aloe which forms a dense, rounded shrub with succulent grey foliage. Spikes of delicate red flowers with yellow tips cover the bush in spring and autumn. Plant it in well-drained, compost-enriched soil and water well in summer; keep dry in winter. Prune this aloe back by about a third to a half in autumn to keep it neat and to encourage bushiness. It is easily propagated from cuttings, which must be kept fairly dry to prevent rot.

Natural distribution: It grows in the eastern Cape and Lesotho.

Flowering time:
Spring and autumn

Anisodontea scabrosa   MALVACEAE
Pink mallow

1,8 m × 1,8 m to

A rewarding shrub which flowers for a long time, the pink mallow is fairly fast growing and erect with three-lobed, dull, soft green leaves and masses of small-ish – approximately 2 cm in diameter – pink-mauve flowers, marked with dark pink streaks. Mass plant to form a ground cover, plant in an informal border, or use as a temporary filler until slower shrubs have grown and established themselves. The pink mallow grows easily in any soil, but add plenty of compost for better results. Water well in summer but less in winter. Prune the plant back by about a third in autumn to keep it neat. Propagate from seed or from cuttings.

Natural distribution: It grows along the coastal strip from the south-western Cape through the southern and eastern Cape to Port St Johns in the Transkei.

Flowering time:
Spring to autumn

Athanasia crithmifolia   ASTERACEAE

Klaas-Louw bush

1 m × 1 m

Flowering time:
Spring

This fast-growing shrub has grey-green foliage and masses of tiny yellow flowers arranged in flat heads. Plant the Klaas-Louw bush in large groups. It also makes a good temporary filler. Plant it in light, well-drained, compost-enriched soil, and water well in winter. At the coast it will tolerate full sun, but inland prefers light shade for part of the day. Cut the plant back after flowering. Propagate from seed sown in autumn or spring, or from cuttings. In very cold areas it is preferable to plant the seed in August/September. Protect seedlings from frost.

Natural distribution: It grows in the south-western Cape.

Athanasia trifurcata   ASTERACEAE

Kouterbossie

1,5 m × 1,5 m

Flowering time:
Spring

The kouterbossie is fairly fast growing and has attractive grey foliage and flat heads of tiny yellow flowers. Plant this shrub in groups of three to five, or mass plant to form a ground cover. It also makes a good temporary filler until slower shrubs have grown and established themselves. Plant it in light, well-drained, compost-enriched soil and water well in winter but less in summer. Cut the plant back after flowering. Propagate from seed sown in autumn or spring, or from cuttings. Protect seedlings from frost.

Natural distribution: It grows in the south-western and south-eastern Cape.

Barleria albostellata   ACANTHACEAE

Grey barleria

1,75 m × 1 m   to

Flowering time:
Spring and
throughout summer

The grey barleria is fairly fast growing, has attractive woolly grey foliage and heads of tubular white flowers and forms a dense, rounded shrub. Plant in groups of three to five, in light shade under trees, or in an informal border, in good, well-drained soil, adding plenty of compost. Water well in summer, but less in winter. Deadhead the bush to keep it neat. Propagate the grey barleria from seed.

Natural distribution: It occurs in the woodland of the northern Transvaal and Zimbabwe.

Barleria obtusa   ACANTHACEAE

Bush violet

1 m × 1 m   to

Flowering time:
Autumn

This is a fast-growing shrub with small, soft, oval leaves covered in silky hairs, and masses of tubular blue-mauve or white flowers. Plant in a protected position in good, well-drained soil, adding plenty of compost, and water well in summer. Prune the plant back hard after flowering. It is easily propagated from seed or from cuttings; pinch out young shoots to encourage bushiness.

Natural distribution: It grows on rocky koppies and in grassland, from the eastern Cape to the Transkei, Natal, Swaziland and the Transvaal.

Barleria repens   ACANTHACEAE

Small bush violet

50 cm × 50 cm   to

Flowering time:
Autumn

This is a fast-growing shrub with slightly shiny, soft, green foliage and tubular blue-mauve flowers. Mass plant in partial shade under trees to form a ground cover, or plant along the edge of an informal border, or in a lightly shaded rockery. This shrub requires good, light, well-drained soil, with plenty of compost added. Water well in summer but less in winter. Prune the plant back after flowering to keep it neat. It is easily propagated from cuttings; pinch out young shoots to encourage bushiness.

Natural distribution: It grows in northern Natal.

Barleria rotundifolia   ACANTHACEAE

Spiny yellow barleria, Yellow barleria

1 m × 1 m    to

Flowering time:
Summer

Of moderate growth rate, this spiny shrub has small, shiny green leaves, and attractive tubular yellow flowers. Plant it in groups of three to five, in light shade under trees or use it to form a low-growing, thorny hedge or barrier. It could also be planted in a rockery, or along a lightly shaded pathway. The spiny yellow barleria requires good, well-drained soil with plenty of compost added, and must be watered well in summer. Propagate from seed or from cuttings.

Natural distribution: It grows in the Transvaal lowveld.

Chironia baccifera GENTIANACEAE

Christmas berry

45 cm × 45 cm

A fast-growing shrub, the Christmas berry has small, narrow, fleshy, dark green leaves and starry, bright pink flowers, followed by red berries. Plant it approximately 30 cm apart, and place the plants in groups, either at the edge of a pond, in a rockery or as a border along the front edge of a flowerbed. The soil must be good, light, well drained and contain plenty of compost. Keep moist throughout the year. The plants are at their best for two to three seasons, after which they should be replaced. Propagate from seed sown in spring.

Natural distribution: It grows in Natal and the Cape Province.

Flowering time:
November to January

Coleonema album RUTACEAE

White confetti bush

1 m × 0,75 m

With its moderate growth rate, fine, heath-like foliage and masses of tiny white flowers, the white confetti bush may be planted singly or in groups and is suitable for a large rockery or an informal border. It is wind resistant and tolerant of coastal conditions. Plant this shrub in light, well-drained soil containing plenty of compost. Water well in autumn and winter. The plant can be lightly pruned, if necessary. It is easily propagated from seed or from cuttings.

Natural distribution: It grows in the south-western Cape.

RIGHT The flowers of *Coleonema pulchrum*, which are similar to those of *C. album*.

Flowering time:
Winter and spring

Coleonema pulchellum RUTACEAE

Dark pink confetti bush

1,5 m × 1,5 m

This shrub has a moderate growth rate and fine, heath-like foliage with masses of small bright pink flowers. Plant singly or in groups. It may be used to form a hedge or planted in a large rockery or an informal border. The dark pink confetti bush is wind resistant and tolerant of coastal conditions. Plant it in light, well-drained soil containing plenty of compost. Water well in autumn and winter. The plant can be lightly pruned, if necessary. It is easily propagated from seed or from cuttings.

Natural distribution: It grows along the southern Cape coast.

Flowering time:
Winter and spring

Coleonema pulchrum   RUTACEAE

Pink confetti bush

1,5 m × 1,5 m

Of moderate growth rate and with fine, heath-like foliage and masses of tiny pink flowers, the pink confetti bush can be planted close together to form a hedge or screen, or used in a rockery or a shrub border. The plant is wind resistant and tolerant of coastal conditions. It requires light, well-drained soil containing plenty of compost. Water well in autumn and winter. The pink confetti bush can be lightly pruned, if necessary. It is easily propagated from seed or from cuttings.

Natural distribution: It grows in the south-western Cape, and as far east as Uitenhage.

Flowering time:
Winter and spring

Crassula ovata   CRASSULACEAE

(= *C. portulacea*)

Pink joy

1,8 m × 1,5 m

This fast-growing plant forms a large, rounded shrub with succulent, dark green leaves. In winter it is covered in masses of star-shaped, pale pink flowers. Plant the shrub in a sheltered position to prevent frost damage to the flowers. It is wind resistant and tolerant of coastal conditions, and ideal for a rockery, or for an informal shrub border in hotter, drier areas. It grows easily in any well-drained soil – add plenty of compost and water sparingly in summer. Propagate the pink joy from cuttings, which must be kept fairly dry to prevent rot.

Natural distribution: It grows in the south-eastern Cape and the Little Karoo.

Flowering time:
May to July

Dietes bicolor   IRIDACEAE

Yellow wild iris

1 m × 1 m

This fast-growing, drought-resistant plant forms a large clump of strap-shaped, light green leaves, each nearly a metre long and softly drooping at the ends. The flowers, which are lemon yellow and spotted with black, are carried on long stalks. Plant the yellow wild iris in large groups, or singly, as an accent plant at the edge of steps or next to a pond. It grows in any soil, but add plenty of compost, and water regularly throughout the year. It is easily propagated from seed sown in September, or by dividing up large clumps, which spread by means of rhizomes.

Natural distribution: It occurs in and around Bathurst in the eastern Cape.

Flowering time:
October to January

Dietes grandiflora   IRIDACEAE
Wild iris

1 m × 1 m   to

The wild iris is a fast-growing, drought-resistant plant which forms large clumps of stiff, strap-shaped, dark green leaves, each approximately a metre long. The large white-orange-and-mauve flowers are carried on long stalks. Mass plant this shrub in light shade under trees to form a ground cover, or use singly as an accent plant next to a pond, steps or an attractive rock. This plant is slightly more tolerant of drought and poor soil than the previous species. It is easily propagated from seed sown in September, or by dividing up large clumps, which spread by means of rhizomes.

Natural distribution: It occurs from Kentani in the eastern Cape to the Durban area in Natal.

Flowering time:
November to January

Dyschoriste rogersii   ACANTHACEAE
Blue joy, Blue surprise

50 cm × 50 cm

This is a fairly fast-growing, small, sparse shrub, each stem of which is covered in tiny blue flowers. Mass plant, about 20 cm apart, to form a ground cover in a large sunny bed, or plant in a rockery or an informal shrub border. The blue joy requires good soil, containing plenty of compost, and must be watered well in summer. Cut the plant back after flowering to keep it neat. Propagate this shrub from cuttings.

Natural distribution: It grows in the northern and eastern Transvaal and in Swaziland.

Flowering time:
Spring to autumn

Eriocephalus africanus   ASTERACEAE
Wild rosemary

1,75 m × 1,75 m

The wild rosemary is fast growing and has aromatic, semisucculent grey-green foliage. Masses of small white flowers, borne at the ends of the branches, are followed by woolly white seedheads. Plant this shrub in groups of three to five, or mass plant on a sunny bank to form a ground cover. Water well throughout the year. Propagate the wild rosemary from seed sown in March, or from cuttings.

Natural distribution: It is found throughout the Cape Province, but especially near the coast.

Flowering time:
June to October

Eumorphia prostrata   ASTERACEAE
Silver cloud

0,5 m × 1 m

As its common name implies, this fast-growing shrub has soft, silver-grey foliage and small white flowers. Mass plant the silver cloud to form a ground cover on a bank or steep slope. This plant must have very well-drained soil or it will tend to die back in the rainy season (or if overwatered). Propagate from cuttings.

Natural distribution: It grows in the Natal Drakensberg, Lesotho and the north-eastern Cape.

Flowering time:
January to April

Euphorbia caput-medusae   EUPHORBIACEAE
Medusa's head

30 cm × 30 cm

This spineless, dwarf succulent with cream-green flowers at the ends of the stems has a moderate growth rate. It contains a milky sap which may irritate the skin and eyes. Plant it in a rockery or in a container, in light, well-drained soil containing compost and coarse riversand. Water sparingly. Propagate this succulent from cuttings, which must be planted in coarse riversand and kept fairly dry to prevent rot.

Natural distribution: It occurs on rocky outcrops in the south-western Cape.

Flowering time:
Summer

Euphorbia schinzii   EUPHORBIACEAE
Schinz's euphorbia

30 cm × 30 cm

This is a slow-growing, spiny, dwarf succulent which produces yellow flowers along its stems. It contains a milky latex which may irritate the eyes and skin. Plant Schinz's euphorbia in a rockery or group it together with a few other small succulents in a container to form a miniature rock garden. The soil must be light and very well drained, and must contain compost and coarse riversand. Propagate this succulent from cuttings planted in coarse riversand and kept fairly dry to prevent rot.

Natural distribution: It grows on rocky outcrops in the Transvaal, from Pretoria eastwards to Lydenburg.

Flowering time:
August or September

Euryops pectinatus   ASTERACEAE
Grey euryops, Golden daisy bush

1 m × 1 m

This is an attractive, fast-growing, free-flowering daisy bush which has soft, grey-green foliage and bright yellow daisy flowers. Plant it in groups of three to five, or along the edge of a shrub border. The soil must be well drained and contain plenty of compost. Water well in winter, cut off dead flowerheads after flowering, and prune the bush back lightly. Replace the plant every four to five years. It may be propagated from seed or from cuttings – cuttings will produce a quicker result.

Natural distribution: It grows in the south-western Cape.

Flowering time:
Winter and spring

Euryops speciosissimus   ASTERACEAE
Clanwilliam euryops

1 m × 1 m

The Clanwilliam euryops is fast growing and has finely divided, soft, green foliage and large yellow daisy flowers. Plant it singly or in groups. As this shrub tends to be rather bare at the base, it is best planted behind other lower growing plants to conceal this. The soil must be light, well drained and contain plenty of compost. Water well in winter and cut the plant back hard after flowering. Propagate from seed or from cuttings, and pinch out young shoots to encourage bushiness.

Natural distribution: It grows in the Clanwilliam area in the south-western Cape.

Flowering time:
Spring

Euryops virgineus   ASTERACEAE
Honey euryops

1,5 m × 1,5 m

Fast growing, the honey euryops has fine, dark green foliage and masses of small, honey-scented yellow flowers. Plant it close together, in large groups. The soil must be light, well drained and contain plenty of compost. Prune the plant back hard after flowering, otherwise it will become very untidy. It may be propagated from seed or from cuttings but the latter will grow faster and produce flowers sooner.

Natural distribution: It grows in the southern and eastern Cape and Lesotho.

Flowering time:
Winter and spring

Felicia amelloides   ASTERACEAE

Blue felicia, Blue marguerite

50 cm × 50 cm

Flowering time:
Spring and summer

Fast growing and with slightly hairy leaves and blue daisy flowers, this shrub may be planted along the front of a border, or in a rockery. The blue felicia prefers light, well-drained soil with plenty of compost. Clip back after flowering to encourage the plant to produce a further crop of flowers. Propagate from seed or from cuttings.

Natural distribution: It occurs from Riversdale to Bathurst in the Cape Province.

Felicia filifolia   ASTERACEAE

Wild aster

1 m × 1 m

Flowering time:
September

A moderate growth rate, fine, light green, needle-like foliage and masses of pale mauve flowers in spring characterise the wild aster. Plant it in groups in an informal border, or in a rockery, in any light, well-drained soil, adding plenty of compost; water moderately in summer. Prune the plant back lightly after flowering to keep it neat. It is easily propagated from seed sown in March or September.

Natural distribution: It grows on hillsides and mountainsides, in both the summer and winter rainfall regions of the Cape, and in Natal, the Orange Free State, Lesotho, the Transvaal and Namibia.

Freylinia tropica   SCROPHULARIACEAE

Blue freylinia

1,5 m × 1 m

Flowering time:
Mainly spring

This is a delicate, sparse shrub with pale green foliage, small blue flowers and a moderate growth rate. Plant the blue freylinia in groups, close together, in a protected position, or in a container on a patio. The soil must be good, light, well drained and contain plenty of compost. This shrub requires water regularly throughout the year, but less in winter. Trim the plant to keep it neat, and to encourage bushiness. Propagate from seed or from cuttings.

Natural distribution: It grows in the northern Transvaal.

Freylinia undulata   SCROPHULARIACEAE
Mauve honey-bell bush

1,5 m × 1,5 m

This shrub has heath-like foliage, bears large heads of tubular pink-mauve flowers at the tips of the stems and is of moderate growth rate. It is suitable for a mixed border. The soil must be light and well drained and contain plenty of compost. Water well in winter and spring in the summer rainfall regions. As this shrub has a rather sprawling habit it must be pruned to keep it neat. Propagate from seed or from cuttings.

Natural distribution: It grows in Namaqualand and in the south-western and south-eastern Cape.

Flowering time:
Late winter or spring

Geranium incanum   GERANIACEAE
Carpet geranium

30 cm × 30 cm

This fast-growing plant has finely divided, lacy foliage and small, flat, saucer-shaped mauve flowers. Mass plant to form a ground cover, or plant in a rockery or overhanging a terraced wall. Keep the soil – which must be light, well drained and contain plenty of compost – moist in summer and winter. Prune the carpet geranium back after flowering, or when untidy, to keep it neat and encourage a new batch of flowers. This plant usually seeds itself freely, so older plants can eventually be removed, leaving the younger ones in their place. It can also be propagated from seed or from cuttings.

Natural distribution: It occurs near the Cape coast from Stellenbosch to about Knysna.

Flowering time:
Spring to winter

Helichrysum splendidum   ASTERACEAE
Cape gold

1,5 m × 1,5 m

The Cape gold is a fast-growing, dense, erect shrub with silver-grey foliage and heads of small yellow flowers in spring. Plant it in groups of three to five, or mass plant in a sunny position to form a ground cover. The soil must be light, well drained and contain plenty of compost. Water moderately and cut the plant back after flowering. Propagate from cuttings.

Natural distribution: It grows in the eastern Cape, Lesotho, Natal, Swaziland, the north-eastern Orange Free State and the northern and eastern Transvaal.

Flowering time:
Spring

Hemizygia transvaalensis LAMIACEAE
Pink salvia

1 m × 1 m

Fairly fast growing, the semideciduous pink salvia has soft foliage and terminal spikes of pink-mauve flowers. It is very attractive in full flower and is suitable for a mixed border or for planting in light shade under trees. The soil must be good, well drained and contain plenty of compost. Water well in summer and trim the plant back after flowering. Propagate from seed or from cuttings and protect young plants from frost.

Natural distribution: It occurs in lightly wooded grassland, in the eastern Transvaal and Swaziland.

Flowering time:
November onwards

Hibiscus praeteritus MALVACEAE
Dwarf red hibiscus, Miniature red hibiscus

1,5 m × 1,5 m

This is a delicate, sparse, fast-growing, semideciduous shrub with small, red, hibiscus-like flowers. Plant very close together, in groups of five or more. The soil must be good, light, well drained and contain plenty of compost. Water well in summer and pinch out the tips of new shoots to encourage branching. Propagate the dwarf red hibiscus from seed.

Natural distribution: It occurs in the bushveld of the northern and eastern Transvaal, Botswana and Namibia.

Flowering time:
Spring to winter

Hypoestes aristata ACANTHACEAE
Ribbon bush

1,5 m × 1 m

The ribbon bush is fast growing and has soft, hairy, dark green leaves and spikes of tubular mauve or pink flowers. Plant in light shade, under trees, in light, well-drained soil containing plenty of compost. Water well in summer and prune the plant back hard after flowering. Propagate from seed sown in August, or from cuttings.

Natural distribution: It grows in the northern and eastern Transvaal, north-western Natal and the south-eastern and eastern Cape.

Flowering time:
May onwards

Lebeckia sericea FABACEAE

Silver pea

1,5 m × 1,5 m

This is a fast-growing shrub with soft, shiny grey-green foliage and small, yellow, sweetpea-like flowers. Plant singly or in groups of three to five. In the summer rainfall area this plant must be grown in very well-drained soil, preferably in a raised bed, or in a rockery – too much rain or moisture in summer can kill it. Water well in winter. Propagate the silver pea from seed.

Natural distribution: It grows in dry and rocky places in Namaqualand and the south-western Cape.

Flowering time:
March

Leucadendron salignum PROTEACEAE

Geelbos

1,5 m × 1,5 m

The geelbos is a fairly fast-growing, dense, rounded shrub with light green to yellowish foliage, which may be tinged with red. Male and female flowers are borne on separate plants. The female flowers are produced as small cones and those of the male plant as fluffy yellow cones. The bracts surrounding these flowers are yellow in winter and spring. Plant the geelbos in an airy, sunny position, in well-drained, acid soil. Water well in summer and winter, especially in the summer rainfall area. Provide a thick mulch of pine needles or compost, but do not apply artificial fertiliser or disturb the roots by digging. Propagate this shrub from seed or from cuttings.

Natural distribution: It grows in the south-western and southern Cape.

RIGHT The flowers of the male plant appear as small, fluffy yellow cones.

Flowering time:
Late winter and spring

Leucospermum cordifolium PROTEACEAE

Nodding pincushion

1,5 m × 2 m

Of moderate growth rate, the nodding pincushion forms a neat, symmetrical bush and has large salmon-pink 'pincushion' flowers. These make excellent cut flowers and last for up to four weeks in a vase. Plant this shrub on a sloping bank or in a raised rockery for better drainage, in a sunny, airy position and water well, summer and winter, especially in the summer rainfall area. The soil must be light and well drained, with the addition of plenty of compost or peat. These plants will not do well in heavy clay soil unless it has been lightened by adding large quantities of riversand and compost or peat. Provide a thick mulch of pine needles or compost, but do not apply artificial fertiliser or disturb the roots by digging. The life span of the individual plants is seldom more than 10 years. Propagate from seed, and protect young plants from frost.

Natural distribution: It grows in the south-western Cape.

Flowering time:
Winter to early summer

Limonium capense PLUMBAGINACEAE
Pink statice

30 cm × 30 cm

This shrub has a moderate growth rate, small, oval, leathery leaves and heads of tiny, papery pink flowers. These make excellent cut flowers and last for up to two weeks in a vase. Plant the pink statice in a rockery or on a sloping bank, in very well-drained, compost-enriched soil and water throughout the year, especially in the summer rainfall area. Propagate by division of the larger clumps or from seed sown in autumn or spring. Young plants grow fairly slowly.

Natural distribution: It grows along the coast near Langebaan in the western Cape.

LEFT AND RIGHT *Limonium* sp., which is similar to *L. capense.*

Flowering time:
Spring to summer

Limonium perigrinum PLUMBAGINACEAE
Sea lavender

50 cm × 50 cm

The sea lavender has a moderate growth rate and bears its oval, leathery leaves at the base of the plant. Clusters of tiny rose-pink flowers are carried on wiry stems. This shrub is suitable for a rockery or for the edge of a border and should be planted in sandy, well-drained and compost-enriched soil. Water throughout the year, especially in the summer rainfall area. Propagate the sea lavender by division of the larger clumps or from seed sown in autumn or spring. Young plants grow fairly slowly.

Natural distribution: It occurs along the south-western Cape coast.

Flowering time:
Midwinter to midsummer

Lobostemon fruticosus BORAGINACEAE
Agtdaegeneesbos

1 m × 1 m

The narrow, oval, hairy leaves of this shrub grow all the way up the soft-wooded stems, which are topped by bell-shaped blue or sometimes pink flowers. The agtdaegeneesbos has a moderate growth rate and is suitable for a rockery or mixed border. It prefers well-drained, compost-enriched soil and must be watered throughout the year, especially in the summer rainfall region. At the coast it is fairly drought resistant. Fresh seed sown in March takes about five weeks to germinate, and seedlings and young plants must be protected from frost.

Natural distribution: It is common in the south-western Cape.

RIGHT The blue flower of *Lobostemon* sp., which is similar to *L. fruticosus.*

Flowering time:
Spring to early summer

Maytenus tenuispina CELASTRACEAE

Bell maytenus

1,5 m × 1,5 m

This spiny shrub, with its masses of tiny, sweetly scented yellow-green flowers and attractive bell-shaped reddish fruits which remain on the plant for a long time, may be used to form a hedge. It is frost-hardy and drought resistant. Plant the bell maytenus in good, well-drained soil, adding plenty of compost, and water well in summer. Propagate from seed.

Natural distribution: It grows in the Cape, Transvaal, Swaziland, the Orange Free State and Botswana.

Flowering time:
November or December

Melianthus comosus MELIANTHACEAE

Kruidjie-roer-my-nie

1,5 m × 1 m

This is a fast-growing, drought-resistant shrub with attractive, feathery, dark green foliage and orange sweetpea-like flowers. These are followed by inflated seed pods which are green at first, becoming brown and papery as they age. The kruidjie-roer-my-nie is suitable for a mixed border and grows easily in any soil, but add plenty of compost for better results. Water well in summer. This shrub tends to become 'leggy' and needs to be pruned back once in a while to keep it neat, and encourage new growth. Propagate from seed sown in March or August.

Natural distribution: It grows in the south-western, southern and eastern Cape, the Orange Free State, Lesotho and Namibia.

Flowering time:
September

Myrsine africana MYRSINACEAE

Cape myrtle

1,5 m × 2,5 m

The Cape myrtle is a neat, slow-growing, moisture-loving shrub with attractive, small, shiny red-brown leaves and tiny, inconspicuous flowers. These are followed by slightly fleshy purplish berries. Plant the Cape myrtle in dappled shade under trees, or in a mixed shrub border, in well-drained, compost-enriched soil. Water regularly. Propagate from seed or from cuttings, which tend to be slow to root.

Natural distribution: It is found in wooded kloofs and among clumps of bushes throughout South Africa.

Flowering time:
Spring

Nylandtia spinosa   POLYGALACEAE
Tortoise berry

1 m × 1 m

The tortoise berry is an erect, stiffly branched, spiny shrub of moderate growth rate, which is a mass of beautiful pinkish sweetpea-like blooms in the flowering season. These are followed by edible scarlet berries. Plant this shrub in a rockery or in a mixed border, in well-drained, sandy soil, adding plenty of compost, and water moderately throughout the year. Propagate from fresh seed.

Natural distribution: It occurs in Namaqualand and along the south-western, southern and eastern Cape coast.

Flowering time:
Late winter or early spring

Orphium frutescens   GENTIANACEAE
Orphium

50 cm × 45 cm

This is a fast-growing shrub with narrow, leathery, light green leaves and shiny cyclamen-pink flowers. Plant in large groups, approximately 20 cm apart, at the edge of a pond, or in a rockery. The soil must be well drained and compost enriched. Pinch out the growing tips to encourage bushiness, and water plants throughout the year, especially in the summer rainfall area. This plant is easily propagated from seed sown in August (inland), or in March (in the Cape).

Natural distribution: It occurs in the coastal areas of the south-western and southern Cape.

Flowering time:
November to February

Orthosiphon labiatus   LAMIACEAE
Pink sage

1,5 m × 1,5 m   to

The pink sage is a semideciduous, fast-growing shrub with soft, hairy, heart-shaped leaves and spikes of two-lipped, light pinkish-mauve flowers. It is suitable for an informal border or may be mass planted under trees to form a ground cover. Provide rich, well-drained soil, adding plenty of compost, and water well in summer. Cut the plant back hard after flowering. It is easily propagated from seed or from cuttings.

Natural distribution: It occurs on rocky koppies, in the eastern and northern Transvaal, Swaziland and eastern Natal.

Flowering time:
Early summer until autumn

Paranomus reflexus   PROTEACEAE

Yellow bottlebrush

1,8 m × 1,8 m

A fast-growing, erectly branched shrub with slender, feathery leaves, the yellow bottlebrush carries its broad spikes of lemon-yellow flowers at the tips of the stems. Plant it in groups of three to five in well-drained soil, with plenty of compost or peat added, in a sunny, airy position. Mulch with pine needles, and water well in summer and winter, especially in the summer rainfall area. At the coast the yellow bottlebrush is drought resistant during summer. Propagate it from seed.

Natural distribution: It grows in the Port Elizabeth and Humansdorp areas in the Cape Province.

Flowering time:
May to August

Pelargonium tetragonum   GERANIACEAE

Square-stemmed pelargonium, Succulent pelargonium

1 m × 2 m

This neat, spreading shrub with its succulent, cylindrical blue-grey stems and masses of large white flowers with red markings has a moderate growth rate. Plant the square-stemmed pelargonium in a very well-drained position, preferably in a raised rockery or on a steep slope, especially in the summer rainfall region where too much rain causes the stems to rot. The soil should be sandy and very well drained, with plenty of compost added. Water sparingly in winter. Propagate this shrub from cuttings, which must be kept very dry to prevent rot.

Natural distribution: It grows in the Cape Province.

Flowering time:
September and October

Pentas lanceolata   RUBIACEAE

Pentas

1,5 m × 1 m   to

The pentas is a fast-growing and soft-wooded shrub with mint-like foliage and flattish heads of small, starry flowers which range in colour from white, cerise, pale and deep pink to shades of red, lilac, magenta and purple. This rewarding shrub grows very easily in well-drained, compost-enriched soil. Water regularly and prune lightly after each flowering, to encourage the plant to produce more blooms. It is easily propagated from cuttings.

Natural distribution: It occurs in tropical Africa and Madagascar.

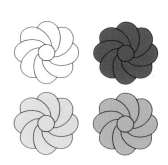

Flowering time:
Spring to autumn

Phaenocoma prolifera   ASTERACEAE
Cape everlasting

1 m × 0,5 m

This plant is fast growing, but has a fairly short life span. It is erect and stiffly branched and has minute grey-green leaves. Papery, daisy-like flowers are carried on the tips of the stems. Suitable for a rockery or raised bed, the Cape everlasting must be planted approximately 40 cm apart, in groups of at least five plants. It requires very well-drained soil in the summer rainfall region, and, in these areas, should be watered only in winter. It is easily propagated from seed sown in autumn.

Natural distribution: It occurs in the south-western Cape, from the Peninsula eastwards to Mossel Bay.

Flowering time:
Spring to autumn

Phygelius capensis   SCROPHULARIACEAE
Cape fuchsia

1 m × 0,5 m

This plant is a fast-growing, water-loving shrub which sends up numerous stems from the base. The soft-textured, dark green leaves are oval and pointed and the drooping, tubular red flowers are borne on tall spikes. The Cape fuchsia will thrive planted next to a pond or stream and recover well in spring if damaged by frost. It likes a rich, loamy soil, and plenty of water in summer. Propagate from seed or from cuttings.
   Phygelius aequalis (river bell) is very similar to the shrub described above, and will reach a height of 2 m.

Natural distribution: It occurs in forests and along rivers, in the northern and eastern Transvaal, Swaziland, Natal, Lesotho, the north-eastern Orange Free State and the eastern Cape.

Flowering time:
Summer

RIGHT   The flower of *Phygelius aequalis*, which is similar to that of *P. capensis*.

Plectranthus ecklonii   LAMIACEAE
Mauve plectranthus

1,5 m × 1,5 m

A fast-growing, soft-wooded shrub, the mauve plectranthus has large, oval, soft-textured, dark green leaves and spikes of two-lipped, tubular purple flowers. Pink- and white-flowered forms are also available. Plant this shrub in groups in light shade under trees in well-drained, compost-enriched soil, with plenty of moisture in summer. Plant it in a protected position in cold gardens. Cut the plant back by half, or more, after winter. The mauve plectranthus is easily propagated from cuttings.

Natural distribution: It grows in the southern and eastern Cape, Natal, Zululand and the eastern Transvaal.

Flowering time:
Autumn

Plectranthus fruticosus   LAMIACEAE

Pink fly bush

1,25 m × 0,5 m   to

Flowering time:
December to February

The pink fly bush is a fast-growing, soft-wooded shrub, with large, soft-textured, heart-shaped leaves and long spikes of pink or bluish-purple flowers. Plant it in groups under trees or on the shady side of the house in light, well-drained and compost-enriched soil. Water well in summer. Cut the plant back after flowering to encourage new growth. It is easily propagated from cuttings.

Natural distribution: It grows in the forests of the mist belt, from Knysna through to Natal, Swaziland and the northern Transvaal.

LEFT *Plectranthus fruticosus* 'James'. **RIGHT** The flower of *Plectranthus fruticosus* 'Ngoya'.

Plectranthus saccatus   LAMIACEAE

Stoep jacaranda

50 cm × 50 cm   to

Flowering time:
Midsummer

This fast-growing, soft-wooded shrub has small, roundish, light green leaves and sprays of pale purple flowers. It makes an excellent ground cover when planted in light shade under trees, and also grows very well in a container indoors, next to a north-facing window. Plant it in a protected position in cold gardens. The soil should be light and well drained with plenty of compost added. Water well in summer. The stoep jacaranda is easily propagated from cuttings.

Natural distribution: It grows in the eastern Cape, Natal and Zululand.

Protasparagus densiflorus 'Meyersii'

ASPARAGACEAE

Foxtail fern, Cat's tail asparagus

45 cm × 60 cm      to

Flowering time:
Summer

Of moderate growth rate, this plant is an erect-growing perennial with foxtail-shaped 'fronds'. It has small, shiny, slightly fleshy berries – red when ripe – which birds love. The foxtail fern is an attractive foliage plant for a rockery, or may be mass planted in light shade under trees to form a ground cover. It also makes an excellent container plant for outdoors, and seems to prefer more sun than shade. Once established, it is fairly drought resistant, but always looks better if planted in good, compost-enriched soil and well watered. Cut this shrub back to ground level if burnt by frost – the plant will send up new 'fronds' in spring. Propagate from seed or by dividing larger clumps.

Natural distribution: It grows in the Transvaal, the Orange Free State, Natal and the Cape.

Rhus magalismontana   ANACARDIACEAE
Dwarf grey karee

75 cm × 75 cm

Flowering time:
October to November

The growth rate of this miniature shrub is unknown. It has attractive grey leaves, with its spring foliage being a soft apricot to red colour. The dwarf grey karee is suitable for a rockery or informal border. As this plant has not been widely cultivated, little is known of its requirements but it probably needs well-drained soil – it always occurs on rocky koppies in nature. Propagate from seed.

Natural distribution: Widespread, the dwarf grey karee occurs in rocky places in the south-eastern Transvaal, south-eastern Botswana, the northern Cape and in Vredefort in the Orange Free State.

Ruspolia hypocrateriformis var. *australis*
ACANTHACEAE
Red ruspolia

1,5 m × 1,5 m

Flowering time:
Summer

This semideciduous shrub has a moderate growth rate, large, soft-textured, light green leaves and showy spikes of bright red flowers. An attractive, free-flowering shrub, it is suitable for warmer gardens. Plant it in groups of three to five. The soil must be good, well drained and contain plenty of compost. Water well in summer. Prune the plant back hard after flowering, or if damaged by frost. Propagate from seed or from cuttings.

Natural distribution: It grows in the northern Transvaal and Botswana.

X Ruttyruspolia 'Phyllis van Heerden'   ACANTHACEAE
Ruttyruspolia

1,5 m × 1,5 m

Flowering time:
Summer

This attractive, free-flowering, semideciduous shrub has a moderate growth rate and a slightly sprawling/scrambling habit. The light green foliage is soft textured and the plant bears long spikes of rose pink flowers. Suitable for warmer gardens, the ruttyruspolia needs well-drained, compost-enriched soil. Water well in summer and prune the plant back after flowering, or if damaged by frost. Propagate from cuttings.

Natural distribution: This plant is a hybrid.

Salvia africana-lutea   LAMIACEAE

Beach salvia, Brown salvia

1,8 m × 1,8 m

This is a fairly fast-growing shrub with soft, grey foliage, and yellow flowers which soon fade to brick-red and then brown. They contain nectar which attracts sunbirds. The beach salvia is suitable for an informal shrub border. Fairly tolerant of coastal conditions, it requires light, well-drained soil containing plenty of compost and must be well watered in summer. Prune the plant to keep it neat. Propagate from cuttings, or from seed sown in spring.

Natural distribution: It grows in Namaqualand and the south-western and eastern Cape.

Flowering time:
Spring and summer

Salvia chamelaeagnea   LAMIACEAE

Blue salvia

1 m × 1 m

A fairly fast-growing, much-branched, sprawling shrub with soft, light green leaves and spikes of pale blue flowers, the blue salvia is suitable for a mixed border, or may be mass planted to form a ground cover. It is easy to grow and requires good, light, well-drained soil with the addition of plenty of compost. Water well in summer and prune the plant to keep it neat. Propagate from cuttings, or from seed sown in spring.

Natural distribution: It grows in Namaqualand and the south-western Cape.

Flowering time:
Summer

Strelitzia reginae   STRELITZIACEAE

Crane flower

1,5 m × 1,5 m  to

This slow-growing shrub forms sturdy clumps of grey-green banana-like leaves and bears large orange-and-blue flowers that make excellent cut flowers. It is wind resistant and grows well in coastal gardens. In frosty areas the crane flower should be planted against a north- or west-facing wall. Plant it in good, rich soil and water regularly. It flowers well only when properly established, so do not divide or transplant unnecessarily. Propagate the crane flower from seed. Although large clumps may also be split, they will take a long time to re-establish and flower again.

Natural distribution: It grows in the bush around Port Elizabeth in the eastern Cape and in northern and southern Natal.

Flowering time:
Autumn, winter and spring

Sutherlandia frutescens FABACEAE

Cancer bush

1,25 m × 1 m

The cancer bush is a fast-growing shrub with a short life span. It has silver-grey foliage, sweetpea-shaped, bright orange flowers and attractive inflated pinkish pods. Suitable for a rockery or mixed border, it should be planted close together in groups of five or more. It is easy to grow, in any type of soil, and should be watered well in winter, especially in the summer rainfall areas. This shrub seeds itself freely, so older plants can be removed when past their best.

Natural distribution: It grows in the Cape, especially in the Karoo, and in Lesotho, Natal, the Orange Free State, Botswana and Namibia.

Flowering time:
Late winter to summer

Tecomaria capensis BIGNONIACEAE

Cape honeysuckle

,5 m × 2,5 m

The Cape honeysuckle is a fast-growing, sprawling shrub with soft, shiny, dark green foliage, and spikes of trumpet-shaped flowers which are either yellow or salmon. It may be planted to form an attractive hedge in warmer areas, or included in a mixed border. Wind resistant, this shrub will grow well in coastal gardens. Plant it in any soil, in sun or partial shade. Prune the plant to keep it neat. The yellow Cape honeysuckle seems to form a neater, less sprawling bush. Propagate from cuttings.

Natural distribution: It grows in coastal areas from the eastern Cape to Natal, and in Swaziland and the north-eastern Transvaal.

Flowering time:
Spring and autumn

Thorncroftia longiflora LAMIACEAE

Mauve wild sage

m × 0,5 m

Fairly drought resistant and fast growing, the semideciduous mauve wild sage has soft, semisucculent leaves and delicate spikes of tubular, pale mauve flowers. Plant this shrub in a rockery or in a mixed border, or mass plant to form a ground cover under trees. It is easily grown in well-drained, compost-enriched soil. Trim the plant back after flowering to keep it neat and encourage new growth. Propagate from seed or from cuttings.

Natural distribution: It grows in the eastern Transvaal and Swaziland.

Flowering time:
February or March

Thorncroftia succulenta   LAMIACEAE
Wild sage

1 m × 0,5 m

Fast growing and semideciduous, the wild sage is an erect, soft-wooded shrub with soft, semisucculent leaves, and spikes of tubular purple-pink flowers. Plant this shrub in large groups in a mixed border, or under trees – the plants make a beautiful show when in full flower. The soil must be well drained and compost enriched. Water moderately in summer. Trim the wild sage back after flowering to keep it neat and to encourage new growth. Propagate the plant from seed or from cuttings.

Natural distribution: It grows in the northern and eastern Transvaal.

Flowering time:
Autumn

Thunbergia natalensis   ACANTHACEAE
Dwarf thunbergia

1 m × 1 m

The dwarf thunbergia is a fast-growing, erect, soft-wooded shrub with slightly hairy leaves and large, tubular blue to blue-mauve flowers, each with a white to yellow throat. Mass plant this shrub in a lightly shaded position under trees to form a dense ground cover. It requires good, light, well-drained soil containing plenty of compost and, as it prefers moist conditions, should be watered well in summer. Cut the plant back to ground level if damaged by frost – it will recover rapidly in spring. Propagate from seed or from cuttings.

Natural distribution: It grows in the Cape, Natal, Swaziland and the northern and eastern Transvaal.

Flowering time:
October to December

Aloe arborescens ASPHODELACEAE

Krantz aloe

3 m × 3 m

This fast-growing, rounded shrub which has large, succulent blue-grey leaves and spikes of tubular, brilliant red flowers is an excellent accent plant for a rockery. The flower spikes brighten a winter garden, and produce nectar which attracts sunbirds. The krantz aloe is an easily grown plant which needs well-drained, compost-enriched soil. It can tolerate a fair amount of neglect and adapts well to both the summer and winter rainfall areas. Water moderately in summer. Propagate from end-of-stem cuttings, which must be kept fairly dry to prevent rot. Coarse river sand is the best rooting medium for cuttings. Aloes can also be propagated from seed, but this is a long and fairly difficult process. The seed takes approximately three to four weeks to germinate and seedlings require adequate moisture and protection from frost while still young. The plant will flower three to five years after the seed was sown.

Natural distribution: It occurs mainly in high mountainous areas from the Cape Peninsula eastwards along the coast to Natal and Zululand, and inland to Swaziland and the eastern and central Transvaal.

National tree number 28.1

Flowering time:
May to July

Aloe ferox ASPHODELACEAE

Bitter aloe

3 m × 1 m

This is a slow-growing succulent, with a single, erect stem topped with large, thorny, succulent leaves. The spikes of tubular orange-red flowers are carried on showy, candelabra-like inflorescences. The bitter aloe is an excellent accent plant for a rockery and must be planted in well-drained and compost-enriched soil. Water moderately in summer. The dry, dead, lower leaves must be removed to keep the plant neat. Propagate this aloe from seed and protect the young plants from frost.

Planting a selection of aloes is an excellent way to introduce a spectacular display of colour into your garden during the winter and will also attract sunbirds which are very fond of the nectar. There is a large variety of species available from which to choose. As they flower at different times, a wise selection can provide a continuous display of colour throughout autumn and winter. Bear in mind that some aloes are completely frost-hardy while others cannot tolerate frost at all. Most are very tough and will adapt to difficult conditions. Remember to check whether the aloes originate in a summer or winter rainfall region and water them accordingly.

Natural distribution: It occurs in bush scrub and on hillsides, in the eastern Cape, Lesotho and southern Natal.

National tree number 29.2

Flowering time:
Late summer to spring

Aloe marlothii   ASPHODELACEAE

Flat-flowered aloe, Mountain aloe

3 m × 1 m

Flowering time:
Winter

This slow-growing succulent has a single, erect stem topped with large, thorny, succulent leaves. It bears horizontal spikes of tubular orange or red flowers which produce nectar that sunbirds love. The flat-flowered aloe is a good accent plant for a rockery. Plant it in well-drained, compost-enriched soil and remove dry, dead, lower leaves to keep the plant neat. Water moderately in summer. Propagate from seed and protect the young plants from frost.

Natural distribution: It occurs in warm valleys and on rocky hillsides, in Swaziland, the Transvaal (except the extreme south) and Mozambique.

National tree number 29.5

Bauhinia galpinii   FABACEAE

Pride-of-De Kaap

3 m × 4 m

Flowering time:
Summer to autumn

This fast-growing shrub – which may be evergreen under favourable conditions – has roundish, two-lobed, leathery, light green leaves, and bright orange orchid-like flowers. The pride-of-De Kaap, which in full flower is one of our most beautiful shrubs, is suitable for an informal hedge, a mixed border, or a rockery. It grows well in any type of soil, to which plenty of compost has been added. The plant is fairly drought resistant in winter, and does not require much water at that stage but must be watered well in summer. Although it does tend to scramble and spread into other shrubs, it may be pruned to keep it neat. Propagate from seed and protect the young plants from frost.

Natural distribution: It occurs in woodland and riverine bush, in the far northern and eastern Transvaal, Swaziland and northern Natal.

National tree number 208.2

Bauhinia tomentosa   FABACEAE

Yellow bell bauhinia

2 m × 3 m

Flowering time:
December to March

This shrub, which has a moderate growth rate, may be evergreen in a mild climate. It has small, two-lobed, leathery, light green leaves and bell-shaped yellow flowers with a black marking in the throat. An attractive shrub suitable for a rockery or mixed border, the yellow bell bauhinia also makes a lovely bonsai, planted in a small container in well-drained soil. Prune the plant to keep it in shape. Propagate from seed and protect the young plants from frost.

Natural distribution: It occurs in woodland, riverine bush, and coastal dune bush, in eastern Natal, Zululand, the north-eastern Transvaal, Mozambique and Zimbabwe.

National tree number 208.1

Bowkeria citrina   SCROPHULARIACEAE

Yellow shell-flower bush

2,5 m × 2 m    to

Flowering time:
November to June

Of moderate growth rate, this shrub has quite attractive, soft-textured, lemon-scented, light green foliage, and small, shell-shaped yellow flowers. It is suitable for a mixed border, or for planting in light shade under trees and will do well next to a pond or stream. Plant the yellow shell-flower bush in well-drained, compost-enriched soil and keep it fairly well watered. Propagate from cuttings.

Natural distribution: It occurs along streams and on the margins of evergreen forests, in southern Swaziland, the extreme north of Natal and the south-eastern Transvaal.

Brillantaisia subulugurica   ACANTHACEAE

Giant salvia

2 m × 2 m    to

Flowering time:
Summer

This is a vigorous, fast-growing shrub with attractive, large, soft-textured, slightly shiny, dark green leaves and long spikes of large, blue-mauve, salvia-like flowers. To grow well, the giant salvia needs full sun for at least part of the day – too much shade makes it long and lanky and it does not flower well. As it is frost-tender it needs to be planted in a very protected position. Water well in summer. Trim the plant back lightly after flowering, and cut back by half (or more) after winter to keep it neat and encourage bushiness. It is easily propagated from cuttings.

Natural distribution: It grows in Zimbabwe and tropical Africa.

Burchellia bubalina   RUBIACEAE

Wild pomegranate

2,5 m × 1 m   to

Flowering time:
Late spring to summe

The wild pomegranate is a neat, slow-growing shrub with glossy, dark green foliage, and begins bearing clusters of small, tubular orange flowers while still young. It is an attractive ornamental and will tolerate partial shade, but needs to be planted in a position where it is protected from cold winter winds. It prefers rich loam soil, with the addition of plenty of compost or peat. Propagate the wild pomegranate from seed sown in October, or from cuttings of half-ripe shoots. The seed takes about four to six weeks to germinate and young plants must be protected from frost.

Natural distribution: It occurs in the forests of the east coast, extending from Swellendam in the Cape to Natal, and in the eastern and northern Transvaal.

National tree number 688

Carissa bispinosa   APOCYNACEAE

Num-num

2,5 m × 1,5 m    to

Fast growing and with glossy, dark green foliage and sweetly scented, white, jasmine-like flowers, the num-num produces edible, plum-sized red fruits. Plant specimens a metre apart to form an impenetrable hedge – they are well armed with thorns – or use as an ornamental in an informal border. Plant the num-num in light, well-drained soil with the addition of plenty of compost. It can be lightly pruned to keep it neat. Propagate from seed.

Natural distribution: It grows along the coast from Cape Town to Natal, and in the Transvaal, the Orange Free State, Lesotho, Swaziland and Zimbabwe.

Flowering time: Summer

Chrysanthemoides monilifera   ASTERACEAE

Bush-tick berry

2 m × 2,5 m

This is a very fast-growing, drought-resistant, spreading, soft-wooded shrub with grey-green foliage, yellow daisy flowers and edible purple berries. Plant the bush-tick berry singly, or in large groups to form a ground cover. It may also be planted as a temporary filler, until slower shrubs have grown and established themselves. It grows easily in any soil; add plenty of compost, and water regularly. This shrub is easily propagated from cuttings.

Natural distribution: It grows in the south-western, southern and eastern Cape, Lesotho, Natal, the eastern Orange Free State and the south-eastern Transvaal.

National tree number 736.1

Flowering time: Spring

Cyathea dregei   CYATHEACEAE

Tree fern

3 m × 2 m

The tree fern is very slow growing and has a sturdy, fibrous, dark brown trunk topped by large, arching, light green fronds. It is an excellent accent plant for a water garden. Plant the tree fern in good, light, well-drained, compost-enriched soil and keep the stem and roots moist at all times. This is a protected species, but plants can be legally obtained. It can be propagated from ripe spores but it is much easier to purchase a plant from a nursery.

Natural distribution: It grows in grassland and along the edges of streams, and sometimes in forests, from the southern and eastern Cape northwards through the Transkei, Natal, Lesotho and Swaziland to the northern and eastern Transvaal, Zimbabwe and Mozambique.

National tree number 1

Foliage plant

Cyperus papyrus   CYPERACEAE

Papyrus

2 m × 1 m

A very fast-growing, aquatic or marsh garden plant which spreads vigorously by means of rhizomes, the papyrus forms clumps of tall, bare stems, each topped by a head of thread-like flower spikelets. It is an excellent ornamental for the edge of a pond, but may become invasive if not kept in check by chopping back new growth when necessary. Plant the papyrus anywhere in the garden, i.e. not necessarily near water, but water it well and cut off old spikes to keep it neat. Propagate by the division of rhizomes.

Natural distribution: It grows in northern Natal, the northern Transvaal, Botswana and Namibia.

Foliage plant

Cyphostemma juttae   VITACEAE

Tree grape

2 m × 2 m

The tree grape is a slow-growing, succulent shrub with a huge swollen trunk and large blue-grey leaves. The flowers are inconspicuous, but the red to purple fruits are carried in large grape-like bunches. This is an ideal accent plant for a rockery in a warm garden, or it may be planted in a large container on a sunny, protected patio. The soil must always be very well drained, preferably with plenty of riversand added; do not overwater. Propagate the tree grape from seed, and possibly from cuttings or truncheons.

Natural distribution: It grows in Namibia.

National tree number 456.1

Flowering time:
November

Diospyros austro-africana   EBENACEAE

Fire-sticks

2 m × 2 m

This is a slow-growing shrub with grey-green foliage and small, bell-shaped pink-cream flowers. The spherical, fleshy fruits are slightly hairy, are red to black when ripe and are eaten by birds. A neat plant, this shrub is suitable for a mixed border. Plant it in light, well-drained soil, adding plenty of compost, and water well in summer. Propagate from seed.

Natural distribution: It occurs in a wide variety of habitats, in the central, south-western and eastern Cape, southern Natal, Lesotho, the Orange Free State and the south-western Transvaal.

Flowering time:
September or October

Dracaena hookeriana   DRACAENACEAE

Dragon tree

2 m × 1,5 m

Flowering time:
November to February

The dragon tree is usually single stemmed, with large, leathery, strap-shaped, dark green leaves, and has a moderate growth rate. Very small yellow-green flowers are carried on tall spikes, and are followed by orange berries. This is an attractive foliage plant for a very protected position and makes an excellent container plant for indoors or for a shady patio. It will tolerate fairly poor light conditions and must not be situated in direct sunlight. Plant it in well-drained, compost-enriched soil, and water moderately. Propagate from seed or from stem cuttings. Seed should be sown in an organic potting mix and kept moist until it has germinated. This takes approximately three weeks. The seedlings grow reasonably fast and when about 10 cm high they should be transplanted into small individual containers filled with equal parts of coarse riversand, compost, organic potting soil and good garden soil (preferably loam) to which approximately 5 ml (1 teaspoon) each of superphosphate, bonemeal and slow release 3:2:1 fertiliser has been added. Water well and then allow the soil to become fairly dry before watering again. Stand each container on a layer of pebbles in a drip tray to ensure good drainage.

Natural distribution: It occurs in a variety of habitats – shady places in the dry bushveld, dune forest undergrowth and mountain forests – from Port Elizabeth eastwards to Natal, Zululand, Swaziland and the eastern and northern Transvaal.

National tree number 30.9

Elegia capensis   RESTIONACEAE

Broom reed

2,5 m × 1,5 m

Foliage plant

The broom reed – which has a moderate growth rate – forms a large clump of bamboo-like stems, each with rings of soft, feathery, needle-like leaves at regular intervals along the stem. An attractive foliage plant, it is ideal for a water garden. As it is a neat plant, which does not shed its foliage, it may also be planted next to a swimming pool. Plant the broom reed in sandy, compost-enriched soil and cut back older, untidy stems at ground level to keep it neat. It can be propagated from seed, but this is difficult to germinate.

The broom reed is one genus within the large restio family, which is a typical part of the western Cape fynbos and which occurs from the sandy coastal regions to the foothills of the mountains. The restios have a characteristic, tufted, reed-like appearance and vary from a few centimetres to well over a metre in height. They are particularly suitable for low-maintenance feature planting and combine well with proteas, pincushions and ericas. *Thamnochortus insignis* and *Chrondopetalum tectorum*, both known as thatch reed, and traditionally associated with the thatched roofs typical of Cape Dutch architecture, are two popular plants in this range which are commercially available. Plant them in well-drained soil and water well in winter in the summer rainfall area.

Natural distribution: It grows in the south-western Cape.

Grewia flava   TILIACEAE
Brandy bush

2,5 m × 2,5 m

Flowering time:
October to March

The brandy bush is a fast-growing, drought-resistant shrub with soft, hairy grey-green leaves and sweetly scented, starry yellow flowers. Its edible reddish-brown fruit has only a thin layer of flesh, but has a pleasant, sweet, slightly astringent flavour, and contains some protein and a high percentage of sugar. Birds love the fruits. Suitable for a mixed shrub border, or a large rock garden, the brandy bush should be planted in well-drained soil. Its leaves provide valuable fodder for game and stock in drier areas. Propagate this shrub from seed.

Natural distribution: It occurs in deciduous woodland and dry bushveld, in the northern Cape, northern Orange Free State, north-western Natal, Swaziland, the western and south-western Transvaal, Botswana, Namibia and Zimbabwe.

National tree number 459.1

Halleria elliptica   SCROPHULARIACEAE
Wild fuchsia

2,5 m × 2,5 m

Flowering time:
Autumn

This is a fast-growing, drought-resistant shrub with light green foliage and drooping clusters of tubular red flowers followed by fleshy fruits, which attract birds. The wild fuchsia is suitable for a mixed border, in a slightly protected position, or may be mass planted under trees to form a ground cover. Plant it in well-drained, compost-enriched soil and keep it reasonably moist for best results. Propagate from seed or from cuttings.

Natural distribution: It grows in the south-western Cape.

Hymenolepis parviflora   ASTERACEAE
(= *Athanasia parviflora*)

Coulter-bush

2,5 m × 2 m   to

Flowering time:
November

Suitable for a large garden, this is a fast-growing, soft-wooded shrub with finely divided grey-green foliage, and masses of tiny yellow flowers carried in large, flat heads. Plant this shrub in groups of at least five in well-drained soil, with plenty of compost added. The coulter-bush tends to become somewhat bare at the base as it ages, so plant it behind other lower growing plants to conceal this. Water well in winter, especially in the summer rainfall area. Prune the shrub back lightly after flowering to keep it neat. These plants are at their best for about three years, after which they should be replaced. The coulter-bush is easily propagated from cuttings, or from seed sown in April, or in August in colder areas. Seedlings must be protected from frost.

Natural distribution: It grows in the coastal areas of the Cape.

Hypericum revolutum   CLUSIACEAE

Curry bush

3 m × 3 m

A large, attractive, fast-growing shrub with arching branches, the curry bush has bright yellow flowers, each with a tuft of stamens in the centre. The leaves, which are narrow and pointed and arranged neatly along the stems, give off a scent of curry after rain. Suitable for an informal shrub border, this shrub is easily grown in any well-drained soil, with plenty of compost added – it prefers full sun, but will tolerate light shade for part of the day. The curry bush tends to sprawl, so prune it back fairly hard at the end of winter to keep it neat and encourage new growth. Propagate from cuttings, or by removing young suckers from the root area.

Natural distribution: It grows on forest margins, from the eastern Cape, through Natal and Swaziland, to the north-eastern Transvaal.

National tree number 484

Flowering time:
Mainly spring, and some
flowers throughout summer

Lebeckia cytisoides   FABACEAE

Wild broom

2 m × 1,5 m

A very showy species, this is a sparsely branched, fast-growing shrub with grey-green foliage and dense spikes of sweetpea-shaped bright yellow flowers. Its most important requirement is very well-drained soil – therefore a position in a rockery or raised bed is ideal – and some water in winter. Unfortunately the wild broom is not tolerant of the wet summers in the summer rainfall area but does very well in gardens which have dry summers, and is drought resistant at the coast. Trim the plant back after flowering and propagate from seed.

Natural distribution: It grows in the drier areas of the western Cape, from Namaqualand to Swellendam.

Flowering time:
Spring

Leonotis leonurus   LAMIACEAE

Wild dagga

2 m × 1,5 m

This colourful perennial is a fast-growing, drought-resistant shrub with long, softly hairy, tapering leaves with serrate edges. The velvety, bright orange flowers are carried in whorls at the top of each stem. Suitable for a mixed border, the wild dagga is very easy to grow, but will do best in well-drained loam with plenty of compost added. Water well in summer but keep almost dry in winter. Cut the plant right back at the end of winter. Propagate from seed, from cuttings or by dividing up large clumps.

Natural distribution: It occurs amongst rocks in grassland and is widespread in South Africa.

Flowering time:
Autumn

Leonotis leonurus   LAMIACEAE
White wild dagga

2 m × 1,5 m

A white-flowered form of the previous species, this shrub is fast growing and drought resistant, with long, softly hairy, tapering leaves with serrate edges. The velvety cream-white flowers are carried in whorls at the top of each stem. Suitable for a mixed border, the white wild dagga is easy to grow, in a well-drained loam soil with plenty of compost added. Water well in summer but keep almost dry in winter. Cut the plant right back at the end of winter. Propagate from seed, from cuttings or by dividing up large clumps.

Natural distribution: The white wild dagga grows amongst rocks in grassland and can occur in the same regions as the orange-flowered wild dagga. It is, however, very rare and is seldom found in nature.

Flowering time:
Autumn

Leucospermum tottum   PROTEACEAE
Fire-wheel pincushion

3 m × 3 m

The fire-wheel pincushion has a moderate growth rate. It is a neat, rounded shrub with dark green foliage and pink-red 'pincushion' flowers. This very attractive plant is drought resistant in the south-western Cape but should be watered well in winter and summer in the summer rainfall area. It requires well-drained, acid soil, in a sunny, airy position. Provide a thick mulch (preferably of pine needles) and do not apply artificial fertilisers or disturb the root area by digging. This shrub may be propagated from seed, but it is probably easier to buy plants from a nursery.

Natural distribution: It grows in the south-western Cape.

Flowering time:
September to November

Mackaya bella   ACANTHACEAE
Forest bell bush, Mackaya

3 m × 2 m    to

This shrub, which thrives when planted near water or in light shade under trees, is reasonably fast growing. It has beautiful, glossy, dark green foliage and trumpet-shaped pale mauve flowers and may also be grown as an ornamental in a large container. It prefers light, well-drained soil, with plenty of compost added. Water well in summer, but very little in winter. Pinch out the growing tips of young plants to encourage bushiness. The forest bell bush is easily propagated from cuttings.

Natural distribution: It occurs in evergreen forest, often along the edges of streams, from the Transkei through Natal, Zululand and Swaziland to the eastern and north-eastern Transvaal.

National tree number 681.1

Flowering time:
Spring

Maerua cafra   CAPPARACEAE
Bush-cherry

3 m × 3 m   to

A slow-growing, drought-resistant shrub, the bush-cherry has dense, dark green foliage, and a very neat habit. Each flower has a tuft of long, threadlike white stamens. The fruits are rounded and resemble plums. This shrub is suitable for a mixed border, or for planting in shade under trees but should be planted in a protected position in cold gardens. The soil should be well drained and compost enriched. Propagate the bush-cherry from seed or from cuttings.

Natural distribution: It occurs in scrub, wooded grassland and forest, from Humansdorp in the eastern Cape, through Natal and Swaziland to the Transvaal and Zimbabwe.

National tree number 133

Flowering time:
September or October

Maytenus polyacantha   CELASTRACEAE
Kraal spike thorn

2 m × 3 m

This is a fast-growing, dense, spreading shrub with long, straight spines and small, leathery, dark green leaves. The white flowers are carried in small bunches and the red-brown fruits contain small black seeds with yellow arils. This drought-resistant shrub may be planted to form a dense, impenetrable hedge. It will grow in any soil, but remember to add plenty of compost. Prune the plant to keep it neat. Propagate from seed.

Natural distribution: It usually grows in dry mixed woodland, from the eastern Cape through the Orange Free State to the central Transvaal.

Flowering time:
Midsummer

Melianthus major   MELIANTHACEAE
Giant honey flower, Touch-me-not

2,5 m × 3,5 m

The honey flower is a fast-growing, vigorous, invasive plant with attractive divided blue-green leaves which are up to 75 cm long. The rusty red flower spikes are carried above the foliage. Its lush-looking, ornamental foliage makes it a good accent plant for a stream or pond. It should be planted in a hot, open position where there is plenty of room for it to spread – these plants grow very easily and may sucker and become a nuisance if not controlled. If cut back by frost, the honey flower will shoot again in spring. It is easily propagated from seed.

Natural distribution: It occurs from the north-western to the eastern Cape.

Flowering time:
Spring

Myrica serrata   MYRICACEAE

Lance-leaved waxberry

3 m × 1,5 m

Flowering time:
August or September

This shrub, which has a moderate growth rate, may even grow into an attractive small tree 3-4 m high. It has long, narrow, light green leaves, and flowering spikes with a reddish tinge. The small, spherical blue-black seeds have a waxy coating. The lance-leaved waxberry thrives when situated next to a stream or pond and should be planted in good garden soil, with plenty of compost, and be kept well watered. Propagate from seed.

Natural distribution: It grows along streams, in forests, swamp forests and coastal flats, from the Cape Peninsula eastwards along the coast to Natal and Zululand. It also grows in the eastern Transvaal, Zimbabwe, Botswana, Namibia and Swaziland.

National tree number 38

Ochna serrulata   OCHNACEAE

Small-leaved plane, Mickey Mouse bush

2,5 m × 2,5 m

Flowering time:
September or October

This slow-growing shrub has narrow glossy leaves which are a beautiful pinkish-bronze colour in spring. The bright yellow flowers, each with a tuft of stamens in the centre, are followed by black fruits which are suspended below bright red sepals and resemble little Mickey Mouse faces. The small-leaved plane is an attractive shrub for a mixed border. Plant it in good garden soil with plenty of compost, and keep it fairly moist throughout the year. Prune the plant lightly to give it a nice compact shape. Propagation is difficult as the seed only germinates if very fresh, but cuttings of half-ripe shoots can be taken in summer.

Natural distribution: It occurs on forest margins, and on rocky hill slopes, from Caledon in the Cape eastwards along the coast to Natal and Zululand, and inland to Swaziland and the eastern and north-eastern Transvaal.

National tree number 479.1

Plumbago auriculata   PLUMBAGINACEAE

Cape leadwort

3 m × 3 m

Flowering time:
Throughout summer

This fast-growing, drought-resistant shrub with its small, delicate, light green leaves and masses of powder-blue phlox-like flowers makes an attractive, informal hedge, or, if planted en masse, forms a good ground cover for a large garden. Plant the Cape leadwort in any soil, adding plenty of compost, and water well in summer but keep fairly dry in winter. The plant can be pruned to keep it neat as it tends to spread and scramble. It will recover if damaged by frost. Propagate from seed or by lifting suckers from the root area, and protect young plants from frost.

Natural distribution: It occurs in the eastern Cape, Natal, the Orange Free State and the Transvaal.

Podalyria calyptrata   FABACEAE

Sweetpea bush

3 m × 3 m

Flowering time:
Spring

The sweetpea bush is a fast-growing shrub with shiny grey-green foliage, and is particularly beautiful when in full bloom and covered in masses of sweetly scented, mauve, sweetpea-like flowers. The attractive grey foliage adds interest to a mixed shrub border. Plant the sweetpea bush in light, well-drained soil which contains plenty of compost and water well in winter, especially in the summer rainfall region. Pinch back to encourage a bushy shape. Propagate this shrub from seed.

Natural distribution: It occurs in mountainous areas, along streams and at forest margins in the Cape, from Table Mountain eastwards to Caledon and Bredasdorp.

National tree number 225

Polygala myrtifolia   POLYGALACEAE

Bloukappies

3 m × 3 m

Flowering time:
Throughout the year

This attractive, free-flowering shrub is a very fast-growing, drought-resistant plant with soft, light green foliage and masses of magenta-pink flowers throughout the year. It makes a good hedge or screen plant and grows easily in any type of soil – be sure to give it plenty of compost and water. The plant can be lightly pruned if necessary and is easily propagated from seed.

Natural distribution: It occurs in a variety of habitats – from moist evergreen forest and open grassy hillsides to dune bush and sand dunes – from Clanwilliam southwards to the Cape Peninsula, and then eastwards to Natal and the Orange Free State.

Polygala virgata   POLYGALACEAE

Purple broom

2 m × 1 m

Flowering time:
Winter and spring

A fast-growing shrub with long, narrow, dark green leaves and spikes of purple sweetpea-like flowers, the purple broom tends to become very 'leggy', so plant it behind other shrubs, e.g. *Felicia filifolia*, and always close together, in groups of at least three or more plants. Young plants are very sparse, with single stems, but they fill out after a couple of years, to carry a dense, rounded crown of branches. The purple broom grows easily in any soil which contains plenty of compost. Water regularly and prune back severely if the plant becomes untidy – it will bush out again from that point. Propagate from seed sown in autumn or spring.

Natural distribution: It occurs in the south-western and eastern Cape, Lesotho, Natal, Swaziland, the Orange Free State and the Transvaal.

Protea cynaroides   PROTEACEAE
King protea

1,8 m × 1 m

This magnificent protea, which has a moderate growth rate, is well worth growing. It bears its broad leaves on red leaf stalks and has the largest flower head of all proteas, measuring nearly 30 cm across. Plant the king protea in well-drained, acid soil – it will not succeed in heavy clay soil – in a sunny, airy position. Water regularly throughout the year, especially in the summer rainfall area. Mulch well with pine needles, but do not apply artificial fertiliser or manure and do not disturb the root area by digging. Propagation from seed is difficult; it is probably easier to buy plants from your local nursery.

Natural distribution: It grows from the south-western Cape to Grahamstown.

Flowering time:
Autumn to spring

Protea grandiceps   PROTEACEAE
Peach protea

2 m × 1,5 m

This protea forms a neat, rounded bush and is very slow growing. It bears broad grey-green leaves with red margins, and flower heads with beautiful peach-pink bracts. The peach protea requires well-drained, acid soil – it will not succeed in heavy clay soil – in a sunny, airy position. Water regularly throughout the year, especially in the summer rainfall area. Mulch well with pine needles, but do not apply artificial fertiliser or manure and do not disturb the root area by digging. Propagation from seed is difficult; rather buy plants from your local nursery.

Natural distribution: It grows from the Cape Peninsula to Uitenhage.

Flowering time:
Spring to autumn

Protea magnifica   PROTEACEAE
Woolly-bearded protea

1,8 m × 1,8 m

The woolly-bearded protea is slow growing and forms a spreading, rounded shrub with broad grey-green leaves. The flower heads are up to 20 cm across, filled with a mass of soft white hairs and tipped with black in the centre. The outer bracts vary from soft pink to a deep rose in colour. The plant requires well-drained, acid soil, in a sunny, airy position. It will not succeed in heavy clay soil unless plenty of riversand and compost are added, and the bed is raised, e.g. in a rockery. Water regularly throughout the year, especially in the summer rainfall area. Mulch well with pine needles, but do not apply artificial fertiliser or manure and do not disturb the root area by digging. Propagation from seed is difficult; it is easier to buy plants from your local nursery.

Natural distribution: It grows from the Cederberg to Houwhoek in the Cape.

National tree number 86.1

Flowering time:
June to November

Pterocelastrus echinatus　CELASTRACEAE
White cherrywood

3 m × 2 m　

The white cherrywood is of moderate growth rate and suitable for a mixed border. In warm coastal areas this plant may grow into a tall, graceful tree, but in the Transvaal highveld it forms a bushy shrub or low tree. It has thick, leathery, glossy, dark green foliage and compact clusters of small white to cream flowers followed by attractive orange fruits which are spiky in appearance. Plant this shrub in well-drained, compost-enriched soil and water regularly. Propagate from seed.

Natural distribution: It occurs in forest, on forest margins and rocky hillsides, and sometimes along the edges of streams, from the Transkei to Natal, Zululand, Swaziland and the central, eastern and northern Transvaal.

National tree number 405

Flowering time:
February to November

Senecio barbertonicus　ASTERACEAE
Succulent bush-senecio, Yellow bush-senecio

2 m × 2 m　

A good drought-resistant plant for a hot rockery, this is a fast-growing, rounded shrub with long, narrow, succulent, needle-like leaves. The small yellow daisy flowers are carried in heads at the tips of the branches. This shrub grows easily in any well-drained soil with plenty of compost added. Water moderately in summer and propagate from cuttings, which must be kept fairly dry to prevent rot.

Natural distribution: It occurs amongst rocks in grassland, in the northern, north-eastern, central and southern Transvaal, Swaziland, Natal, Zimbabwe and Mozambique.

Flowering time:
Summer

Tecomaria capensis　BIGNONIACEAE
Cape honeysuckle

3 m × 3 m　

This beautiful free-flowering shrub is fast growing, drought resistant and very easy to grow. It has slightly glossy, dark green foliage and spikes of tubular orange or red flowers, which produce nectar that will attract sunbirds to your garden. There is also a smaller, yellow-flowered form. The Cape honeysuckle is suitable for a mixed border or an informal hedge. Plant it in good garden soil, adding plenty of compost, and water regularly in summer. It has a tendency to spread and scramble, but may be pruned to keep it neat. If cut back by frost, the plant will recover quickly in spring. Propagate from cuttings, or by removing suckers from the root area of the plant. Protect young plants from frost.

Natural distribution: It occurs on the margins of evergreen forest, in bush and scrub, and along streams, from the eastern Cape coast through the Transkei to Natal and Zululand, and also in Swaziland and the eastern and north-eastern Transvaal and Mozambique.

National tree number 673.1

Flowering time:
Spring and autumn

Tetradenia riparia   LAMIACEAE
Ginger bush

2 m × 1,5 m  to

Flowering time:
Late winter

The ginger bush is a fast-growing shrub with semisucculent stems and soft, heart-shaped leaves. The tall spikes of pale mauve flowers are carried at the tops of the stems. The shrub grows easily in light, well-drained soil containing plenty of compost. In frosty gardens it should be planted in a very protected position, otherwise frost will damage the flowers. Water well in summer but keep fairly dry in winter. Prune the plant back hard after flowering to keep it neat and encourage new growth. It is easily propagated from cuttings.

Natural distribution: It occurs in Natal, Swaziland, Zululand, the northern and eastern Transvaal, Zimbabwe, Botswana and Namibia.

Turraea obtusifolia   MELIACEAE
Honeysuckle tree

2,5 m × 2 m   to

Flowering time:
Spring

The honeysuckle tree is semideciduous and of moderate growth rate and in coastal areas it may grow into a small bushy tree up to 3 m high. It has glossy, dark green foliage and masses of white honeysuckle-like flowers, followed by decorative red berries. Plant this shrub close together in groups of three to five in good garden soil, adding plenty of compost, and water regularly. Propagate from seed. Young plants grow slowly.

Natural distribution: It grows in coastal bush, often on dunes, in bushveld and woodland, and on rocky koppies, from the eastern Cape northwards to Zululand and inland through the Transvaal to Botswana and Zimbabwe.

Typha capensis   TYPHACEAE
(= *T. latifolia*)

Bulrush

2 m × 0,5 m

Foliage plant

A striking accent plant for a water garden, the bulrush is fast growing and forms clumps of long, strap-shaped leaves, and bears cylindrical, velvety-brown inflorescences. It will only grow where the soil is under water, or very wet. The bulrush spreads by means of rhizomes and can, if necessary, be controlled by chopping back new rhizomes. An untidy plant can be cut back to ground level, or dead, dry leaves may be removed throughout the year. Propagate by dividing up large clumps.

Natural distribution: It grows along streams and on the edges of dams, and is widespread in South Africa.

Xylotheca kraussiana   FLACOURTIACEAE

African dog rose

2,5 m × 2,5 m  to

Flowering time:
Summer

This beautiful little shrub has a moderate growth rate and glossy, dark green foliage. It bears large, attractive, lightly scented, flattish white flowers with a tuft of yellow stamens in the centre. Plant the African dog rose in a very protected spot in frosty gardens. It should also make a good container plant for a sheltered patio. Plant it in well-drained soil enriched with plenty of compost and water regularly, for best results. Propagate from seed, and possibly from cuttings.

Natural distribution: It occurs on coastal dunes, in coastal forest and on forest fringes, and sometimes on grassy slopes, from the Transkei through Natal and Zululand into Mozambique.

National tree number 493

Aloe bainesii   ASPHODELACEAE

Tree aloe

8 m × 6 m

Flowering time:
June

A distinctive and striking accent plant, or decorative garden tree which is fairly easily grown, the tree aloe has a moderate growth rate. A tall bare stem is topped by a rounded crown of long, narrow, succulent, dark green leaves. It bears spikes of tubular rose-pink to orange flowers. Plant this aloe in very well-drained soil and do not overwater. It is easily propagated from cuttings or from truncheons, which must be kept fairly dry to prevent rot.

Natural distribution: It grows in dense bush, forested ravines, and on rugged, rocky mountainsides, from East London through the Transkei, Natal, Zululand, Swaziland and the eastern Transvaal to Mozambique.

National tree number 28

Aloe plicatilis   ASPHODELACEAE

Fan aloe

3 m × 3 m

Flowering time:
August to October

A good rockery plant of moderate growth rate, this aloe often becomes tree-like in appearance as it ages. It is a much-branched shrub with a short, thick stem, and grey leaves that are arranged in a fan-like fashion. It bears unbranched spikes of tubular scarlet flowers. Plant the fan aloe in well-drained, acid soil, water in winter in the summer rainfall area and keep fairly dry in summer. Propagate from seed, or from truncheons.

Natural distribution: The fan aloe is a winter rainfall species from the south-western Cape which grows on rocky mountain slopes, from Franschhoek to the Elandshoek Mountains – a high rainfall area.

National tree number 29.6

Apodytes dimidiata   ICACINACEAE

White pear, Bird's-eye

4 m × 3 m

Flowering time:
October to April

A dense, rounded shrub of moderate growth rate and with leathery, glossy, dark green leaves and sprays of small white flowers, this neat, decorative shrub is suitable for a mixed border or may be used as a screen plant. In the warmer coastal areas it becomes a graceful small tree with a compact, rounded crown of ornamental foliage. The striking fruit – a shiny, flattened, fleshy black berry with a bright red succulent heel – is eaten by many birds. Plant the white pear in good garden soil, enriched with plenty of compost. Propagate from seed, although this may take up to a year to germinate. Young plants grow slowly for the first year, but increase their growth rate thereafter.

Natural distribution: It grows in evergreen forest, coastal evergreen bush, open woodland, and on grassy mountain slopes, from the Cape Peninsula eastwards to George and Knysna and northwards to Natal, Zululand, Swaziland and the south-eastern and northern Transvaal.

National tree number 422

Buddleja auriculata LOGANIACEAE
Weeping sage

4 m × 4 m

Flowering time:
Late winter or
early spring

A fast-growing, dense shrub – yet neat, shapely and graceful – the weeping sage would look particularly attractive planted near water. It has beautiful glossy foliage with leaves that are deep green above and silver below, and spikes of tiny, tubular, sweetly scented cream, orange or lilac flowers, borne on the ends of the 'weeping' branches. Frost and drought resistant, it makes an excellent hedge or screen plant. It grows easily in any soil, but add plenty of compost and fertiliser, and water regularly for better results. It tolerates pruning, but this is usually unnecessary if enough room for spread has been allowed when planting. The weeping sage is easily propagated from hardwood cuttings.

Natural distribution: It grows on mountain slopes, in rocky ravines, and on forest margins, from Somerset East through the mountains of the eastern Cape, to Natal, Zululand, Swaziland and the eastern Transvaal.

National tree number 636.5

Buddleja saligna LOGANIACEAE
False olive

4 m × 3 m

Flowering time:
Late spring to autumn

This hardy evergreen would make an excellent hedge, screen, windbreak or waterside plant. In moister, warmer areas it may even form a small tree up to 8 m high. It is a fast-growing, drought-resistant, dense, bushy shrub with long, narrow grey-green leaves and terminal sprays of minute, sweetly scented white to cream flowers. The false olive grows easily in any soil – add plenty of compost for better results – and will tolerate light pruning. It is easily propagated from seed or from cuttings.

Natural distribution: It grows on dry hillsides, in mixed scrub and wooded valleys, on the margins of forests, along streams and in coastal bush throughout South Africa.

National tree number 636

Buddleja salviifolia LOGANIACEAE
Sagewood

5 m × 4 m

Flowering time:
Spring

This fast-growing, semideciduous shrub – which is drought and frost resistant – has silver-grey foliage and large, terminal bunches of attractive, sweetly scented, white to cream or lilac to purple flowers. Although the sagewood can be used as a hedge or screen plant, it is not as dense as the previous two species. While it does also have drooping foliage, it is much untidier than the weeping sage. The sagewood grows easily in any soil, but adding compost will give better results. Prune the plant to keep it tidy, and propagate from cuttings.

Natural distribution: It grows in evergreen forest, on rocky mountain slopes and along streams, in all the provinces of South Africa, and in Lesotho, Swaziland, Zimbabwe and Mozambique.

National tree number 637

Carissa edulis APOCYNACEAE

Small num-num

3 m × 3 m

An attractive ornamental shrub, which may also be planted close together (about a metre apart) to form an impenetrable hedge, the small num-num is dense and thorny, with glossy, dark green foliage, and masses of fragrant, white, jasmine-like flowers. The small, oval red fruits are edible. This shrub is fast growing, and if planted under trees it may scramble up into the tree-tops. Plant it in good garden soil, enriched with compost, and water regularly. Prune the plant to keep it neat, if necessary, and propagate from seed.

Natural distribution: It grows in warm woodland and scrub, from Swaziland northwards into the eastern and north-eastern Transvaal and Zimbabwe. It also grows in north-eastern Namibia and north-western Botswana.

Flowering time:
Spring

Carissa macrocarpa APOCYNACEAE

Amatungulu, Natal plum

3 m × 2 m  to

This is a fast-growing, attractive, ornamental shrub which is wind resistant and tolerant of coastal conditions. Although the amatungulu usually forms a dense, thorny shrub, it may also grow into a small tree up to 4 m high. It has glossy, dark green foliage and starry, sweetly scented white flowers that are larger than those of the previous species. The large oval red fruits are edible and rich in vitamin C. Plant this shrub close together – about a metre apart – to form a dense, impenetrable hedge which can be pruned if necessary. It grows fairly easily in good garden soil enriched with compost. Water regularly and propagate from seed.

Natural distribution: The amatungulu grows in coastal bush, coastal forest and on sand dunes, from Humansdorp in the eastern Cape to Natal, Zululand and Mozambique.

National tree number 640.1

Flowering time:
Spring to midsummer

Cassinopsis ilicifolia ICACINACEAE

Holly cassinopsis, Orange-thorn

4 m × 4 m  to

Of moderate growth rate, this is a thorny, scrambling shrub with attractive glossy green foliage, and almost oval, bright orange fruits, which are enjoyed by birds. The holly cassinopsis thrives in light shade under trees, but also grows well in full sun. Plant it in good garden soil, enriched with compost, and water regularly. Young plants grow slowly at first, but once established, will grow rapidly. Prune the shrub to keep it neat, if necessary. Propagate from seed, which may be slow to germinate.

Natural distribution: It grows on the edge of evergreen forest, in riverine bush, wooded kloofs and along streams, from the southern and eastern Cape to the eastern Orange Free State, Lesotho, western Natal, Zululand, Swaziland, the eastern Transvaal and Zimbabwe.

National tree number 420

Flowering time:
September to November

Clerodendrum glabrum   VERBENACEAE

White cat's whiskers

5 m × 5 m

A fairly fast-growing shrub – which may be evergreen under favourable conditions – this plant has dark green foliage and dense clusters of small, fragrant white flowers tinged with pink. Suitable for a shrub border, in warm moist areas it may grow into a small tree up to 8 m high, with a leafy, often drooping crown. White-eyes, Layard's bulbuls and other birds love the fruits, which take the form of round, smooth, shiny, pea-sized whitish 'berries'. Plant this shrub in good garden soil, enriched with compost, and water well. Propagate from seed or from cuttings.

Natural distribution: It grows in open woodland, along rivers, in coastal forest and bush, and on coastal dunes, from the eastern Cape through Natal, Zululand and Swaziland to the southern, south-eastern and northern Transvaal, Boswana, Mozambique, Zimbabwe and northern Namibia.

National tree number 667

Flowering time:
Spring to summer

Combretum celastroides subsp. *orientale*

COMBRETACEAE

Savanna bushwillow

3 m × 3 m

The savanna bushwillow has a moderate growth rate and is usually a neat, bushy, rounded shrub, but may sometimes form a small tree up to 6 m high. Its dark green foliage turns a deep red colour in winter; it should therefore be placed where this can be seen to advantage. The spikes of tiny greenish-yellow flowers are followed by small winged fruits, which become bright red before drying to golden-brown. Plant the savanna bushwillow in deep soil, enriched with compost. Propagate from seed.

Natural distribution: It grows in dry woodland, on rocky koppies, and often on Kalahari sand, in northern Namibia, northern Botswana, north-western Zimbabwe, and in the Kruger National Park around Punda Maria.

National tree number 534

Flowering time:
December to March

Combretum padoides COMBRETACEAE

Thicket bushwillow

5 m × 8 m

This fast-growing, dense shrub is suitable only for very large gardens in warmer areas, where it could make an excellent hedge, screen, or windbreak. It has shiny, light green foliage and spikes of small cream flowers. Plant the thicket bushwillow in good garden soil, enriched with compost, and water regularly, although once established it is fairly drought resistant. As the plant tends to sprawl and spread over a large area, prune it, if necessary, to keep it in check. Propagate from seed.

Natural distribution: It grows on the margins of evergreen forest, in woodland, along riverbanks and in forested ravines, from Swaziland to the eastern and north-eastern Transvaal, Mozambique and Zimbabwe.

Flowering time:
December to February

Cordia ovalis BORAGINACEAE

Sandpaper tree

5 m × 4 m

Of moderate growth rate, this is a hardy, drought-resistant shrub which may be planted in drier gardens. It is a dense, compact, rounded shrub with leathery, deep green leaves which are rough above – like sandpaper – and velvety below. The small, sweetly scented greenish-yellow flowers are followed by edible, fleshy fruits – the sticky pulp has a bitter-sweet flavour – which are bright orange-red when ripe, and are eaten by a variety of birds. Plant the sandpaper tree in well-drained, compost-enriched soil and water moderately. Propagate from seed.

Natural distribution: It grows in hot, dry bush and woodland, often on rocky hillsides, sometimes in sandy soil on riverbanks, from the northern and north-eastern Transvaal to Zimbabwe.

National tree number 654

Flowering time:
October to May

Crotalaria capensis FABACEAE

Cape rattlepod, Cape laburnum

3 m × 2 m

A very fast-growing shrub, the Cape rattlepod could be planted as a hedge, or in an informal shrub border. It has soft, dark green foliage, and long spikes of large, golden yellow, sweetpea-like flowers. The yellowish pods, which are ridged, inflated and pendulous, become light brown when ripe. The Cape rattlepod requires good, compost-enriched soil and regular water. Propagate from seed.

Natural distribution: It grows in a wide variety of habitats – in forests, on forest margins, along streams and in woodland – in the coastal strip stretching from the Cape Peninsula through the eastern Cape to Natal and Zululand, and in the southern Orange Free State, Swaziland, the eastern and northern Transvaal, Zimbabwe and Mozambique.

National tree number 224.1

Flowering time:
Spring

Dodonaea angustifolia SAPINDACEAE

Cape sand olive

4 m × 3 m

Flowering time:
April to August

This fast-growing, drought- and wind-resistant shrub makes a good hedge or screen plant and sometimes grows into a small tree of up to 5 m high. Its bark is dark grey and stringy and its leaves are covered in a gummy substance that makes them shine. Small yellow-green flowers are followed by decorative, winged greenish-red fruits. The Cape sand olive is easily propagated from seed, and young plants, like the older ones, grow fast if given good soil and plenty of water.

Natural distribution: It grows in a variety of habitats, from arid, semidesert regions to the margins of moist evergreen forest, extending from Namibia through the south-western and eastern Cape, to Natal, Zululand and the south-eastern Transvaal.

National tree number 437.1

Dombeya burgessiae STERCULIACEAE

Pink wild pear

4 m × 4 m  to

Flowering time:
Autumn to winter

Very fast growing, this attractive ornamental forms either a large bushy shrub or a small tree up to 4 m high. It has large, soft, heart-shaped leaves and rounded heads of white to pale pink flowers. Plant the pink wild pear in a protected north-facing position, in good garden soil, enriched with compost, and water regularly in summer but less in winter. Propagate from seed.

Natural distribution: It grows on forest margins, along streams, in open woodland, and on rocky hillsides, from central Natal, Zululand and Swaziland through the eastern and northern Transvaal to Mozambique and Zimbabwe.

National tree number 468.1

Dombeya cymosa STERCULIACEAE

Small-flowered dombeya

5 m × 3 m

Flowering time:
March to May

The small-flowered dombeya forms a rounded shrub or a small tree with gracefully drooping branches and is particularly beautiful when in full flower. Of moderate growth rate, it would make an attractive ornamental for the garden. It has a smooth cream to brown bark and in autumn bears masses of small, sweetly scented white flowers, from which an excellent honey is made. Plant this shrub in well-drained, compost-enriched soil and water regularly in summer. Propagate from seed.

Natural distribution: It grows along streams, in coastal bush, on forest margins, and on rocky koppies, from the eastern Cape through Natal, Zululand and Swaziland to the eastern Transvaal and Mozambique.

National tree number 469

Dovyalis caffra FLACOURTIACEAE

Kei apple

4 m × 3 m

Flowering time:
November to January

The Kei apple, which may be evergreen under favourable conditions, is a drought-resistant, spiny shrub of moderate growth rate that may be planted close together to form an impenetrable hedge. It has waxy, oval, light green leaves and small cream-green flowers that are followed by large, edible apricot-coloured fruits. These are rich in vitamin C and can be eaten fresh or made into a tasty jam. Birds love them, especially loeries and blackeyed bulbuls. Plant this shrub in good soil, with plenty of compost. If necessary, it can be heavily pruned to keep it neat. The Kei apple is easily propagated from very fresh seed.

Natural distribution: It grows in hot, dry country, in open bush and wooded grassland, on rocky koppies and on the edges of dune forest, from the eastern Cape through Natal and Zululand to Swaziland, the eastern, central and northern Transvaal and Zimbabwe.

National tree number 507

Duvernoia aconitiflora ACANTHACEAE

Lemon pistol-bush

3 m × 3 m   to

Flowering time:
Summer

This reasonably fast-growing, rounded shrub should be planted in a fairly protected position in an informal shrub border, or in light shade under large trees. It bears masses of two-lipped, pale lemon-yellow flowers that are carried on spikes at the tips of the branches. Sunbirds are attracted by the nectar in the flowers, which are followed by club-shaped, velvety brown fruits. Plant the lemon pistol-bush in good, compost-enriched soil, and water regularly in summer. Propagate from seed.

Natural distribution: It grows in the Transvaal lowveld and in Swaziland.

Duvernoia adhatodoides ACANTHACEAE

Pistol bush

3 m × 2 m   to

Flowering time:
Summer

This fast-growing plant usually forms an attractive bushy shrub with large, dark green leaves and showy, fragrant white flowers, but under favourable conditions it may grow into a small tree up to 6 m high. The club-shaped fruits burst open with a sharp explosive sound – hence the common name 'pistol bush'. It thrives in a lightly shaded, moist position. Plant it in good, compost-enriched soil, and water regularly for best results. Propagate from seed.

Natural distribution: It grows in coastal forest, and along streams, from the eastern Cape to Zululand, and in the extreme south-eastern Transvaal.

National tree number 681

Ehretia rigida   BORAGINACEAE

Hottentot's lilac

4 m × 4 m

Flowering time:
Spring

This many-stemmed shrub has a slightly 'weeping' habit – its arching branches spread and curve stiffly downwards, giving it a rigid, tangled and untidy appearance. It is fast growing and drought and frost resistant. Clusters of small, sweetly scented lilac flowers are followed by berries which are orange-red to black when ripe. Birds love them and eat them as soon as they ripen. Plant this shrub in any compost-enriched soil and water moderately. It usually has to be pruned to keep it looking neat. Propagate from seed or cuttings.

Natural distribution: It grows in a wide variety of habitats in all four provinces of South Africa, and in Zimbabwe, Mozambique, Botswana, Namibia, Lesotho and Swaziland.

National tree number 657

Ensete ventricosum   MUSACEAE

African wild banana

6 m × 3 m  to

Foliage plant

The very fast-growing African wild banana is a good accent plant for a water garden. It has a stout, fleshy stem topped by large, banana-like leaves. This foliage will be destroyed in areas of severe frost, but the plant will recover rapidly in spring. The cream flowers are enclosed in maroon bracts, making a showy bunch up to 1,5 m long. The fruits look rather like bananas, but contain masses of hard black seeds resembling dried peas. Plant the African wild banana in good garden soil, add plenty of compost, and water well. It has a lifespan of about eight years – it flowers and fruits once, then dies. Propagate from seed.

Natural distribution: It grows in high rainfall forest, in mountain kloofs and near mountain streams in the north and north-eastern Transvaal.

National tree number 31

Gardenia cornuta   RUBIACEAE

Natal gardenia

4 m × 4 m

Flowering time:
Spring

This rounded, ornamental shrub, which is of moderate growth rate, has decorative flowers and fruits and may be planted in a mixed shrub border or alongside a pond or stream. It has shiny, light green leaves, and showy, sweetly scented white flowers followed by large, shiny, oval fruits that are yellow when ripe. The Natal gardenia prefers slightly acid soil, and lots of water. Mix in plenty of compost when preparing the soil for planting. Propagate from seed; young plants grow slowly.

Natural distribution: It grows in grassland and in open woodland, in north-eastern Natal, Zululand and Swaziland.

National tree number 690.1

Gardenia thunbergia RUBIACEAE

Starry gardenia

5 m × 3 m

Flowering time:
Summer

The beautiful, slow-growing starry gardenia may form a shrub or a small tree up to 5 m high, and is well worth cultivating. Plant it near a pond or stream where its glossy, dark green foliage and sweetly scented, starry white flowers will enhance the setting. It has distinctive egg-shaped grey fruits speckled with whitish encrustations. The fruits are very hard and woody and remain on the tree for a long time. The starry gardenia requires acid soil and good drainage and plenty of compost should be added to the soil when preparing the planting hole. This shrub is easily propagated from seed or from truncheons. Young plants grow slowly.

Natural distribution: It grows in evergreen forest and woodland, from the eastern Cape through Natal to Zululand.

National tree number 692

Grewia occidentalis TILIACEAE

Cross-berry

5 m × 3 m

Flowering time:
Summer

This fast-growing shrub or small tree may be evergreen under favourable conditions and is suitable for an informal border. It bears starry pink flowers and small, edible, four-lobed fruits that birds, particularly speckled mousebirds, love. Plant the cross-berry in good, compost-enriched soil and water well in summer. As the plant can sometimes look untidy, prune it to keep it neat, if necessary. Propagate from seed – fresh seed germinates best. Young plants transplant readily and grow fast.

Natural distribution: It scrambles in evergreen forest, or is a shrub or small tree on forest margins, in open woodland, in coastal bush and on wooded hillsides, in all four provinces of South Africa, and also in Swaziland, Lesotho, Zimbabwe and Mozambique.

National tree number 463

Greyia sutherlandii GREYIACEAE

Natal bottlebrush

5 m × 3 m

Flowering time:
August to October

The Natal bottlebrush is a beautiful shrub when in full flower, carrying showy, brilliant red bottlebrush flowers at the ends of bare branches. The bark is reddish grey and smooth and the leaves are large and almost circular. It grows fairly fast, given good soil and water, but must be planted in a protected spot. The soil must be well drained and compost enriched and the plant must be watered regularly in summer. It prefers little or no water in winter, and does not seem to like a hot, humid climate. The Natal bottlebrush is easily grown from seed sown in September, or from cuttings or suckers.

Natural distribution: It grows on rocky mountainsides, from the eastern Cape through the eastern Orange Free State, Natal and Swaziland to the eastern Transvaal.

National tree number 446

Holmskioldia tettensis   VERBENACEAE

Chinese-hat plant

4 m × 3 m

Flowering time:
Summer

Fairly fast growing, the Chinese-hat plant forms a much-branched shrub or shrubby tree up to 5 m high. It has small triangular leaves and is a mass of soft pink-mauve in full flower with its blue flowers topped with pink-mauve calyxes, which resemble Chinese hats. Plant this shrub in a protected position in sandy soil mixed with plenty of compost, and water well in summer. It prefers a warm, moist summer and a dry, mild winter. In the winter rainfall area, it must be planted in a very well-drained position. Prune the plant to keep it neat, and propagate from seed or from cuttings.

Natural distribution: It grows in riverine bush and open woodland, and on rocky koppies, from Zululand to the eastern and north-eastern Transvaal.

National tree number 668

Leucospermum reflexum   PROTEACEAE

Rocket pincushion

3 m × 3 m

Flowering time:
July to December

This ornamental shrub, with its attractive soft grey foliage and striking, rocket-shaped, salmon to orange 'pincushion' flowers, is fast growing and spreading. It prefers well-drained, acid soil, in a sunny, airy position. Water well in summer and winter, especially in the summer rainfall area. Mulch well with pine needles, but do not apply artificial fertiliser and do not disturb the root area by digging. Propagate the rocket pincushion from seed. Unless carefully handled, seedlings damp off easily.

Natural distribution: It always grows along streams or in seepage areas, in hot, arid mountain fynbos in the Clanwilliam area.

Nuxia floribunda   LOGANIACEAE

Forest elder

3 m × 4 m

Flowering time:
Autumn and winter

The fast-growing forest elder forms a medium-sized tree in warm, moist areas – where it is at its best – or a shrub in colder gardens, where it is usually cut back by frost. It has shiny, light green leaves and large sprays of small, sweetly scented cream flowers. Plant this shrub in a very protected position, in deep, rich soil, adding plenty of compost, and water well throughout the year. Propagate from seed or from cuttings – young plants grow fast.

Natural distribution: It grows in evergreen forest, and on forest margins, often along the edges of streams, from the Knysna forests through Natal and Zululand to the eastern and northern Transvaal and Zimbabwe.

National tree number 634

Nymania capensis   MELIACEAE

Chinese lantern

4 m × 2 m

This decorative, slow-growing shrub would do well in hot, dry gardens – it is drought resistant and can tolerate extreme heat and cold. It has tiny, leathery leaves and attractive, dark pink, bell-like flowers followed by papery, pink, balloon-like seed pods. The Chinese lantern requires poor, well-drained soil and is difficult to cultivate in the Transvaal, although it may survive for a couple of years in a container placed in a dry position. It cannot tolerate overwatering or too much rain, but water sparingly in winter. It is easily propagated from seed.

Natural distribution: It grows in hot, dry areas, all over the Karoo and northwards to Namaqualand and Namibia. It also grows near Humansdorp and Uitenhage in the eastern Cape.

National tree number 295

Flowering time:
July onwards

Oncoba spinosa   FLACOURTIACEAE

Snuff-box tree

3 m × 3 m

Slow growing and spiny, with glossy, dark green leaves and large fragrant white flowers, this attractive shrub may grow into a small evergreen tree up to 5 m high under favourable conditions. The flowers are followed by large, decorative fruits, about 6 cm in diameter, which have hard shells and become reddish brown when ripe. These contain an edible, unpleasant tasting, mealy-like pulp and many small seeds. The hard-shelled fruits are used to make rattles and armbands for children and also snuff boxes – hence the common name. Planted close together this shrub makes an excellent throny hedge or barrier and it can also be planted in an informal shrub border or at the edge of a pond or stream. Plant the snuff-box tree in light, well-drained soil, adding plenty of compost, and water throughout the year. Propagate from seed sown in September, or from cuttings.

Natural distribution: It grows along streams and in hot, open woodland, sometimes becoming thicket-forming, from eastern Natal, Zululand and Swaziland to the eastern and north-eastern Transvaal, Zimbabwe, Mozambique and Botswana.

National tree number 492

Flowering time:
Spring and summer

Pavetta lanceolata   RUBIACEAE

Forest bride's bush

5 m × 4 m

Of moderate growth rate, the forest bride's bush forms a dense shrub and, under favourable conditions, i.e. in warm, moist areas, may also become a small tree up to 6 m high. It has glossy, dark green foliage and large sprays of small white flowers, which produce nectar that attracts sunbirds. The small, round, pea-sized fruits are black when ripe. Plant this shrub in light, well-drained soil, adding plenty of compost, and water well throughout the year. Prune the plant to keep it neat. Propagate from seed and possibly from cuttings as well.

Natural distribution: It grows in coastal and inland forests, from Port Elizabeth in the eastern Cape to Natal, Zululand, the eastern and north-eastern Transvaal and Mozambique.

National tree number 718

Flowering time:
Summer

Phoenix reclinata   ARECACEAE

Wild date palm

6 m × 4 m

This is a fairly fast-growing palm with attractive, glossy, dark green fronds. Small cream flowers are borne in long sprays with male and female flowers on separate plants. Masses of edible orange-brown fruits (dates) are carried on short branches and are eaten by birds. The wild date palm tends to sucker from the base, forming a multistemmed plant, so allow plenty of room for it to spread. It will also make a good container plant at the edge of a pool. Plant this palm in good soil, adding plenty of compost, and water well throughout the year. Plants in containers need plenty of water and should be fed regularly with slow-release 3:2:1 fertiliser. Trim off the older leaves at the bottom when they begin to turn yellow to keep the palm looking neat. Specimens growing in the garden look their best when they are bare stemmed and surrounded by younger, lush-looking sucker plants. This palm is easily propagated from seed, which may be slow to germinate. Young plants grow slowly.

Natural distribution: It grows along riverbanks in low-lying, open grassland, from Port Elizabeth in the eastern Cape to Natal, Zululand, the eastern Transvaal, Mozambique, Zimbabwe, northern Botswana and northern Namibia.

National tree number 22

Flowering time:
Summer

Portulacaria afra   PORTULACACEAE
Spekboom

4 m × 3 m

The spekboom grows fairly fast and may be used as a hedge, as an ornamental succulent tree for a rockery or planted to check soil erosion. It has a succulent, glossy red-brown trunk and bears a dense crown of succulent leaves and stems. The small, star-shaped pink flowers are followed by tiny, papery, three-winged fruits. This shrub is exceptionally beautiful in full flower, when it is a mass of pink. The leaves are edible and have a pleasant acid flavour – in drier areas the plant provides excellent fodder for stock and game. Plant the spekboom in well-drained soil, adding plenty of compost, and propagate from cuttings, which must be kept fairly dry to prevent rot.

Natural distribution: It grows on dry, rocky koppies and in succulent scrub, in the eastern Cape (especially on Karoo hills), along the coast of Natal, and in dry areas of the eastern Transvaal.

National tree number 104

Flowering time:
October to November

Protea compacta   PROTEACEAE
Bot River protea

3 m × 2 m

This protea grows easily and flowers well – the flowers are a clear pink colour. It requires well-drained, acid soil in an airy, sunny position. Water well during summer and winter, especially in the summer rainfall area. Provide a thick mulch of pine needles or other organic matter, but do not apply artificial fertilisers or manure and do not disturb the root area by digging. The Bot River protea can be propagated from seed. Unless carefully handled, seedlings tend to damp off, so it may be easier to buy the plant from a nursery. Young bushes must be well staked.

Natural distribution: It grows in coastal regions from Knysna in the southern Cape to the Caledon and Bredasdorp areas in the south-western Cape.

Flowering time:
May to September

Protea neriifolia   PROTEACEAE
Blousuikerbos

3 m × 3 m

Fast growing, this shrub forms a neat, dense, rounded bush. The flowers, which vary in colour from pale salmon to a deep rose pink, make excellent cut flowers and last for up to three weeks in a vase. The plant requires well-drained, acid soil in an airy, sunny position. Water well in summer and winter, especially in the summer rainfall area. Provide a thick mulch of pine needles or other organic matter, but do not apply artificial fertilisers or manure and do not disturb the root area by digging. The blousuikerbos can be propagated from seed, but as seedlings tend to damp off easily, it may be more convenient to buy a plant from your local nursery.

Natural distribution: It grows in the coastal mountains of the southern Cape.

National tree number 93.1

Flowering time:
Autumn and winter

Protea repens   PROTEACEAE

Sugarbush protea

3 m × 3 m

This fast-growing plant forms a dense, rounded shrub. The flowers vary in colour from almost white to pink and contain a sticky nectar. The plant requires well-drained, acid soil in an airy, sunny position. Water well in summer and winter, especially in the summer rainfall area. Provide a thick mulch of pine needles or other organic matter, but do not apply artificial fertilisers or manure and do not disturb the root area by digging. The sugarbush protea can be propagated from seed. Unless carefully handled, seedlings tend to damp off, so it may be easier (and quicker) to buy plants from a nursery.

Natural distribution: It grows in a variety of habitats and is widespread in the south-western and southern Cape.

National tree number 94.2

Flowering time:
Autumn to spring

Protea roupelliae   PROTEACEAE

Drakensberg protea

5 m × 4 m

Of moderate growth rate, the Drakensberg protea has silver-blue foliage and a tree-like habit. The flower bracts are deep pink, fading to white, and the centres are filled with creamy hairs. The plant requires well-drained, acid soil in an airy, sunny position. Water well in summer. Provide a thick mulch of organic matter, preferably pine needles, but do not apply artificial fertilisers or manure and do not disturb the root area by digging. The Drakensberg protea can be propagated from seed, but as young seedlings damp off easily, it may be quicker to buy a plant from a nursery.

Natural distribution: It grows on grassy hillsides and on mountain slopes, from the eastern Cape to the extreme eastern Orange Free State, the Natal Drakensberg, Swaziland and the central, eastern and northern Transvaal.

National tree number 96

Flowering time:
Summer

Rhamnus prinoides   RHAMNACEAE

Dogwood

4 m × 4 m

This fairly fast-growing plant may form a dense, bushy shrub – sometimes scrambling into surrounding plants – or a small tree up to 6 m high. It has dark brown bark and attractive, dense, shiny, dark foliage. Small greenish flowers are followed by spherical, fleshy fruits the size of a pea, which are purple when ripe and are eaten by birds. The dogwood grows easily in most soils and may make a good waterside plant. It is easily propagated from seed.

Natural distribution: It grows on the margins of evergreen forest, along riverbanks and in riverine bush, from Swellendam, through the eastern Cape, the Orange Free State and Lesotho, to the Transkei, Natal, Swaziland, the eastern and north-eastern Transvaal and Zimbabwe.

National tree number 452

Flowering time:
October to December

Rhigozum obovatum   BIGNONIACEAE

Karoo gold, Yellow pomegranate

3 m × 2 m

This twiggy, spiny shrub, of moderate growth rate, has very small blue-green leaves and trumpet-shaped golden yellow flowers and should be planted in a well-drained position, e.g. in a rockery. Rigid and upright, this little bush is rather dull and bare-looking for most of the year, but is spectacular in full flower, when it is a mass of bright yellow, and is well worth planting. Although the Karoo gold tolerates drought and neglect, the results are better if plenty of compost is added to the soil, and the plant is well watered in winter. It is easily propagated from seed.

Natural distribution: It grows in hot, dry, rocky areas in the northern and eastern Cape, the southern Orange Free State and southern Namibia.

National tree number 675

Flowering time:
Spring or early summer

Rhus batophylla   ANACARDIACEAE

Redberry rhus, Grey rhus

3 m × 4 m

The redberry rhus has a moderate growth rate and is suitable for an informal shrub border. The plant branches freely from the base and has attractive, strongly toothed grey leaves and small yellow-green flowers, followed by long spikes of deep red fruits, which remain on the bush for a long time and which birds love. These bright red spikes stick out above the grey foliage and are very decorative. This shrub is fairly tender to frost and would do better in warmer gardens. Plant it in good, well-drained soil, adding plenty of compost, and water well in summer. Prune the plant to keep it neat, if necessary. Propagate from seed.

Natural distribution: It grows on rocky koppies in the Lydenburg area of the Transvaal.

Flowering time:
October or November

Rothmannia globosa   RUBIACEAE

Bell gardenia, September bells

4 m × 3 m

This is a beautiful ornamental shrub, of moderate growth rate, which may grow to be a small, slender tree up to 6 m high under favourable conditions. It has glossy, dark green foliage and masses of large, sweetly scented, bell-shaped cream flowers. The round green fruits – approximately 2,5 cm in diameter – become hard, woody and brown when ripe. Plant the bell gardenia in good, well-drained garden soil, adding plenty of compost, and water throughout the year. Propagate from seed.

Natural distribution: It grows in coastal and dune bush, along riverbanks, and on the margins of evergreen forest, from the eastern Cape through the Transkei to Natal, Zululand, Swaziland and the eastern Transvaal.

National tree number 695

Flowering time:
Spring to summer

Ruttya fruticosa   ACANTHACEAE

Jammy mouth

4 m × 4 m

This is a large, bushy, rounded shrub which may scramble up into surrounding trees if allowed and may also be trained over a carport or strong pergola to provide shade. Semideciduous and of moderate growth rate, it has glossy, dark green foliage and showy, tubular yellow or orange flowers, each with a shiny dark patch on its lip. Plant the jammy mouth in good garden soil, adding plenty of compost and water well in summer. Prune the plant back hard after flowering to keep it neat. Propagate from semi-hardwood cuttings.

Natural distribution: It grows in East Africa.

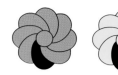

Flowering time:
Summer

Scutia myrtina   RHAMNACEAE

Cat thorn, Droog-my-keel

6 m × 8 m

The very fast-growing cat thorn usually occurs as a sprawling shrub or vigorous climber, but may form a small tree up to approximately 8 m high. It has strong, curved thorns and attractive, glossy, dark green foliage which may be used as stock fodder. The inconspicuous, fragrant flowers are followed by small, round, fleshy fruits, which are purple-black when ripe, and are eaten by humans and birds. Plant this shrub in any soil, adding plenty of compost, and water well throughout the year. Propagate from seed.

Natural distribution: It grows on the margins of evergreen forest, in coastal and evergreen bush, and on steep wooded hillsides, from the Cape Peninsula eastwards to Knysna and northwards through the Transkei and Orange Free State, Natal, Zululand and Swaziland, to the central and northern Transvaal, Zimbabwe and Mozambique.

National tree number 451

Flowering time:
October to January

Sparrmannia africana   TILIACEAE

Cape stock-rose

4 m × 2 m    to

This fast-growing plant is an attractive, bushy, soft-wooded ornamental which may form a small tree up to 6 m high under favourable conditions. It has smooth greenish-grey to light brown bark. The large, rounded leaves are covered in hairs that may produce a skin irritation. Showy white flowers with a central mass of golden stamens are followed by spherical capsules covered in bristles. The Cape stock-rose will grow very easily in good, compost-enriched soil, but should be planted in a protected position in colder gardens, and must be watered regularly. Propagate from seed or from cuttings.

Natural distribution: It usually grows in moist places, on the margins of evergreen forest, on hillsides, and along riverbanks, in the George, Knysna, Uniondale and Humansdorp areas in the Cape Province.

National tree number 457

Flowering time:
June to November

Strelitzia nicolai   STRELITZIACEAE

Natal wild banana

8 m × 4 m

A fast-growing shrub with tall, bare stems topped by large banana-like leaves, this is a good accent plant. It tends to sucker from the base, so allow plenty of room for it to spread. The large 'bird-of-paradise' flowers are blue-purple-and-cream, and they produce nectar that attracts sunbirds, in particular the olive sunbird. Plant this shrub in a protected position in areas that receive frost, in good soil, adding plenty of compost, and water regularly throughout the year in all areas. Propagate from seed, or by removing suckers.

Natural distribution: It grows in coastal bush and forest, from East London in the eastern Cape to the Zululand-Mozambique border. It also grows in Zimbabwe and Mozambique.

National tree number 34

Flowering time:
Spring to summer

Tarchonanthus camphoratus   ASTERACEAE

Camphor bush

5 m × 5 m

A fast-growing, drought-resistant and frost-hardy plant, the camphor bush may form a dense bushy shrub or a small tree up to 6 m high. It is wind resistant and very tolerant of coastal conditions. The leathery grey-green foliage has an aromatic, camphor-like smell. Terminal sprays of small creamy flowers are followed by tiny fruits covered in what looks like cottonwool – these white woolly sprays are very decorative. Plant this shrub in any compost-enriched soil and water regularly. It is easily propagated from seed.

Natural distribution: It grows in a wide variety of habitats, from arid semidesert to moist coastal forest, in all four provinces of South Africa, and in Lesotho, Swaziland, Zimbabwe, Botswana and Namibia.

National tree number 733

Flowering time:
April to June

Tarchonanthus trilobus   ASTERACEAE

Three-lobed camphor tree

5 m × 4 m

Of moderate growth rate, this plant may form a small tree or rounded shrub with attractive, dark green foliage and a cracked, flaky grey-brown bark. The oblong, aromatic, puckered leaves are three-lobed at the tips and have velvety white undersurfaces. The honey-scented cream flowers occur in short sprays at the tips of the branches. The young fruits are less woolly than those of the previous species. Plant this shrub in good, well-drained soil, adding plenty of compost, and water regularly. Propagate from seed.

Natural distribution: It grows on the margins of evergreen forest, and on wooded hillsides, from the Transkei through Natal and Zululand to the eastern and northern Transvaal.

National tree number 736

Flowering time:
August to February

Turraea floribunda   MELIACEAE

Wild honeysuckle

5 m × 3 m

The wild honeysuckle is an excellent ornamental for the garden with its distinctive, decorative fruits – it is also beautiful in full flower. Of moderate growth rate, it may grow into a small tree up to 5 m high in warm, moist climates. The shrub has soft, light green foliage and bears attractive, sweetly scented, cream-green, honeysuckle-like flowers. The shiny, roundish, deeply ribbed fruits split along the ribs into segments which curl back to expose the bright, shiny orange-red seeds inside, the open fruits appearing like woody flowers. Plant the wild honeysuckle in a very protected position in cold gardens, in good, compost-enriched soil, and water regularly in all areas. Propagate from seed.

Natural distribution: It grows in wooded ravines, open woodland, coastal bush, and along streams, from the eastern Cape through Natal to Zululand. It also grows in Mozambique and Zimbabwe.

National tree number 296

Flowering time:
Spring to early summer

Vepris lanceolata   RUTACEAE

White ironwood

6 m × 5 m   to

Of moderate growth rate, the white ironwood is a good screen plant. In open woodland it tends to form a dense shrub, more or less triangular in shape, but in deep forest it becomes a tall, graceful tree with a gently rounded crown. It has shiny, light green foliage and sprays of tiny yellowish flowers. The small, slightly fleshy fruits become black when ripe, and are eaten by redwinged starlings and Layard's bulbuls. Plant the white ironwood in good garden soil, adding plenty of compost, and water regularly. Once established, the plant is fairly drought resistant. Propagate from seed.

Natural distribution: It grows in coastal bush, evergreen forest, dry forest, and on sand dunes, from the eastern Cape through the Transkei, Natal and Zululand to Swaziland, the eastern and central Transvaal, and Mozambique.

National tree number 261

Flowering time:
December to March

3 HERBACEOUS PERENNIALS, GROUND COVERS AND BULBS

Herbaceous perennials, ground covers and bulbs have been grouped together in this chapter for practical purposes as these plants all serve to round off the layout of a garden on a relatively permanent basis. As most of these plants are at their best when used in large groups to provide a spectacular display of seasonal colour, the items in this chapter have been arranged according to flower colour, making it easy for the gardener to select those that match a specific colour theme. Several aquatic plants and a variety of attractive foliage plants, mainly ferns, have also been included here.

To ensure healthy plant and root growth thorough preparation of the soil prior to planting is essential. It is particularly important to add as much organic matter as possible to the soil. In loose, sandy soil the organic matter helps to retain water and in heavy clay soil it serves to aerate the soil and improve drainage. Organic material also encourages the development of beneficial micro-organisms as well as earthworm activity, which improves the texture of the soil.

Having marked the outlines of a proposed flowerbed, dig the bed over to a depth of about 50 cm, breaking up all large clods of soil. Spread a thick layer of compost – about 30 dm^3 (one bag) per square metre – evenly over the surface and sprinkle approximately 125-190 ml each of superphosphate and slow-release 3:2:1 fertiliser per square metre on top of the compost. Dig the whole bed over again to work in the compost and fertiliser.

Water thoroughly after planting and thereafter two or three times a week in very hot, dry and/or windy weather and once a week in cooler weather. A good, deep watering is much more beneficial than numerous short sprinklings. If a bed contains only shallow-rooted plants such as annuals and ground covers, saturating the top 10 cm of the soil should suffice, but a bed which also contains shrubs and trees needs much deeper watering. Allow the top 5-7 cm of soil to dry out before watering again. Constantly oversaturated soil prevents air reaching the roots and could result in root rot, thus killing the plants. It is important to remember that plants originating in the winter rainfall region have to be watered through the winter if grown in the summer rainfall area and vice versa.

Plants should be fertilised at six- to eight-weekly intervals throughout the growing season, using slow-release 3:2:1 for foliage plants and 3:1:5 for flowering plants. Bulbs should be fed from the time that they stop flowering until they become dormant. Always mulch flowerbeds with a 10 cm thick layer of organic matter and replenish regularly.

Most of the plants discussed in this chapter will thrive for several years if rejuvenated from time to time. Bulbs such as watsonias, nerines and March lilies form new side bulbs as the plants grow older and the clump slowly increases in size. After several years the quality and number of flowers on such old clumps start to diminish. At this stage the whole clump can be lifted with a fork after the flowering season and the bulbs separated by hand and replanted or stored in a dry, dark place until the following planting season. The same applies to plants with fleshy, swollen roots, such as agapanthus, wild garlic, irises and red-hot pokers. Separate the sections by hand or with a knife and replant immediately.

Carpeting ground covers will form a dense mat which may eventually die back in patches and look untidy. At this stage some of the more vigorous types can be rejuvenated by cutting back most of the growth above ground in early spring. Spike the soil between the plants carefully with a fork to aerate it, apply mulch and fertiliser and water in well.

Aloe striata   ASPHODELACEAE
Coral aloe

1 m × 1 m

This fast-growing, drought-resistant plant is one of the most attractive aloes. It has a basal rosette of thornless grey-green leaves and a branched inflorescence of tubular, deep coral red flowers which produce nectar that attracts sunbirds. Suitable for a rockery in both summer and winter rainfall areas, it should be planted in very well-drained, sandy soil with the addition of plenty of compost. Propagate the coral aloe from seed or by removing young suckers, and protect young plants from frost.

Natural distribution: It grows on dry, rocky hillsides in the southern and eastern Cape.

Flowering time:
Winter to spring

Aloe wickensii   ASPHODELACEAE
Wickens's aloe

1 m × 1 m

This striking aloe is a fast-growing, drought-resistant plant which forms large clumps of succulent grey leaves. Tubular red-and-yellow flowers are carried on branched inflorescences. Wickens's aloe is very easily grown in well-drained, compost-enriched soil, but in frosty areas it should be planted in a protected position. Water in summer and keep dry in winter. Propagate this aloe from seed and protect young plants from frost.

Natural distribution: It grows on rocky koppies in the northern and eastern Transvaal.

Flowering time:
June or July

Antholyza ringens   IRIDACEAE
Rat's tail

30 cm × 30 cm

This small cormous plant has a moderate growth rate and strongly ribbed or pleated leaves. The tubular scarlet flowers are carried on a stalk that resembles a rat's tail. Curious and unusual, this plant would do well in a rockery. Plant corms in groups of at least 10-20 (15 cm deep), in very well-drained, compost-enriched soil, and water well in winter. They are dormant in summer and should be kept as dry as possible. Propagate this plant from seed.

Natural distribution: It grows in coastal areas of the south-western Cape.

Flowering time:
Spring

RIGHT *Antholyza plicata*, which is related to *A. ringens*.

Aptenia cordifolia MESEMBRYANTHEMACEAE
Aptenia

15 cm × 60 cm   to

Flowering time:
Spring to summer

Vigorous, fast-spreading and drought resistant, this ground cover has semisucculent, light green leaves and small, dark rose-pink flowers. It is an excellent ground cover for planting under trees, or on a steep bank or slope where it will help to hold the soil. Plant it in any soil, adding plenty of compost, and water moderately throughout the year. The aptenia is easily propagated from cuttings.

Natural distribution: It grows in the Cape, Natal, Swaziland and the Transvaal.

Babiana villosa IRIDACEAE
Red babiana

25 cm × 25 cm

Flowering time:
September

Of moderate growth rate, the red babiana is a cormous plant with ribbed leaves and fragrant, deep red flowers. Plant corms in March – in groups of at least 12-15, about 5 cm apart and 15 cm deep – in a rockery. Babianas must always be planted deeply, i.e. to a depth of 15-20 cm, in well-drained, compost-enriched soil. Although they will tolerate clay soil, riversand and plenty of compost must be added if planting in this medium. In the summer rainfall area they must be well watered in winter, and they must always be kept reasonably dry in summer. If drainage is good, the corms can be left in the ground for three to four years, but if poor, they must be lifted and stored in a cool, dry place until the following March. In the Cape they can be left permanently in the ground. Propagate the red babiana from seed or by removing offsets from the 'parent' corms.

Natural distribution: It grows in the Tulbagh area of the south-western Cape.

Cotyledon orbiculata CRASSULACEAE
Pig's ear

1 m × 0,5 m

Flowering time:
Summer

The fast-growing pig's ear usually forms a small shrub with roundish, succulent grey-green leaves, each with a red margin. The bell-shaped orange-red flowers are borne on branched inflorescences. This drought-resistant plant prefers full sun – it is a good plant for a rockery in hot, dry areas, or for a container on a sunny patio – but can tolerate light shade for a short part of the day. Plant it in light, well-drained, compost-enriched soil, and water in summer but keep dry in winter. It is easily propagated from seed or from cuttings, which must be kept fairly dry to prevent rot.

Natural distribution: It grows in grassland and on rocky koppies, from Namaqualand and the western, southern and eastern Cape through Natal, Lesotho, Swaziland and the Orange Free State to the eastern, central and northern Transvaal and Namibia.

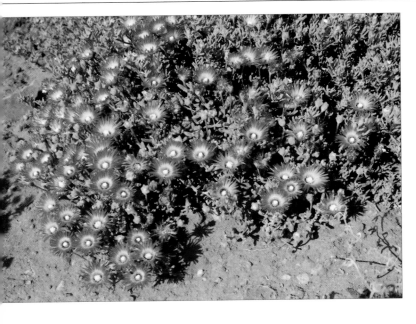

Crassula coccinea CRASSULACEAE

Red crassula

60 cm × 40 cm

Of moderate growth rate, the red crassula has erect stems with symmetrically arranged, succulent leaves, and rounded heads of tiny, tubular, dark red flowers. A good rockery or container plant, it prefers light, well-drained, compost-enriched soil, water in winter and a dry summer. Propagate the red crassula from seed or from cuttings (which should be allowed to dry out a little before planting in riversand), and protect young plants from frost.

Natural distribution: It grows on the mountains in the south-western Cape.

Flowering time:
Late summer

Crassula perfoliata CRASSULACEAE

Sickle crassula

30 cm × 30 cm

The sickle crassula – which is of moderate growth rate – has succulent, sickle-shaped grey-green leaves, hence its common name. Rounded heads of tiny, star-shaped, bright red flowers are borne at the tips of the stems. Plant this succulent in groups of at least 10-15 plants, in a rockery or in a large container on a sunny patio. The soil must be light, well drained and compost enriched. Water in summer and keep dry in winter. Propagate this plant from seed or from cuttings (which should be allowed to dry out a little before planting in riversand), and keep fairly dry to prevent rot.

Natural distribution: It grows on dry, rocky koppies in the eastern Cape, the Transkei, Natal, Swaziland and the northern and north-eastern Transvaal.

Flowering time:
January or February

RIGHT *Crassula* sp., which has a flower very similar to that of *C. perfoliata.*

Drosanthemum speciosum

MESEMBRYANTHEMACEAE

Red ice-plant

60 cm × 60 cm

This is a fast-growing shrublet, with small, succulent leaves, and red or orange 'vygie' flowers that have pale yellow centres. Plant it in a well-drained rockery or on a bank, to form a ground cover. Water moderately in winter but keep fairly dry in summer. This plant is at its best for about three years, after which it should be replaced. Propagate from seed or from cuttings planted in riversand – the latter do not root easily.

Natural distribution: It grows in the south-western Cape.

Flowering time:
Spring

Gazania krebsiana ASTERACEAE

Gazania

25 cm × 30 cm

Flowering time:
Spring and summer

The fast-growing gazania forms a basal clump of grey-green leaves and carries its daisy-like flowers on longish stalks above the foliage. These shiny, brightly coloured, blotched and striped flowers (which only open in the sun) come in an incredible range of colours. Mass plant close together to form a ground cover, in light, well-drained, compost-enriched soil, and water well in winter and spring – keep them fairly dry in summer or the plants may rot. Propagate the gazania from seed or by division of clumps. The plants will also selfseed. They hybridise freely, resulting in a new range of beautifully marked, brilliantly coloured flowers. These younger plants can be left to replace the older ones which need to be removed after about three years. The older clumps may also be lifted, divided and the younger portions replanted, but it is usually better to make cuttings from the younger stems. The cuttings can be rooted in coarse riversand or in a mixture of riversand and organic potting soil. When the cuttings have developed strong roots they are ready to be planted into the garden.

Natural distribution: It grows in the drier areas of the Karoo and Namaqualand in the Cape Province, and in Lesotho, Natal, Swaziland, the Orange Free State, the Transvaal and Botswana.

Gerbera jamesonii ASTERACEAE

Barberton daisy

40 cm × 30 cm

Flowering time:
September to November

The Barberton daisy has a moderate growth rate and is a perennial with a basal clump of leaves, and daisy flowers carried on long stalks. Single and double hybrids are available in a wide variety of beautiful colours, and they make excellent cut flowers for the vase. Plant this daisy in a rockery or a slightly raised bed, with well-drained soil, and do not disturb or divide unnecessarily as flowering may be affected. This plant is easily grown and needs little attention once established. Add plenty of compost to the soil, fertilise, and water well in summer. Remove dead flowers regularly to encourage further blooms and keep fairly dry in winter. Propagate the Barberton daisy from fresh seed of less than three months old, or by division of the clumps in spring or autumn.

Natural distribution: It grows in well-drained soil in the grassland of the eastern Transvaal.

LEFT *Gerbera jamesonii*.
CENTRE AND RIGHT (ABOVE AND BELOW) *Gerbera jamesonii* hybrid.

Haemanthus coccineus AMARYLLIDACEAE
March flower

25 cm × 25 cm

Flowering time:
Autumn

The March flower bears a 'brush' of bright red flowers, surrounded by waxy red bracts, which appears before the strap-shaped leaves. Plant this bulb with its neck just below the soil surface, in groups under trees or in a rockery or a raised bed (in frosty gardens it must have a position sheltered from the morning sun), in light, well-drained, compost-enriched soil. Water about once a week throughout winter in the summer rainfall area. Do not disturb unnecessarily as flowering may be affected. This plant has a moderate growth rate and, as it is dormant in summer, it must be kept dry during this period. Propagate from very fresh seed, planted just below the soil surface, or by removing offsets from the 'mother' bulb.

Natural distribution: It grows in shaded kloofs and rock crevices – as well as on flats in the shelter of bushes and shrubs in the winter rainfall area – from southern Namibia to the Cape Peninsula and eastwards to Grahamstown.

Homoglossum priorii IRIDACEAE
Flames

40 cm × 20 cm

Flowering time:
Autumn

Of moderate growth rate, this is a cormous plant with strap-shaped leaves and red gladiolus-like flowers. Plant it in groups for a striking display – in a very well-drained position – approximately 5 cm deep and 10 cm apart. Add plenty of compost to the soil and water well in winter, especially in the summer rainfall area. Keep fairly dry in summer when the plant is dormant. Propagate from seed or by removing offsets from the 'mother' corm.

Natural distribution: It grows on mountainsides and sandy flats in the southwestern Cape.

LEFT AND CENTRE *Homoglossum priorii.* **RIGHT** *Homoglossum huttonii.*

Kalanchoe blossfeldiana CRASSULACEAE
Red kalanchoe

30 cm × 30 cm   to

Flowering time:
Winter to spring

This is a fast-growing succulent with glossy, dark green leaves and masses of tiny red flowers, carried in large, flattish heads. Many attractively coloured hybrids are available and, as this beautiful succulent grows well in a container, it can be brought indoors in winter to provide colour for a couple of months. In frost-free areas it can be grown outdoors in a rockery in light, well-drained, compost-enriched soil. Water the kalanchoe moderately and propagate it from seed or from cuttings.

Natural distribution: It grows in Madagascar.

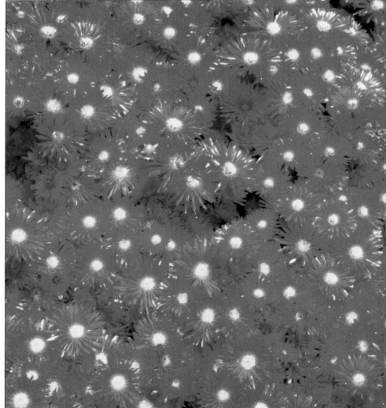

Kniphofia praecox   ASPHODELACEAE
Red-hot poker

1,5 m × 1,5 m

Flowering time:
Winter

The red-hot poker has a moderate growth rate and forms large clumps of strap-shaped leaves, with its flowers carried on tall, stout stalks in poker-shaped heads. The closely packed buds are bright orange, but become yellow as they open. This plant looks attractive situated next to a dam or stream, or in a mixed border. Plant it in good, well-drained, compost-enriched soil. It is easy to grow provided it receives sufficient water in the growing season. Do not move or divide it unless absolutely necessary, as flowering may be affected. Propagate the red-hot poker from seed (which may take up to six weeks to germinate) or by the division of larger clumps, which spread by means of rhizomes. Sow the seed in trays any time from spring to autumn. The seedlings are planted into the garden when they are five to six months old (or about 15 cm high) and should be kept moist at all times to ensure success. The plant takes two to three years to flower well. Older clumps should only be divided when the quality of the flowers they produce begins to deteriorate. Lift the clump and divide it with a spade. Discard older portions and replant the younger rhizomes immediately. Water well and keep the plant moist until it has re-established itself.

Natural distribution: It grows in marshy places, from the eastern Cape through Natal to the eastern Transvaal.

Lampranthus coccineus
MESEMBRYANTHEMACEAE
Red vygie

45 cm × 60 cm

Flowering time:
Spring

This is a moderately fast-growing plant with a trailing habit, which has small, cylindrical, succulent leaves and bright red 'vygie' flowers. Mass plant to form a ground cover in a rockery or on a steep bank. They make a spectacular show in the flowering season and should be mixed with other colourful vygies to produce a vibrant effect. The flowers only open fully on bright, sunny days. Plant the red vygie in well-drained, compost-enriched soil and water moderately from autumn to spring. Propagate from seed or from cuttings taken in summer.

Natural distribution: It grows in the south-western Cape.

Nerine sarniensis AMARYLLIDACEAE
Guernsey lily, Red nerine

45 cm × 30 cm

This bulbous plant, of moderate growth rate, has strap-shaped leaves and rounded heads of bright red flowers carried on stout stalks. The flowers have a sparkling iridescence and the petals curl back delicately. Plant groups of bulbs 6-10 cm apart in a rockery, with the neck of each bulb above soil level, and leave undisturbed for at least three years. Plant in good, well-drained, compost-enriched soil and water well in winter, especially in the summer rainfall area. If the bulbs cannot be kept dry in summer, they must be lifted, stored, and replanted the following February. Propagate this plant from very fresh seed or by removing offsets from the 'mother' plant.

Natural distribution: It grows high up in the mountains of the Cape Peninsula and the south-western Cape.

Flowering time:
March

Scadoxus puniceus AMARYLLIDACEAE
Paintbrush, Blood lily

50 cm × 30 cm

This plant has a moderate growth rate and bears a brush-like head of scarlet flowers from among the glossy, strap-shaped leaves. The beautiful flowers are followed by fleshy red berries, which are eaten by birds. Plant the paintbrush – not too deeply – in shade under trees, in good, well-drained, compost-enriched soil, and do not disturb unnecessarily as flowering may be affected. Water it regularly in summer and keep reasonably dry in winter. Propagate this plant from fresh seed.

Natural distribution: It grows in open grassland, or under trees in lightly wooded areas, in the southern and eastern Cape, Natal, and the eastern Transvaal.

LEFT AND CENTRE *Scadoxus multiflorus*, which is similar to *S. puniceus*.
RIGHT (ABOVE AND BELOW) *Scadoxus puniceus*.

Flowering time:
Spring

Schizostylis coccinea IRIDACEAE
Scarlet river lily

50 cm × 20 cm

The scarlet river lily has a moderate growth rate and strap-like leaves. Beautiful star-shaped scarlet flowers with satiny petals are carried on long stalks. As its name implies it should be planted near water – it likes moist conditions. Plant it in good, compost-enriched soil and water regularly, especially during summer. Do not disturb unnecessarily as flowering may be affected. The best time to transplant, if necessary, would be from January to April. Propagate this lily from seed or by dividing the rhizomes – it is important to leave at least five to six plants per clump.

Natural distribution: It grows along the edges of streams in the eastern Cape, Transkei, Lesotho, the Natal midlands and uplands, the eastern Orange Free State, Swaziland and the southern and eastern Transvaal.

Flowering time:
December to January

Sparaxis hybrids IRIDACEAE
Harlequin flower

20 cm × 10 cm

Flowering time:
Spring

This is a fast-growing, cormous plant with blade-like leaves and brightly coloured, cup-shaped, velvety flowers, carried on wiry stems. The flowers range in colour from cream to the most luminous reds and purples, often with blotches or markings in contrasting colours. Plant the corms, about 10 cm apart in large groups in well-drained soil with plenty of compost, in March, and water well in winter, especially in the summer rainfall area. The corms can be left in the ground year-round as they do not rot easily, but make sure the soil is well drained if the plant is cultivated in the summer rainfall area. Propagate the harlequin flower from seed sown in March, or by removing offsets from the 'mother' corms.

Natural distribution: It grows in the south-western Cape.

Tritonia crocata IRIDACEAE
Blazing star

20 cm × 15 cm

Flowering time:
Spring to summer

Fast growing, this tritonia species has a fan of stiff, pointed leaves and carries several bright orange-red flowers at the top of a long and slender stalk. Plant the corms about 7 cm deep in fairly large groups in a rockery in good, well-drained, compost-enriched soil. Water well in winter, especially in the summer rainfall area, and keep fairly dry in summer – the corms may be left in the soil year-round as they do not rot easily. Propagate this plant from seed or by removing offsets from the 'parent' corm.

Natural distribution: It grows in the south-western Cape.

Veltheimia bracteata HYACINTHACEAE
Bush lily

45 cm × 45 cm

Flowering time:
July to September

The bush lily has a moderate growth rate and is a bulbous plant which bears heads of tubular pink-red flowers that are carried on long stalks. The flowers resemble those of the aloe and last for about a month. The attractive, wavy, glossy green leaves, which are broad and strap shaped, die back in midsummer and, after a short dormancy period of a couple of weeks, are replaced by new leaves. Plant the bush lily in groups under trees, or in a container on a shady patio. Do not disturb unnecessarily as flowering may be affected. Plant in good, well-drained, compost-enriched soil and water regularly throughout the year, but more in winter, especially in the summer rainfall area. The plants will be unharmed by severe frost if overhanging branches protect them from the early morning sun. Propagate the bush lily from seed or by removing offsets from the 'parent' bulbs.

Natural distribution: It grows in the forests of the eastern Cape, Transkei and Natal.

Watsonia galpinii   IRIDACEAE

Galpin's watsonia

75 cm × 20 cm   to

Flowering time:
February or March

Of moderate growth rate, this is a small watsonia with brilliant orange-scarlet flowers that are carried on long, slender stalks. It prefers moist conditions throughout the year. Plant the corms about 5-7 cm deep in good, well-drained, compost-enriched soil and leave undisturbed for at least four to five years. When the quality of the flowers begins to deteriorate the clump may be lifted, divided and immediately replanted. Propagate Galpin's watsonia from seed or by removing offsets from the 'parent' corms.

Natural distribution: It grows in moist places near George in the southern Cape.

LEFT *Watsonia angusta*, which has a growth habit similar to that of *W. galpinii*.

Ixia spp.   IRIDACEAE

Ixia

30 cm × 10 cm

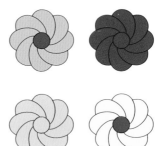

Flowering time:
Spring

Many hybrids of this fast-growing plant are available in different colours. It has fine, grassy leaves and dense clusters of star-shaped flowers carried on tall, wiry stems. For a mass of colour, plant large groups (at least 30-50 corms per group) in autumn, with each corm at a depth of approximately 4 cm. Plant in well-drained, compost-enriched soil and water well in winter, especially in the summer rainfall area. Keep dry in summer when the plants are dormant or, after the foliage has died, lift the corms and store them in a dry place. Propagate the ixia from seed sown in March, or by removing offsets from the 'mother' corms.

Natural distribution: It grows in the south-western Cape.

LEFT AND CENTRE (ABOVE) *Ixia* sp.   CENTRE (BELOW) *I. orientalis*.
RIGHT (ABOVE) *I. maculata*.   RIGHT (BELOW) *I. viridiflora*.

Aloe vanbalenii   ASPHODELACEAE

Van Balen's aloe

1 m × 0,5 m

Flowering time:
August to September

Van Balen's aloe has succulent, strap-shaped olive-green leaves, which sometimes have a red tinge, and tubular creamy-yellow flowers carried at the tips of tall stalks. Of moderate growth rate, it is ideal for rockeries, or steep, dry slopes. It requires good, well-drained, compost-enriched soil, and should be watered in summer and kept fairly dry in winter. Propagate this aloe from seed or by removing young offsets from the 'mother' plant. Protect young plants from frost.

Natural distribution: This aloe grows in Zululand and the south-eastern Transvaal.

Arctotheca calendula   ASTERACEAE
Cape weed

10 cm × 40 cm

Very fast growing and hardy, this is an excellent, fairly drought-resistant ground cover. Its leaves are green above and grey below and it produces yellow daisy-like flowers throughout the year. Plant the Cape weed in any garden soil, add plenty of compost, and water moderately. The plant spreads by means of runners and is propagated by lifting the rooted runners. It is said to be an annual in some parts of the Cape.

Natural distribution: The Cape weed grows in Namaqualand and the south-western Cape.

Flowering time:
Throughout the year

Arctotis 'Silver Lining'   ASTERACEAE
Silver arctotis

10 cm × 30 cm

This is a fast-growing ground cover with silver-grey foliage and yellow daisy-like flowers. The leaves have attractive cream borders. Plant this arctotis in a rockery or on a steep slope or a bank – it prefers a well-drained position in full sun, or with very light shade for part of the day. The soil must be light and have plenty of compost added. Water well in winter, especially in the summer rainfall area, and moderately in summer. Propagate this plant from cuttings or by dividing the clumps.

Natural distribution: It grows in the Cape Province.

Flowering time:
Spring, summer and autumn

Bulbine angustifolia   ASPHODELACEAE
Grass bulbine

25 cm × 25 cm

This plant is drought resistant and has a moderate growth rate. Its leaves form a small, grass-like clump approximately 25 cm high. The flowering stalk is about a metre high and carries masses of star-shaped yellow flowers. The grass bulbine is suitable for a rockery and, for a good display, should be mass planted close together in good, well-drained and compost-enriched soil. Water it well in summer and keep on the dry side in winter when the plant is dormant. Propagate it from seed or by the division of large clumps.

Natural distribution: It grows amongst rocks in grassland, in Botswana and the eastern, western, northern and central Transvaal.

Flowering time:
November or December

Bulbine frutescens   ASPHODELACEAE

Stalked bulbine

30 cm × 40 cm

Flowering time:
Spring, summer and autumn

This is a vigorous, spreading, drought-resistant plant requiring little attention. It has succulent, cylindrical grey-green leaves and spikes of star-shaped yellow or orange flowers carried on long stalks. Mass plant to form an excellent ground cover for drier areas. It combines beautifully with dwarf blue agapanthus, which flower at the same time. Although it prefers full sun, it will also tolerate light shade for part of the day. Plant it in any garden soil, adding plenty of compost, and water moderately throughout the year. Deadhead to keep the plant neat and to encourage further flowering. Propagate from seed or cuttings, or by the division of rhizomes.

Natural distribution: It is widespread in the Cape, and also occurs along the Natal coast, and in Lesotho, Swaziland, the Orange Free State and the Transvaal.

Bulbinella latifolia   ASPHODELACEAE

Cat's tail

45 cm × 30 cm

Flowering time:
July or August

The cat's tail is a fast-growing, drought-resistant perennial which develops a thick mass of fibrous roots. The plant forms clumps of broad, tapering leaves and has poker-shaped spikes, about 75 cm high, which carry masses of small, star-shaped yellow or orange flowers. Plant the cat's tail in large groups – in a very well-drained position in the summer rainfall area – in full sun or very light shade. The soil must be good and light and must contain plenty of compost. Place the roots just below the surface of the soil, and water the plant well in autumn and winter, especially in the summer rainfall area. It is dormant from about November to February and should not be watered unnecessarily during this period. Propagate this perennial from seed sown in March, or by the division of larger clumps.

Natural distribution: It grows in vleis in the south-western Cape.

CENTRE *Bulbinella* sp., which is similar to *B. latifolia*.

Carpobrotus edulis   MESEMBRYANTHEMACEAE

Yellow sour fig

0,15 m × 1 m

Flowering time:
Spring

The yellow sour fig is a trailing plant with three-sided, fleshy leaves, which spreads rapidly to form a tough, drought-resistant ground cover. The yellow 'vygie' flowers, which fade to pink as they age, are followed by edible fruits. The plant can be used to hold soil on steep banks, as a ground cover in hot, dry areas, or for roadside planting. It tolerates all soils and grows quickly and easily, rooting as it spreads. Water moderately from autumn to spring, especially in the summer rainfall area. The yellow sour fig is easily propagated from cuttings or by lifting rooted runners.

Natural distribution: It grows along the coast in the south-western Cape.

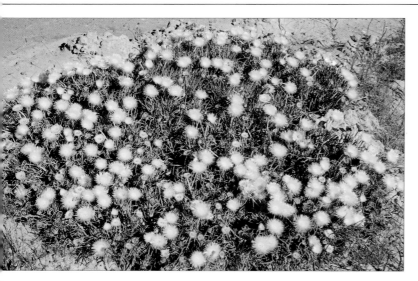

Cineraria saxifraga ASTERACEAE

Wild cineraria

15 cm × 40 cm

Fast growing, the wild cineraria has soft, roundish, light green leaves and masses of small yellow flowers. This delicate ground cover grows well in a container, draping itself over the edges and cascading to the ground. It will also do well in a rockery or on a steep bank, and in addition makes a good ground cover for light shade. Plant the wild cineraria in good, well-drained, compost-enriched soil and water regularly. It is slightly frost-tender and is probably better suited to warmer gardens. Propagate it from cuttings or by removing rooted runners from the 'parent' plant.

Natural distribution: It grows in the eastern Cape and the eastern Orange Free State.

Flowering time:
Spring to autumn

Conicosia pugioniformis

MESEMBRYANTHEMACEAE

Gansies, Snotwortel

15 cm × 40 cm

This fast-growing plant has succulent, cylindrical grey-green leaves and large, shiny, deep yellow 'vygie' flowers. It makes a good ground cover for dry, sandy soils, or for a rockery and may be mass planted on a slope to provide a beautiful splash of colour in spring. Plant it in light, well-drained, compost-enriched soil. Water sparingly in winter in the summer rainfall area. Propagate this plant from seed or from cuttings.

Natural distribution: It grows in sandy soils north of Cape Town as far as Namaqualand.

Flowering time:
Spring

Didelta carnosa ASTERACEAE

Duinegousblom

1 m × 1 m

This well-rounded, fast-growing little bush has attractive silver-grey foliage and yellow daisy-like flowers. Mass plant it to form a ground cover to control the sand in coastal gardens – it is tolerant of sea spray and strong winds and should also do well in gardens away from the coast. Plant the duinegousblom in well-drained sandy soil, adding plenty of compost, and water regularly. Propagate from seed.

Natural distribution: It grows on coastal sand dunes from the south-western Cape to Namibia.

Flowering time:
Summer

Drosanthemum bicolor
MESEMBRYANTHEMACEAE

Bicoloured ice-plant

60 cm × 60 cm

Flowering time:
Spring

This fast-growing shrublet has small succulent leaves and bears bicoloured 'vygie' flowers that have brilliant, shiny red tips and yellow centres. The flowers cover the entire bush in spring and make a spectacular show, although they only open fully on bright sunny days. Mass plant this perennial in a well-drained rockery to form a ground cover. The soil must be light and contain plenty of compost. Water moderately in winter and keep fairly dry in summer. This plant is at its best for about three years, after which it should be replaced. Propagate from seed or from cuttings planted in riversand – the latter do not root easily.

Natural distribution: This plant grows in the south-western Cape.

Dymondia margaretae   ASTERACEAE

Silver carpet

10 cm × 30 cm

Flowering time:
Spring

Fast growing, the silver carpet forms a neat, prostrate, fairly drought-resistant ground cover, with blue-grey foliage and small, yellow daisy-like flowers. If not given a well-drained position the plant tends to rot and die back – in high rainfall areas it should be planted on a steep slope or in a raised rockery. It could also be used to form a ground cover between paving stones or railway sleepers. Plant the silver carpet in light, sandy, well-drained soil, adding plenty of compost. Do not overwater. Propagate from seed or by the division of clumps.

Natural distribution: It grows in the southern Cape.

Eucomis autumnalis   HYACINTHACEAE

Pineapple flower

75 cm × 75 cm

Flowering time:
Summer

This fast-growing plant has strap-shaped leaves and yellow-green flowers which are carried on a spike. At the top of each of these spikes, above the densely packed flowers, is a tuft of leaf-like bracts – the flower stalk thus resembles a pineapple. These are excellent cut flowers and the plant also makes an unusual and attractive ground cover if mass planted under trees. It requires partial, light shade otherwise it will not flower well. Plant the pineapple flower with the neck of the bulb just below the surface, in very well-drained, sandy soil, adding plenty of compost. Water well in summer and keep fairly dry in winter. The bulbs need not be lifted in either the summer or winter rainfall areas, provided the drainage is good. Propagate the plant from seed or by removing offsets from the 'parent' bulbs – replant immediately.

Natural distribution: It grows in grassland in the northern and eastern Cape, Natal, Lesotho, Swaziland, the Orange Free State and the eastern and northern Transvaal.

Freesia hybrids IRIDACEAE
Freesia

20 cm × 15 cm

The fast-growing, sweetly-scented freesia is available in many colours. These are hybrids and the flower colours include cyclamen, purple, yellow, white, orange and different shades of red and pink. Not as fragrant as the originals, they are more spectacular and make excellent cut flowers for the vase. They are easy to grow: mass plant the corms, pointed side up, and about 15 cm apart and 4 cm deep, in April in a sunny position in light, well-drained soil, adding plenty of compost and superphosphate. Water regularly throughout the growing and flowering season, but do not allow the soil to become sodden. All cormous and bulbous plants feed off the nutrients in the corms and bulbs during the growing season. It is, however, important to remember that these plants need to be fed and watered after they have ceased flowering and until the leaves begin to die back to enable the corms to store enough nutrients to produce a good crop of flowers the following season. Take care not to feed with a fertiliser rich in nitrogen as this will stimulate the development of the leaves at the expense of the flowers and result in inferior blooms. When the foliage turns yellow, slowly withhold watering and keep dry until the following season. In gardens with heavy clay soil, lift the corms and store them in a cool, airy place. Inland, plant the corms in partial shade, to keep the early morning winter sun off the plants – this will prevent frost damage. Propagate the freesia by removing offsets from the 'parent' corms – the clumps may be lifted, divided and replanted every three to four years.

Natural distribution: The original plants grew in the south-western Cape.

Flowering time:
Spring

Gazania rigens var. *rigens* ASTERACEAE
Trailing gazania

15 cm × 40 cm

This is a fast-growing ground cover with silver-grey foliage and yellow daisy-like flowers. Very easy to grow, it is tolerant of coastal conditions, and makes an excellent ground cover for large areas. It is particularly suitable for slopes and banks, cascading over terraced walls or planted alongside roads. Plant the trailing gazania in well-drained soil, adding plenty of compost, and water moderately. Propagate from stem cuttings or by lifting rooted runners.

Natural distribution: It grows in coastal areas, usually near rivers, in the south-western Cape.

Flowering time:
Spring and summer

Gazania rigens var. *uniflora*   ASTERACEAE
Trailing gazania

15 cm × 40 cm

Flowering time:
Spring and summer

This plant is similar to the previous species but has smaller flowers. Easy to grow, it is tolerant of coastal conditions and makes an excellent ground cover for large, sunny areas. Use it in large tubs or planting boxes, allow it to cascade over terraced walls or dry banks, or plant it on traffic islands. Plant this trailing gazania in well-drained soil, adding plenty of compost, and water moderately. It may be cut back hard, if necessary, to keep it in check. Propagate from stem cuttings or by lifting rooted runners.

Natural distribution: It grows in coastal areas, usually near rivers, in the south-western Cape.

Helichrysum argyrophyllum   ASTERACEAE
Everlasting

10 cm × 25 cm

Flowering time:
Summer

A fast-growing, dense ground cover with papery, golden yellow, daisy-like flowers, the everlasting forms a low-growing mat and covers the soil with its attractive silver-grey foliage. It is ideal for a rockery, where it can drape itself over the rocks, or for cascading over a terraced wall. Use between stepping stones, or in large containers on a sunny patio, or as a ground cover in a steeply sloping flowerbed. Plant the everlasting in a warm, sunny position in well-drained, sandy soil, adding plenty of compost, and do not overwater. If cut back by frost, it will recover rapidly in spring. Propagate from seed or by lifting rooted runners.

Natural distribution: It grows in the drier areas of the eastern Cape.

Helichrysum cymosum subsp. *cymosum*
ASTERACEAE

Gold carpet

10 cm × 40 cm

Flowering time:
Summer or autumn

A fast-growing ground cover with grey-green foliage and terminal heads of small yellow flowers, the gold carpet lives up to its name by being covered in masses of these flowers in late summer and autumn. It is an excellent and attractive ground cover for hotter, drier areas and would do well on steep banks or in raised rockeries. Plant it in a very well-drained position, in full sun and in sandy soil, adding plenty of compost. Do not overwater – if conditions are too moist and the drainage is bad, this plant tends to die back in large patches. Cut it back, if necessary, to keep it in check. Propagate from cuttings or by lifting rooted runners.

Natural distribution: It grows in the drier areas of the Cape and Natal.

Hypoxis hemerocallidea   HYPOXIDACEAE

(= *H. rooperi*)

Star flower

50 cm × 50 cm

Flowering time:
Spring and summer

This beautiful, hardy plant of moderate growth rate has a large bulb, strap-shaped leaves and starry yellow flowers. Plant it in large groups in a rockery. It comes from the summer rainfall area and flowers freely throughout the summer if the old flower stalks are removed – give a gentle tug and they come out easily. Plant the star flower in full sun in any well-drained garden soil, adding plenty of compost, and water moderately in summer. As the bulbs are dormant in winter, they must be kept fairly dry but need not be lifted if the drainage is good. Propagate this plant from seed.

Natural distribution: It grows in grassland, from the eastern Cape to Natal, the Orange Free State, Lesotho, Swaziland, the Transvaal and Botswana.

Monopsis lutea   LOBELIACEAE

Yellow lobelia

20 cm × 30 cm

Flowering time:
Summer

This is a fast-growing perennial with bright yellow, lobelia-like flowers and small leaves with serrate edges. Plant it in a rockery, or mass plant to form a ground cover. It may also be used as an edging plant for borders or planted in large containers on a sunny patio. The yellow lobelia requires full sun and sandy soil, with the addition of plenty of compost. Water regularly, particularly during autumn and winter. It may die back slightly in the latter season. Propagate from seed sown in March or April.

Natural distribution: It grows in marshy places in the Cape Peninsula.

Nymphoides indica   GENTIANACEAE

Small yellow water lily

30 cm × 80 cm

Flowering time:
November to May

This very fast-growing water lily has rounded, flat leaves and small, starry yellow flowers (the dainty petals have feathery edges) that float on the surface of the water. It is suitable for ornamental ponds and dams. Plant roots in the soil at the bottom of the pond at a depth of about 30-40 cm. The plant may need to be thinned out from time to time. Propagate from seed or by dividing the plants at the end of winter.

Natural distribution: This water lily grows in streams, ponds, rivers and pools throughout South Africa.

RIGHT   The flower of *Nymphoides thunbergiana*, which is very similar to that of *N. indica*.

Othonna carnosa var. *carnosa*   ASTERACEAE

Othonna

10 cm × 60 cm

A very fast-growing, drought-resistant plant with narrow, cylindrical, succulent grey-green leaves, and masses of small, yellow, daisy-like flowers, the othonna is an excellent ground cover for a large sunny rockery, or for holding soil on banks or slopes. It is also ideal for planting on traffic islands, can be grown in large containers, or allowed to cascade over terraced walls. It is very easily grown and requires little attention. Plant the othonna in any soil, adding plenty of compost, and do not overwater. Propagate from cuttings or by lifting rooted runners.

Natural distribution: It grows in the drier areas of the Cape and Lesotho.

Flowering time:
Throughout the year

Oxalis flava   OXALIDACEAE

Yellow oxalis

25 cm × 25 cm

This beautiful little plant is fast growing and has clover-like leaves and starry yellow flowers – which need full sun to open properly – with silky, shiny petals. It has nut-like rhizomes which multiply rapidly so that the plant spreads very quickly under good conditions – therefore position it where this will not be a problem. It is best grown in containers to prevent it becoming weedy. The yellow oxalis grows easily in light, sandy soil. Water regularly in winter, especially in the summer rainfall area, but keep dry in summer. Propagate from seed or by lifting and dividing the clumps.

Natural distribution: It grows in the south-western Cape.

Flowering time:
Winter

LEFT AND RIGHT *Oxalis pes-caprae*, which is similar to *O. flava*.

Senecio tanacetopsis   ASTERACEAE

Lace-leaf senecio

30 cm × 50 cm

Of moderate growth rate, this plant has soft, finely divided silver-grey foliage and small, yellow, daisy-like flowers. Mass plant to form a ground cover in a sunny rockery, or on a sloping bank, or plant along the edge of an informal border. The soil must be good, light and well drained and contain plenty of compost. Water well in summer and trim back after flowering. Propagate the lace-leaf senecio from seed or from cuttings.

Natural distribution: It grows in the eastern Cape, Lesotho, the Natal uplands and the eastern Orange Free State.

Flowering time:
Summer or autumn

Ursinia sericea   ASTERACEAE

Lace-leaf ursinia

50 cm × 50 cm

A fast-growing, bushy plant with attractive, feathery silver-grey foliage and canary-yellow daisy-like flowers, this ursinia could be planted in an informal shrub border, in a rockery, along the edge of a driveway, in low planter boxes or as an accent plant at the base of a flight of steps. It must, however, always be in full sunshine. Plant it in light, well-drained soil, adding plenty of compost, and riversand if necessary. Water regularly in winter, but do not allow the soil to become sodden. Propagate the lace-leaf ursinia from seed sown in March or April, or from cuttings.

Natural distribution: It grows in the south-western Cape.

LEFT *Ursinia* sp., which is similar to *U. sericea*.

Flowering time:
November to February

Wachendorfia thyrsiflora   HAEMODORACEAE

Bloodroot

2 m × 0,5 m   to

Of moderate growth rate, this bulbous plant thrives when planted near water, and is an excellent accent plant for a water garden, with its long showy spikes of starry, deep yellow flowers, and attractive, pleated, strap-shaped foliage. It grows easily in any soil – be sure to add plenty of compost or peat – even heavy clay, and will tolerate some light shade for part of the day. Morning shade will prevent damage to the foliage in frosty gardens. The plant must be very well watered in winter and spring, especially if growing in a flowerbed away from water. This bulb is dormant from about January to March, but does not have to be lifted during this period. Keep it as dry as possible, however, until growth recommences. Propagate from seed or by division of the roots.

Natural distribution: This plant grows in swampy places along the edges of streams, and occasionally in the water, in the eastern, southern and south-western Cape.

Flowering time:
September to November

Agapanthus africanus   ALLIACEAE

Dwarf agapanthus

50 cm × 50 cm   to

The dwarf agapanthus is a fast-growing perennial which forms a clump of strap-shaped leaves and spreads by means of rhizomes. The large, rounded heads of tubular blue or white flowers are carried on stalks above the foliage. Mass plant it under trees to form a ground cover, on steep banks to hold the soil, in large containers on a patio or along the front of a shrub border. This plant is easily grown and can tolerate full sun or light shade. Plant the dwarf agapanthus in good, rich soil, adding plenty of compost and superphosphate. Water well throughout the year, but especially in spring and summer. It is easily propagated from seed, or by dividing larger clumps in February or March.

Natural distribution: It grows from sea level almost to the tops of mountains, from the Cape Peninsula northwards to Paarl and eastwards to Riversdale.

Flowering time:
December to March

Agapanthus inapertus   ALLIACEAE
Drooping agapanthus

50 cm × 50 cm

Flowering time:
Midsummer

This is a clump-forming perennial of moderate growth rate, with strap-shaped leaves, which can be evergreen under favourable conditions. The drooping, tubular, deep blue flowers are carried on long stalks above the foliage. Plant this agapanthus in large groups in a rockery or on a steep bank, in good, light, well-drained soil, with the addition of plenty of compost. Dormant from about May to September, the plant should be kept reasonably dry and should not be lifted out of the ground – if its drainage in the winter rainfall area is good, it will not rot. When growth recommences in September, it must be well watered until the flowering season is over. Propagate the drooping agapanthus from seed, or by dividing clumps in August and replanting immediately.

Natural distribution: It grows on rocky koppies and in grassland, in the central, eastern and northern Transvaal and in Swaziland.

Agapanthus praecox subsp. *orientalis*   ALLIACEAE
Common agapanthus

1,5 m × 0,75 m   to

Flowering time:
December to January

The common agapanthus is a fast-growing, clump-forming perennial with strap-shaped leaves. The large, rounded heads of tubular blue or white flowers are carried on stalks above the foliage. Mass plant it under large trees to form a ground cover, on steep banks to hold the soil, in large containers or planter boxes on a patio, or along the front of a shrub border. This plant is easily grown and can tolerate full sun or light shade. Plant it in good, rich soil, adding plenty of compost and superphosphate. Water well throughout the year, but especially in spring and summer. The common agapanthus is easily propagated from seed, or by dividing larger clumps in February or March. Replant immediately.

Natural distribution: It grows in the eastern Cape.

Aristea major   IRIDACEAE
Aristea

1,5 m × 1 m   to

Flowering time:
October to December

The aristea has a moderate growth rate and forms large clumps of long, strap-shaped leaves. The star-shaped, bright blue flowers are borne on tall spikes above the foliage. Unfortunately, these attractive flowers only open in the morning, closing again by midday. The aristea is suitable for planting next to a stream or pond, or in light shade under trees. It requires good, rich soil with plenty of compost or peat added and regular water throughout the year, but especially during winter and spring. Although an established plant will not easily recover if lifted and divided, it may survive if kept moist throughout the transplanting process. Propagation is from seed sown in March, or by division of clumps.

Natural distribution: The aristea grows in the western Cape.

Babiana disticha   IRIDACEAE

Blue babiana

30 cm × 30 cm

Flowering time:
August

Of moderate growth rate, this cormous plant has ribbed leaves and fragrant, star-shaped, light blue flowers. Plant the corms in March – in groups of at least 12-15, about 5 cm apart and 15 cm deep – in a rockery. Babianas must always be planted deeply, i.e. to a depth of 15-20 cm, for best results. The soil must be well drained, and contain plenty of compost. As this plant requires wet winters, it must be well watered in winter in the summer rainfall area, and kept reasonably dry in summer. If drainage is good, the corms can be left in the ground for three to four years, but if poor, they must be lifted after the flowering season and stored in a cool, dry place until the following March. In the winter rainfall area they can be left permanently in the ground. Propagate the blue babiana from seed or by removing offsets from the 'parent' corms.

Natural distribution: It grows in sandy areas in the south-western Cape.

A variety of mauve-flowered babiana species: **LEFT** *Babiana disticha*. **CENTRE** *Babiana hypogea*. **RIGHT** *Babiana curviscapa*.

Babiana rubrocyanea   IRIDACEAE

Wine cup babiana

20 cm × 20 cm

Flowering time:
July to October

The wine cup babiana has a moderate growth rate and is a cormous plant with ribbed leaves and fragrant royal blue flowers with scarlet centres. Plant the corms in March – in groups of at least 12-15, about 5 cm apart and 15 cm deep – in a rockery. Babianas must always be planted deeply, i.e. to a depth of 15-20 cm, for best results. The soil must be well drained and contain plenty of compost. This species will tolerate clay soil. Originating in the winter rainfall region, the plant must be well watered in winter in the summer rainfall area, and kept reasonably dry in summer. If drainage is good, the corms can be left in the ground for three to four years, but if poor, they must be lifted after the flowering season and stored in a cool, dry place until the following March. In the winter rainfall area they can be left permanently in the ground. Propagate this babiana from seed or by removing offsets from the 'parent' corms.

Natural distribution: It grows in sandy areas of the south-western Cape.

RIGHT The flower of *Babiana stricta* var. *regia*, which is similar to that of *B. rubrocyanea*.

Felicia amelloides   ASTERACEAE

Blue felicia, Blue marguerite

50 cm × 50 cm

Flowering time:
Spring to late autumn

This is a fast-growing shrublet, which has blue flowers with bright yellow centres, and which blooms almost throughout the year. Plant it along the edge of a border or mass plant to form a ground cover under trees. It could also be planted in a rockery or, in fact, anywhere else in the garden. It requires good, well-drained soil, with the addition of plenty of compost, and water throughout the year. Cut the plant back after flowering to keep it neat and to encourage a further batch of flowers. Propagate from seed sown in March or April, or from cuttings.

Natural distribution: It often grows on hillsides, and occurs from Riversdale to Bathurst in the Cape Province.

Lobelia coronopifolia   LOBELIACEAE

Buck's horn lobelia

45 cm × 45 cm

Flowering time:
Almost throughout the year

A fast-growing perennial which flowers almost throughout the year, this lobelia has large – approximately 2 cm long – tubular flowers that open into five gentian-blue petals, the upper two resembling little horns. It is suitable for use in a rockery, as an edging plant in a shrub border, along the edges of a pathway or next to a water feature. Plant this lobelia in good, well-drained, compost-enriched soil and water well throughout the year. Replace the plant after about three years. Propagate from seed sown in August in the cold areas or January in the warm areas, or from cuttings taken in autumn.

Natural distribution: It grows in moist places in the south-western and southern Cape, Natal and the eastern Transvaal.

LEFT AND CENTRE *Lobelia tomentosa*, which has flowers very similar to those of *L. coronopifolia*, and will also grow well in the winter rainfall area. **RIGHT** The flower of *Lobelia coronopifolia*.

Nymphaea capensis   NYMPHAEACEAE

Blue water lily

40 cm × 80 cm

Flowering time:
Spring to late summer

There are many hybrids of this fast-growing water lily available. Its flat leaves float on the surface of the water while the large, showy, starry blue or pink flowers stand 5-8 cm above it. Plant the rhizomes by which the plant spreads in the special containers available for water lilies. Use good garden soil in these containers adding some 3:1:5 fertiliser to the mix. Spread a layer of gravel about 5 cm thick over the surface of the soil to keep it from washing out. Submerge the containers to a depth that is neither too shallow, nor too deep. Propagate this water lily by division of the rhizomes.

Natural distribution: It grows in pools and dams throughout the Cape Province, Natal and Transvaal.

Scilla natalensis   HYACINTHACEAE

Blue squill

1 m × 0,5 m   **to**

This fast-growing plant has a basal tuft of short, broad leaves. Heads of beautiful misty blue flowers, which last well in the garden and make excellent cut flowers for the vase, are carried on long stalks. Plant with the top half of the bulb above soil level, in a sunny position in a rockery or an informal border, though the plants will also thrive in partial shade. Use well-drained, compost-enriched soil and water well in summer. Continue watering and feeding after the flowering season until the foliage begins to yellow. This is essential to ensure that the bulbs store enough nutrients to enable them to flower well the following season. This plant is dormant in winter and should be kept dry during that period. It will grow in the winter rainfall area if given good drainage. Do not transplant or divide unnecessarily, as flowering may be affected for one or two seasons. Propagate the blue squill from seed sown in September, or by removing offsets from the 'parent' clump. These can be removed and replanted in August and new leaves will begin to shoot by September. The offsets grow very easily and can even be planted with very little soil, e.g. in gaps between rocks in a rockery, where the plants will thrive and make a beautiful show.

Natural distribution: It grows in the eastern Cape, Natal, Lesotho, the eastern Orange Free State, Swaziland and the eastern and northern Transvaal.

Flowering time:
Spring

Streptocarpus rexii   GESNERIACEAE

Cape primrose

15 cm × 20 cm   **to**

The Cape primrose is a perennial of moderate growth rate and is usually cultivated as an indoor plant, although it may also be planted in a very protected, moist position outdoors. The rough, hairy leaves form a rosette and the large, foxglove-like flowers, blue-mauve in colour, are carried on long, slender stalks. The plant needs rich, well-drained soil, and must be watered well in summer and less in winter. Propagate from seed, which is very fine, by division of the clumps, or from leaf cuttings. These are made by slitting the veins on the underside of a leaf with a blade or sharp knife and pinning the leaf onto a layer of wet riversand which has been placed in a seed tray. Cover the tray with glass or perspex to maintain the humidity and keep it in a warm staded place. Whole young plants will develop where the leaf has been slit. When these are growing strongly they can be carefully removed and planted into an organic potting soil mixture in individual containers.

Natural distribution: The Cape primrose grows in moist places in forests, in the eastern Cape, southern Natal, the Orange Free State, Swaziland and the eastern Transvaal.

Flowering time:
Summer

Aloe greatheadii var. *davyana*   ASPHODELACEAE

(= *A. davyana* var. *davyana*)

Veld aloe

30 cm × 40 cm

Flowering time:
Throughout winter

This is a fast-growing, drought-resistant plant with a basal rosette of thorny, succulent, strap-shaped leaves. The tubular pink to orange flowers are carried on long stalks above the foliage and produce nectar, which attracts sunbirds into the garden in winter. This aloe is ideal for rockeries or steep, dry banks and may be mass planted for a lovely show of colour. It requires well-drained, compost-enriched soil. Water well in summer and keep dry in winter. Propagate the veld aloe from seed or by removing young suckers.

A beautiful display of colour can be achieved in a dull winter garden by planting a varied selection of aloes. By carefully choosing species which flower consecutively one can have colour from May until August or September. Other recommended winter-flowering species are: *Aloe pretoriensis*, *A. affinis*, *A. parvibracteata* and *A. lutescens* (August). Follow these up with *A. transvaalensis* which flowers in summer.

Natural distribution: It grows on rocky koppies and in grassland, in the central and northern Transvaal and the northern Orange Free State.

Aloe variegata   ASPHODELACEAE

Partridge aloe

25 cm × 25 cm

Flowering time:
Winter to spring

A fast-growing, drought-resistant plant, the partridge aloe has thornless, succulent leaves, which are grey-red with white markings, and a short stalk carrying tubular pink-orange flowers. Plant this aloe in a very well-drained position, and give very little water – it will die if overwatered or too deeply planted. In fact, the foliage should rest on a bed of small coarse stones to ensure that it does not rot, and the soil mix should contain plenty of riversand to ensure good drainage. Propagate the partridge aloe from seed or by removing young suckers.

Natural distribution: It grows in hot, dry areas in the Karoo, north-western and eastern Cape, the south-western Orange Free State and southern Namibia.

RIGHT (BELOW) The seedhead of *Aloe variegata*.

Arctotis laevis ASTERACEAE

Grey arctotis

1 m × 1 m

A fast-growing perennial, with deeply two-lobed bottle-green leaves covered with woolly white hairs, the grey arctotis bears large daisy-like flowers that are yellow to orange. It forms a bushy, rounded shrub and is suitable for planting in a large rockery or an informal shrub border. It is tolerant of coastal conditions, and must be planted in full sun for the flowers to open properly. Plant in ordinary, well-drained garden soil, adding plenty of compost, and water well in winter, especially in the summer rainfall area. Propagate the grey arctotis from seed sown in March and protect young plants from frost.

Natural distribution: It grows on dry hillsides throughout Namaqualand and southwards to Calvinia and Saldanha Bay in the Cape Province.

Flowering time: Spring

Clivia miniata AMARYLLIDACEAE

Bush lily, Fire lily

75 cm × 75 cm   to

This fairly slow-growing clivia forms clumps of strap-shaped, dark green leaves and umbels of showy orange flowers. Plant it near a pond or stream, in shade under trees, or in large containers or tubs on a shady patio. The soil must be light and rich and contain plenty of compost and leaf mould. Water well in summer and about once a week in winter in the summer rainfall area. It will grow in the winter rainfall area provided drainage is good. Do not divide or disturb unnecessarily as flowering may be affected. Propagate this clivia from fresh seed or by carefully dividing the larger clumps and replanting immediately.

Natural distribution: It grows in the forests of the eastern Cape, Transkei, Natal, the eastern Transvaal and Swaziland.

Flowering time: Spring

Clivia nobilis AMARYLLIDACEAE

Drooping clivia, Cape clivia

75 cm × 75 cm   to

Fairly slow growing, this clivia forms clumps of strap-shaped, dark green leaves and umbels of drooping orange flowers that are tipped with green. Plant it near a pond or stream, or in shade under trees. The soil must be light and rich and contain plenty of compost and leaf mould. Water well in summer and about once a week in winter in the summer rainfall area. The drooping clivia will grow in the winter rainfall area provided drainage is good. Do not divide or disturb unnecessarily as flowering may be affected. Propagate it from fresh seed or by carefully dividing the larger clumps and replanting immediately.

Natural distribution: It grows in the coastal areas of the eastern Cape and Transkei.

Flowering time: August to January

Crocosmia aurea IRIDACEAE

Valentine flower

1 m × 0,3 m   to

Flowering time:
Late summer to
early autumn

Fast growing, this cormous plant has gladiolus-like foliage, and showy sprays of large, star-shaped, brilliant orange flowers which make excellent cut flowers for the vase. This plant creates a spectacular show when it flowers in late summer and early autumn. Plant it in large groups in semi-shade under trees or shrubs, where it will receive morning sun and where it can be left undisturbed to multiply – if lifted or divided it may not flower well the following season. The corms must be planted about 4 cm deep and 20 cm apart in August or September, in well-drained, compost-enriched soil. Water well in summer and keep dry in winter when the plant is dormant. Propagate from seed or by dividing larger clumps.

Crocosmia masonorum (golden swans) is very similar to *C. aurea*, except that its flowers are slightly larger.

Natural distribution: *Crocosmia aurea* grows in moist, shady places in the eastern Cape, Transkei, Natal, Swaziland and the eastern and northern Transvaal, whereas *C. masonorum* occurs only in the eastern Cape and Transkei.

RIGHT (ABOVE) *Crocosmia masonorum*.

Crocosmia paniculata IRIDACEAE

Falling stars

1 m × 0,3 m   to

Flowering time:
Spring to summer

Falling stars is a fast-growing, cormous plant with gladiolus-like foliage, and showy sprays of star-shaped orange flowers, slightly smaller than those of the previous two species. They make excellent cut flowers for the vase, as well as a lovely show in the garden. Plant this crocosmia in large groups in semi-shade under trees or shrubs, where it will receive morning sun and where it can be left undisturbed to multiply – if lifted or divided it may not flower well the following season. The corms must be planted about 4 cm deep and 20 cm apart in August or September, in well-drained, compost-enriched soil. Water well in summer and keep dry in winter, when the plant is dormant. Propagate from seed or by dividing larger clumps.

Natural distribution: It grows along the edges of streams in Lesotho, Natal, Swaziland, the Orange Free State and the Transvaal.

Lampranthus aureus MESEMBRYANTHEMACEAE
Orange vygie

45 cm × 60 cm

This moderately fast-growing trailing plant has small, cylindrical, succulent leaves and bright orange 'vygie' flowers, which only open fully on bright, sunny days. Mass plant this vygie to form a ground cover in a rockery or on a steep bank. It makes a beautiful show in the flowering season and should be mixed with other colourful vygies to produce a spectacular effect. Plant it in well-drained, compost-enriched soil and water moderately from autumn to spring. Propagate from seed or from cuttings taken in summer.

Natural distribution: It grows in the south-western Cape.

Flowering time:
Spring

Watsonia pillansii IRIDACEAE
Pillans's watsonia

1,5 m × 0,2 m

A fast-growing plant, Pillans's watsonia forms a clump of strap-shaped leaves, bears tall spikes of showy apricot to pale orange flowers and is suitable for a shrub border. Plant the corms in large groups, 5-7 cm deep, in good, well-drained, compost-enriched soil and water regularly throughout the year, but especially well in summer. Do not disturb for three to four years as flowering may be affected. When the quality of the flowers begins to deteriorate the clump may be lifted, divided and replanted immediately. Cut the leaves back to ground level when the clump becomes untidy or remove dry brown leaves throughout the year. Propagate this watsonia from seed or by removing offsets from the 'parent' corms.

Natural distribution: This plant grows in the southern and eastern Cape.

Flowering time:
Summer to winter

Aponogeton distachyos APONOGETONACEAE
Cape pondweed

Spread: 1 m

A vigorous and rampant grower which spreads by means of rhizomes, the Cape pondweed has broad, strap-like green leaves and sweetly scented white flowers that float on the surface of the water. It is an excellent plant for a pond or dam, particularly as it flowers in winter when little else is in bloom. This plant is edible and is used in the traditional Cape 'waterblommetjiebredie'. Plant the rhizomes in a container in good soil in autumn, and submerge the container in shallow water in the pond or dam until the plant has grown somewhat. It can then slowly be moved into deeper water, to a depth of about 20-30 cm. As this plant grows vigorously, it should be pruned back and divided regularly to keep it in check. Lift the container out of the water in either summer or autumn, divide the rhizomes and replant immediately. The same method is used for propagation.

Natural distribution: It grows in dams and pools throughout the southern and south-western Cape.

Flowering time:
July to October

Asystasia gangetica   ACANTHACEAE

Creeping foxglove

30 cm × 60 cm   to ▢

Flowering time:
Spring and summer

An attractive, fast-growing ground cover, the creeping foxglove has dark green foliage. Its small, fragrant, foxglove-like flowers are cream with purple markings in the throat. It likes moist, lightly shaded to sunny conditions and, mass planted, makes an excellent ground cover under large trees. It will also grow well in a large container or in planter boxes. Any soil is suitable – add plenty of compost and water well in summer but less in winter. Propagate the creeping foxglove from cuttings or by removing rooted runners.

Natural distribution: It grows in the eastern Cape, Natal, Swaziland, the eastern and northern Transvaal, Botswana and Namibia.

Begonia homonyma   BEGONIACEAE

(= *B. caffra*)

Star-leaved begonia

70 cm × 70 cm   to

Flowering time:
Summer

The star-leaved begonia is fast growing and has deeply serrate, almost star-shaped leaves, fairly small white flowers and a thick, succulent main stem. It is a very good foliage plant for indoors or for a patio and excels in a hanging basket where its attractive foliage can cascade gracefully downwards. Use a light, well-drained potting mixture and hang the plant in a position sheltered from winds and extreme cold. Water regularly in the growing season but keep reasonably dry in winter. Propagate from seed or cuttings planted in riversand.

Begonia dregei (wild begonia) is similar to *B. homonyma* but smaller, with a height and spread of about 30 cm. It has ovate, asymmetrical, glossy green leaves with purplish red veins, and white to pale pink flowers. This species can be grown indoors as a container plant or in a protected indoor garden, but will also succeed outdoors under trees in warm, moist areas.

Natural distribution: Both species occur in the eastern Cape and the eastern part of Natal.

Chlorophytum capense   ASPHODELACEAE

Green hen-and-chickens, Spider plant

60 cm × 60 cm   to

Flowering time:
Summer

A good, fast-spreading ground cover, this plant forms clumps of strap-shaped leaves – dark green in colour – and bears spikes of small, star-shaped white flowers. It will do well in a shady position under trees, in a large container on a shady patio or as a container plant indoors. The soil should be light, well drained and contain plenty of compost. Use a mixture of equal parts of organic potting soil and riversand in the containers. Water regularly throughout the year. Propagate from seed or by dividing large clumps.

Natural distribution: It grows in the south-eastern Cape.

LEFT, CENTRE AND RIGHT *Chlorophytum* sp., which is similar to *C. capense*.

Dimorphotheca cuneata ASTERACEAE

Bride's bouquet

50 cm × 60 cm

Flowering time:
Spring

The bride's bouquet, which is a fast-growing, semiwoody perennial, bears masses of white daisy-like flowers. These flowers only open fully on bright, sunny days and, as they face the sun, the plant should be positioned towards the north so that the flowers can be viewed face on. Suitable for a rockery, the bride's bouquet should be mass planted about 25 cm apart, in light, sandy, well-drained soil, adding plenty of compost but no manure, and watered well throughout winter and spring. Replace old bushes every couple of years and propagate from seed.

Castalis nudicaulis (oxeye daisy) is a smaller plant, similar in appearance to the bride's bouquet, and with the same growth requirements. It forms low-growing clumps with a height and spread of about 30 cm. The white daisy flowers have yellow centres and are purple on the undersides of the petals. This species is not as showy as some of the other daisies but may be used in a rockery or informal shrub border or as a ground cover on a dry, sunny bank. Propagate from seed sown in March and protect young plants from frost.

Natural distribution: The bride's bouquet grows in the Cape Province (except the south-western Cape), the southern Orange Free State and Botswana, and the oxeye daisy occurs in the coastal areas of Namaqualand and the south-western Cape.

Eucomis comosa HYACINTHACEAE

Pink pineapple flower

1 m × 0,75 m

Flowering time:
Summer

This fast-growing plant has strap-shaped leaves and white flowers (tinged with pink or purple) carried on a tall spike. At the top of each of these spikes, above the densely packed flowers, is a tuft of leaf-like bracts – causing the flower stalk to resemble a pineapple. These are excellent cut flowers and the plant makes an unusual and attractive ground cover if mass planted under trees. It requires partial, light shade otherwise it will not flower well. Plant the pink pineapple flower with the neck of the bulb just below the surface, in very well-drained, sandy soil, adding plenty of compost. Water well in summer and keep fairly dry in winter when the plant is dormant. The bulbs need not be lifted in either the summer or the winter rainfall areas provided the drainage is good. Propagate the plant from seed or by removing offsets from 'parent' bulbs – replant immediately.

Natural distribution: It grows in Natal, the eastern Transvaal, the Cape, Swaziland and the Orange Free State.

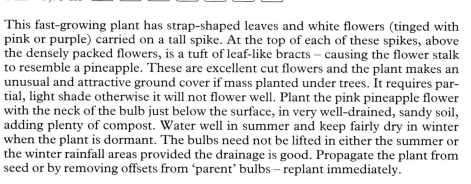

Haemanthus albiflos   AMARYLLIDACEAE
Dappled snowbrush

15 cm × 40 cm   to ⬤

Flowering time:
April to June

This plant, of moderate growth rate, has very attractive, broad, strap-shaped leaves speckled with white, although the speckles are sometimes absent. A 'brush' of white flowers, surrounded by waxy bracts, is carried at the top of a long stalk. Plant the dappled snowbrush in large groups under trees, in large containers on a shady patio, or along the edges of a shady pathway, possibly in front of a sizeable group of clivias. Do not disturb unnecessarily as flowering may be affected. The soil must be good, light and well drained with plenty of compost added. Water regularly throughout the year. Propagate this plant from seed or by removing offsets from the 'parent' bulbs.

Natural distribution: It grows in shady places in forest and woodland, from Still Bay in the southern Cape through the eastern Cape to Zululand.

Osteospermum ecklonis   ASTERACEAE
Blue-and-white daisy bush

0,75 m × 1,5 m

Flowering time:
Spring to late summer

This osteospermum is a fast-growing, drought-resistant perennial which forms a soft, bushy, rounded shrub. It bears large, white, daisy-like flowers, each with a purple centre and is beautiful in full bloom. Mass plant this daisy to form a ground cover, or plant it in a rockery, along the edge of a pathway or in an informal shrub border, in a bright, sunny position. The plant requires light, well-drained and compost-enriched soil. Water moderately throughout the year and propagate from seed, cuttings or from root sections.

Natural distribution: It grows in the eastern Cape.

Plectranthus madagascariensis   LAMIACEAE
Variegated plectranthus

15 cm × 45 cm

Flowering time:
Summer

A very fast-growing ground cover with plain green or green-and-white variegated foliage and spikes of small whitish flowers, this plectranthus spreads by runners which root as they touch the ground. Planted in light or partial shade, it makes an attractive ground cover for warmer gardens. It also grows well in a container indoors and is charming in a hanging basket on a patio. Plant the variegated plectranthus in good, well-drained soil containing plenty of compost, and water regularly. It is easily propagated from cuttings planted in riversand, or by lifting rooted runners.

Natural distribution: It grows in the eastern Cape and southern Natal.

Plectranthus verticillatus   LAMIACEAE
Gossip

10 cm × 50 cm   to ●

A fast-growing ground cover, this plant has attractive, shiny, semisucculent foliage, which is dark green tinged with maroon, and tubular white flowers with purple markings. An excellent choice of ground cover for large areas in partial or light shade under trees, it could also be used near a pond or stream as it enjoys moist conditions. It grows quickly and easily and can be planted in any light, well-drained soil containing plenty of compost. Water regularly. This plectranthus is easily propagated from cuttings planted in riversand, or by lifting rooted runners.

Natural distribution: It grows in the eastern Cape, Natal, Swaziland and the eastern and northern Transvaal.

Flowering time:
Spring to autumn

Protasparagus densiflorus 'Meyersii'
ASPARAGACEAE

Foxtail fern, Cat's tail asparagus

45 cm × 60 cm   to

Of moderate growth rate, the foxtail fern gets its name from its foliage which takes the form of attractive, soft-looking, erect 'fronds' which resemble foxtails and which make this an excellent choice of foliage plant for a water garden or for a large container on a patio. Mass planted, it could be used as a ground cover, or a group of plants could be placed amongst large rocks in a rock garden. It produces small, shiny red berries which attract birds into the garden. Plant the foxtail fern in full sun or partial shade, in good soil containing plenty of compost, and water regularly, although once established, it is fairly drought resistant. Prune away older, yellowing fronds. If cut back by frost, this plant will recover rapidly in spring. Propagate from seed or by dividing larger clumps.

Natural distribution: It grows in the Cape, the Orange Free State, the Transvaal and in Natal.

Flowering time:
Summer

Protasparagus densiflorus 'Sprengeri'
ASPARAGACEAE

Emerald fern

30 cm × 90 cm   to

A fast-growing plant with long, arching 'fronds' of needle-like foliage, the emerald fern has tiny, sweetly scented white flowers, which are followed by small, shiny red berries eaten by many birds. It can be mass planted to form a ground cover, used in hanging baskets, planter boxes or large containers, planted on steep banks to hold the soil or allowed to cascade over terraced walls. Plant the emerald fern in sun or light shade, in good soil, adding plenty of compost, and water regularly, although once established, it is fairly drought resistant. Propagate from seed or by dividing larger clumps.

Natural distribution: It grows in the Cape, the Orange Free State, the Transvaal and in Natal.

Flowering time:
Summer

Sansevieria hyacinthoides DRACAENACEAE
Mother-in-law's tongue

50 cm × 20 cm   to

Flowering time:
December to March

This fast-growing, drought-resistant plant has variegated, tongue-shaped foliage – hence its common name – and sturdy flowering stalks tipped with masses of tiny, whitish flowers. It grows very easily and needs little attention, so is perfect for large gardens or difficult areas and may be mass planted between the rocks in a rockery to form a hardy ground cover. It does well in a container indoors in a well-drained potting mix – be careful not to overwater. Plant the mother-in-law's tongue in sun or partial shade, in any soil, adding plenty of compost, and water sparingly. Propagate from seed, leaf cuttings or by division of the larger clumps.

Natural distribution: It grows amongst rocks under trees, in the eastern Cape, Transkei, Natal, Swaziland, the northern, western and eastern Transvaal, Botswana and Namibia.

Stachys aethiopica LAMIACEAE
Stachys

30 cm × 50 cm

Flowering time:
Spring to autumn

Stachys is a fast-growing ground cover with soft, green foliage and spikes of tiny, tubular white or pale mauve flowers and is particularly attractive when in full bloom. Although it appears delicate, it is in fact fairly hardy. Plant it as a ground cover under large trees or use as an edging along the front of an informal border. Other possibilities are to allow it to cover a shady bank or to grow it in a hanging basket. Plant the stachys in good, well-drained, compost-enriched soil and water regularly. Trim the plant back after flowering to keep it neat. Propagate from cuttings or by lifting rooted runners.

Natural distribution: It grows in the Cape, Lesotho, Natal, Swaziland, the eastern Orange Free State and the Transvaal.

Sutera pauciflora SCROPHULARIACEAE
Trailing phlox

10 cm × 40 cm   to

Flowering time:
Almost throughout the year

The trailing phlox is an attractive, dainty-looking and fast-growing ground cover with small, triangular, dark green leaves and tiny, starry white flowers. Rather more hardy than it looks, it is an ideal ground cover for the edges of water gardens, for planting under trees, for holding soil on slopes, and for planting between stepping stones or sleepers. It prefers partially shaded to sunny positions and spreads fairly vigorously – trim back if necessary. Plant the trailing phlox in any soil, adding plenty of compost, and water regularly. Propagate from cuttings or by lifting rooted runners.

Natural distribution: It grows in the Cape Province.

Watsonia obrienii IRIDACEAE

(= *W. ardernei*)

White watsonia

1 m × 0,2 m

Flowering time:
October or November

The white watsonia has a moderate growth rate, forms a clump of strap-shaped leaves and bears tall, showy spikes of white flowers. Plant it in large groups and do not disturb for three to four years as flowering may be affected. The corms must be planted 5-7 cm deep in March in good, well-drained, compost-enriched soil and watered well in winter, especially in the summer rainfall area. As the plant is dormant in summer, it should be kept fairly dry – the corms will not rot, provided they are in a very well-drained position. Cut the foliage down to ground level when it dies back at the end of the flowering season. Transplanting is best done when the plant is dormant. Propagate it from seed or by removing offsets from the 'parent' corms.

Natural distribution: It grows in the south-western Cape.

CENTRE AND RIGHT *Watsonia* sp., which is similar to *W. obrienii*.

Zantedeschia aethiopica ARACEAE

White arum lily

1,5 m × 1 m

Flowering time:
Spring and midsummer

Suitable for planting along a stream, this is a fast-growing plant which likes moist conditions. It forms a clump of lush, arrow-shaped leaves which are carried on long stalks. The large white flower spathes are borne on long stems above the foliage and make excellent cut flowers for the vase. Usually deciduous from mid-summer to the beginning of autumn, this plant may remain evergreen if grown in moist places. Plant it near a tap, at the edge of a pond or in partial shade (prefer-ably morning shade) under trees, always remembering to water well in winter, spring and early summer. The soil must be good, light and well drained, with the addition of plenty of compost or well-rotted manure. Propagate from seed or by the division of clumps from November to February.

Natural distribution: It grows in marshy or sandy places, from the south-western Cape through the eastern Cape to Natal, Lesotho, the eastern Orange Free State and the northern Transvaal.

RIGHT (BELOW) A green-flowered form of *Zantedeschia*.

Amaryllis belladonna   AMARYLLIDACEAE

Belladonna lily

50 cm × 50 cm

Flowering time:
February or March

The belladonna lily has a moderate growth rate. The large clusters of sweetly scented, trumpet-shaped pink flowers are carried on long red stems and appear before the strap-shaped leaves. They make excellent cut flowers for the vase. Plant the bulbs with their necks at ground level in large groups in a rockery or a mixed border. The soil must be light, well drained and compost enriched. Withhold water in summer when the plants are dormant, leaving the bulbs in the ground if the soil is very well drained. Begin watering again when the leaves appear, and water well throughout winter, especially in the summer rainfall area, to ensure good flowers the following season. Propagate this plant from seed or by dividing large clumps of bulbs.

Natural distribution: It grows in the south-western Cape.

Arctotis stoechadifolia   ASTERACEAE

Trailing arctotis

15 cm × 40 cm

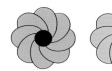
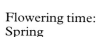

Flowering time:
Spring

A fast-growing plant with grey foliage, the trailing arctotis has large daisy-like flowers that are usually dark pink, but may also be cream or orange. It needs a warm, sunny position as the flowers only open fully in the sun. The plant spreads easily and will quickly cover an area. Ideal for dry banks or slopes, it may also be used as an edging plant along an informal border or allowed to cascade over terraced walls. Plant in any soil – spacing plants about 40 cm apart to get a dense ground cover – adding plenty of compost, and water well in winter. Replace plants every two to three years. Propagate from seed sown in March, or from cuttings taken in spring.

Natural distribution: It grows in rocky or sandy places in Namaqualand and southwards to the Cape Peninsula.

Clematopsis scabiosifolia subsp. *stanleyi*

RANUNCULACEAE

Bush clematis

1,5 m × 1,5 m

Flowering time:
January or February

The bush clematis has a moderate growth rate and attractive, finely divided foliage. It bears large, sweetly scented mauve-pink flowers with wavy petals and a mass of yellow stamens in the centre. These are followed by decorative, feathery seedheads which remain on the plant for a long time. Plant the bush clematis in a warm, sunny position in a rockery or an informal shrub border, in light, well-drained, compost-enriched soil. Keep it dry in winter when the plant is dormant but water well in summer. Cut the plant back to ground level at the end of summer. Propagate from seed sown in September or October – the young plants will flower in the third season.

Natural distribution: It grows in grassland and on koppies, in central, western and southern Transvaal, Botswana and Namibia.

Crassula multicava   CRASSULACEAE
Fairy crassula

20 cm × 30 cm

Flowering time:
July to September

Of moderate growth rate, the fairy crassula has attractive, round, succulent leaves. The large heads of tiny, star-shaped, pale pink flowers form a misty pink mass in the flowering season. Easily grown and requiring little attention, this crassula is ideal for planting in light or partial shade under trees – it also tolerates full sun – and grows well on damp, shady rockeries, rooting as it touches the ground. Severe frost may damage the flowers, but morning shade from overhanging branches may help to prevent this. Plant the fairy crassula in any well-drained soil, adding plenty of compost, and water moderately in summer. It is easily propagated from cuttings.

Natural distribution: It grows in the eastern Cape and southern Natal.

Crinum bulbispermum   AMARYLLIDACEAE
Orange River lily

1 m × 1 m 

Flowering time:
Spring

This fast-growing plant forms a clump of long, strap-shaped grey leaves, which are up to a metre long. The large, white to pink, lily-like flowers are carried in terminal heads on a stout flowering stalk. Each petal has a red stripe down its centre. Suitable for waterside planting, the Orange River lily should be grown in good, rich garden soil, with the addition of plenty of compost or peat. The neck of the bulb must be just below the soil surface. Keep the plant dry in winter but water well in summer – the bulb will even tolerate being submerged in water at times. Do not disturb unnecessarily as flowering may be affected. Propagate this lily from seed – young plants will take about four years to flower – or by removing offsets, which are not readily formed, from the 'parent' bulb.

Natural distribution: It grows along riverbanks – especially those of the Orange River – in the southern, central and eastern Transvaal, Natal, the Orange Free State, north-eastern Cape, Lesotho and Swaziland.

Crinum campanulatum   AMARYLLIDACEAE
Water crinum

45 cm × 45 cm

Flowering time:
Spring

Of moderate growth rate, the water crinum forms a clump of strap-shaped green leaves and bears large, deep pink, lily-like flowers which are carried in a terminal head. An excellent plant for a pond or water garden, it should be grown in a submergible container, filled with compost-enriched soil, and kept underwater, but with the water not more than 5 cm above the level of the soil, all summer. The plant must, however, be kept dry from April to August, otherwise it will not flower – the bulbs must therefore be lifted out of the water and stored in a dry place during this period. Propagate from seed – the young plants will take about four years to flower – or by removing offsets, which are not readily formed, from the 'parent' bulb.

Natural distribution: It grows in shallow dams in the eastern Cape.

Crinum macowanii AMARYLLIDACEAE
River crinum

1 m × 1 m   to

Flowering time:
October to December

The fast-growing river crinum forms a clump of strap-shaped green leaves. The large, bell-shaped pink or white flowers are striped with red and are carried in a head at the tip of a long stalk. This crinum can be planted near water and requires good, rich garden soil, with the addition of plenty of compost or peat. The neck of the bulb must be just below the soil surface. As the plant is dormant in winter it should be kept fairly dry during that season but watered well in summer. Do not disturb unnecessarily as flowering may be affected. Propagate the river crinum from seed – the young plants will take about four years to flower – or by removing offsets, which are not readily formed, from the 'parent' bulb.

Natural distribution: It grows along rivers – especially the Sabie – in the northern Transvaal, and in the eastern Cape, Natal, Namibia and Botswana.

CENTRE The flower of *Crinum delagoense*, which is similar to that of *C. macowanii*. **RIGHT** The fruit of *C. delagoense*.

Crinum moorei AMARYLLIDACEAE
Moore's crinum

1 m × 1 m    to

Flowering time:
Summer

Moore's crinum is fast growing and forms a clump of strap-shaped leaves. New leaves are formed soon after the old ones die down in March or April, and the plant can therefore be described as almost evergreen. It bears flower stalks that are a metre long and that each carry a head of large, pink, lily-like flowers. Plant this crinum in light or partial shade under trees (it combines well with *Agapanthus praecox* subsp. *orientalis*, which flowers at the same time), in good, light, well-drained soil, adding plenty of compost. Water well in summer and do not disturb unnecessarily as flowering may be affected. Propagate Moore's crinum from seed – the young plants take about four years to flower – or by removing offsets, which are not readily formed, from the 'parent' bulb.

Natural distribution: It grows in the forests of the coastal belt from the eastern Cape to Natal.

Diascia integerrima SCROPHULARIACEAE
Twinspur

30 cm × 45 cm

Flowering time:
Summer and autumn

Fast growing, this dainty, bushy perennial has fine foliage and open-mouthed, deep pink, linaria-like flowers with twin spurs. Ideal for the front of a border, as it is seldom without blooms, it may also be planted in groups in a sunny rockery, used as an edging plant along a pathway, planted in large containers on a patio or mass planted – about 20 cm apart. The twinspur is easily grown in any soil. Add plenty of compost, and water regularly. Propagate from seed.

Natural distribution: It has a wide distribution – from the Cape Peninsula to Natal, Lesotho, the Orange Free State and the Transvaal.

Impatiens sylvicola BALSAMINACEAE

Salmon impatiens

20 cm × 20 cm   to

Flowering time:
Midsummer onwards

The fast-growing salmon impatiens has soft, oval leaves, and small salmon-pink to cerise flowers with flat, rounded petals. A lovely ground cover for dappled shade, particularly near a pond or stream – it loves moist conditions – it can also be used in planter boxes on the south side of the house in moist, warm gardens, along the edge of a shady pathway or at the base of a dripping tap. Plant it in light, well-drained, compost-enriched soil and water regularly. It needs a very protected position in frosty areas. Propagate this impatiens from cuttings planted in riversand.

Natural distribution: It grows in the northern and eastern Transvaal.

Lampranthus blandus

MESEMBRYANTHEMACEAE

Pink vygie

45 cm × 60 cm

Flowering time:
Spring

This is a moderately fast-growing trailing plant with small, cylindrical, succulent leaves and pale pink 'vygie' flowers, which only open fully on bright, sunny days. Mass plant to form a ground cover in a rockery or on a steep slope. It will make a spectacular show in the flowering season and should be mixed with other colourful plants to produce a vibrant effect. Plant the pink vygie in well-drained, compost-enriched soil and water moderately from autumn to spring, especially in the summer rainfall area. Propagate from seed or from cuttings taken in summer.

Natural distribution: It grows in the south-western Cape.

Nerine bowdenii AMARYLLIDACEAE

Large pink nerine

45 cm × 20 cm  to

Flowering time:
March or April

The large pink nerine has a moderate growth rate and strap-shaped leaves and bears large, attractive, rounded heads of cyclamen-pink flowers. Plant it with the neck of the bulb above the soil, in groups in a rockery. In coastal areas it can be planted in full sun, but inland it needs to be shaded from the hot afternoon sun. The soil must be light, well drained and compost enriched. The leaves appear in spring – water regularly from then on and particularly well in late summer to prevent leaf loss. The leaves die back during March and April, when the plant is in flower. Leave it undisturbed for at least three years. Thereafter the plants can be divided every three to four years – this is best done in the dormant season from June to August. Propagate from very fresh seed, i.e. as soon as it drops to the ground. These plants will take about three years to flower. Offsets may also be removed from the 'mother' bulb.

Natural distribution: It grows in the eastern Cape, Natal and the Transvaal.

Nerine filifolia   AMARYLLIDACEAE
Grass-leaved nerine

25 cm × 15 cm

Flowering time:
Autumn

This fast-growing nerine has clumps of fine, grass-like foliage, and bears masses of pale pink flowers carried on thin stalks. Plant the bulbs, with their necks above soil level, about 5 cm apart in large groups, either in a rockery, as an edging plant, in large containers on a sunny patio or in planter boxes. Plant the grass-leaved nerine in light, well-drained soil adding plenty of compost, and water regularly as this plant is an evergreen. Propagate from very fresh seed, i.e. as soon as it drops to the ground. These plants will take about three years to flower. Offsets may also be removed from the 'mother' bulbs.

Natural distribution: It grows in open grassland, and in damp places, in the eastern Cape, Transkei, Swaziland, the Orange Free State and the eastern Transvaal.

Oxalis purpurea   OXALIDACEAE
Pink oxalis

7,5 cm × 10 cm

Flowering time:
Spring

The fast-growing pink oxalis has clover-like leaves, and bears pink flowers with yellow centres. Plant the bulbs very close together for a good display but, as they multiply rapidly, it may be best to grow this plant in a container to prevent it from spreading too easily and becoming weedy in the garden. It could also be planted in a hanging basket, between railway sleepers or among cracks in paving stones, or used as a ground cover in a sunny bed, where its spread can be controlled. Easily grown, it prefers well-drained, acid soil and water in winter. It is dormant in summer. Propagate from seed or by the division of clumps.

Natural distribution: It grows in the south-western Cape.

Pelargonium crispum 'Variegatum'   GERANIACEAE
Variegated pelargonium, Crispy-leaved pelargonium

50 cm × 50 cm

Flowering time:
August to April

Of moderate to slow growth rate, this pelargonium tends to have a rather short life span. It has attractive, crinkled, lemon-scented variegated leaves, and white to dark pink flowers with mauve markings. Position the plant so that the green-and-white foliage can be seen to advantage, perhaps in a container on a sunny patio or amongst plants with dark green leaves. Use well-drained, sandy soil, adding plenty of compost, and water well in winter. Propagate this pelargonium from seed or from cuttings planted in riversand.

Natural distribution: It grows on the lower slopes of mountains and hills in the south-western Cape winter rainfall area.

CENTRE (BELOW) AND RIGHT *Pelargonium crispum.*

Pelargonium peltatum　GERANIACEAE
Ivy-leaved pelargonium

0,3 m × 2 m　

A fast-growing plant with a trailing habit, this pelargonium has ivy-shaped leaves and pink, mauve or white flowers. Many cultivars are available, in very bright colours, some of them even two-tone, e.g. red-and-white. Allow the ivy-leaved pelargonium to scramble up into trees, or to cascade over a terraced wall or the edge of a large container. Use it as a ground cover under large trees, as an excellent indoor container plant or grow it in a hanging basket. Plant the ivy-leaved pelargonium in any soil, adding plenty of compost, and water regularly throughout the year. Propagate it from cuttings planted in riversand.

Natural distribution: It grows from the south-western to the eastern Cape.

Flowering time:
Spring and summer

LEFT AND CENTRE *Pelargonium peltatum* hybrid.

Gladiolus spp.　IRIDACEAE
Gladiolus

Height: 20-80 cm　

The indigenous gladioli are fast growing and vary from very small plants to very large. They bear flowers in all shades, often with bright, contrasting markings on their petals and a sweet fragrance. Spectacular hybrids with large, colourful flowers are also available. Three months before the flowering season, plant corms in large groups about 20 cm apart and about 10 cm deep. The soil must be light, well drained and contain plenty of compost. After the leaves have died, lift the corms and store them in a dry place. Propagate gladioli from seed or by removing offsets from the 'parent' corms. Plant them in a separate bed until they reach flowering size, which takes about two years.

Natural distribution: Different species occur in each of the four provinces of South Africa.

Flowering time:
Varies throughout the year
according to the species

FROM LEFT TO RIGHT *Gladiolus dalenii* (orange), *G. carneus* and *G. dolomiticus.*

Watsonia spp.　IRIDACEAE
Watsonia

1,75 m × 0,2 m　

There are many watsonia species available and these vary greatly in size, flowering times, flower colour (ranging from white to pink, orange and mauve) and cultivation requirements. As a general rule, watsonias should be planted in good, well-drained soil, with the addition of plenty of compost. Water the deciduous species only during their growing season and keep them dry when dormant. Evergreen species must be watered throughout the year. Propagate watsonias from seed, by removing offsets from the 'mother' corms or by dividing larger clumps.

Natural distribution: There are about 70 species, growing in the Cape and Transvaal mountains and along the east coast into Natal and Swaziland.

Flowering time:
Varies throughout the year
according to the species

LEFT AND CENTRE *Watsonia* sp. **RIGHT** *W. angusta.*

Carpobrotus deliciosus
MESEMBRYANTHEMACEAE

Purple sour fig

0,15 m × 1 m

Flowering time:
Spring

The purple sour fig is a trailing plant with three-sided, fleshy leaves and large purple 'vygie' flowers followed by edible fruits. As it spreads rapidly to form a tough, drought-resistant ground cover, it can be used to hold the soil on steep banks, in hot, arid areas, or for roadside planting. It tolerates all soils and grows quickly and easily, rooting as it spreads. Water moderately in summer. It is easily propagated from cuttings or by lifting rooted runners.

Natural distribution: It grows on sand dunes along the eastern Cape coast.

LEFT (BELOW) *Carpobrotus dimidiatus*, which is very similar to *C. deliciosus*.

Carpobrotus muirii   MESEMBRYANTHEMACEAE

Real sour fig

0,15 m × 1 m

Flowering time:
Spring

This trailing plant with three-sided, fleshy leaves spreads rapidly to form a tough, drought-resistant ground cover. The large mauve flowers are followed by edible fruits – this species has the best fruits for eating. This plant can be used to hold soil on steep banks, as a ground cover in dry areas, for roadside planting, or be allowed to overhang a terraced wall. It tolerates all soils and grows quickly and easily, rooting as it spreads. Water moderately in summer. The real sour fig is easily propagated from cuttings or by lifting rooted runners.

Natural distribution: It grows in the Riversdale area in the southern Cape.

LEFT AND RIGHT *Carpobrotus acinaciformis*, which is similar to *C. muirii*.

Dicoma zeyheri   ASTERACEAE

Doll's protea

30 cm × 40 cm

Flowering time:
Late summer or autumn

The doll's protea has a moderate growth rate, prickly, whitish, thistle-like flowers and silver-green foliage which lasts well in a vase. Plant it in groups – about 40 cm apart – in a rockery, or use it as an unusual ground cover at the base of trees that are planted in large terracotta containers on a sunny patio. Use well-drained soil, adding plenty of compost, and water regularly in summer. The plant is dormant in winter and should be kept reasonably dry during this period. Propagate from seed.

Natural distribution: It grows on rocky koppies and in grassland, in Natal, Swaziland and the Transvaal.

Dierama pendulum   IRIDACEAE
Harebell

1 m × 1 m

Flowering time:
Spring

The harebell, which has a moderate growth rate, forms large clumps of strap-shaped leaves and bears dainty, drooping, pinkish, bell-like flowers carried on long, slender stalks. Plant it at the edge of a pond – it is an excellent accent plant – or in a rockery (where it must be very well watered), in an informal border, next to a dripping tap, or nestling amongst an attractive clump of rocks. The corms should be planted in groups of 10-15, about 30 cm apart, in good, well-drained soil containing plenty of compost. Although the harebell tolerates full sun at the coast, it likes afternoon shade in the drier inland areas. This is an evergreen and must be watered regularly throughout the year. Leave the corms undisturbed to multiply for a few years. Cut back the old leaves to keep the plant tidy. Propagate from seed or by the division of clumps.

Natural distribution: It grows on mountainsides near Grahamstown and East London in the eastern Cape.

RIGHT The flower of *Dierama cooperi.*

Dissotis canescens   MELASTOMATACEAE
Wild tibouchina

1 m × 1 m

Flowering time:
December to March

The fast-growing wild tibouchina has oval leaves which are velvety in texture, and large, buttercup-shaped magenta-pink flowers carried in spikes at the tips of the branches. As it requires moist soil, it should be planted next to a pond or stream. Other possibilities are next to a dripping tap, or in an informal shrub border (provided it receives the right amount of moisture). Plant the wild tibouchina in good, rich garden soil, containing plenty of compost or peat, and water extremely well in summer. It dies back in winter, and should be kept dry during this time. Propagate from seed or cuttings, or by lifting rooted runners.

Natural distribution: It grows in damp places, from the eastern Cape, Transkei, Natal and Swaziland to the eastern and northern Transvaal.

Dissotis princeps   MELASTOMATACEAE
Royal tibouchina

1 m × 1 m

Flowering time:
Summer

The oval leaves of the fast-growing royal tibouchina are velvety in texture and the large, buttercup-shaped purple flowers, which are slightly larger than those of the previous species, are carried in spikes at the tips of the branches. The plant requires very moist soil, so a position near a pond, stream or dripping tap would be ideal. It can also be planted in an informal border, as long as it receives copious water in summer. It dies back in winter and must not be watered during this period. Plant the royal tibouchina in good, rich garden soil, containing plenty of compost or peat. Propagate from seed or cuttings, or by lifting rooted runners.

Natural distribution: It grows in very wet places in the northern Transvaal, Swaziland, Botswana, Zimbabwe and Mozambique.

Geranium incanum GERANIACEAE

Carpet geranium

30 cm × 30 cm

Flowering time:
Spring, summer and autumn

This fast-growing plant has fine feathery leaves and round, flattish, saucer-shaped mauve flowers. Mass plant the carpet geranium to form a ground cover, or allow it to overhang a terraced wall. It will also do well in large containers or planter boxes on a sunny patio, as an edging plant along the front of an informal border, planted on a large sloping bank, or experiment with a few in a hanging basket. Use light, well-drained soil containing plenty of compost, and water regularly throughout the year. Prune the plant back after flowering to keep it neat and encourage a new batch of flowers. It usually seeds itself freely, so older plants can eventually be removed, leaving the younger ones in their place. It can also be propagated from seed or from cuttings.

Natural distribution: It grows near the Cape coast from Stellenbosch to about Knysna.

Impatiens hochstetteri subsp. *hochstetteri*

BALSAMINACEAE

Mauve impatiens

20 cm × 20 cm   to

Flowering time:
Midsummer onwards

Fast growing, this impatiens has soft, oval leaves and small mauve flowers with flat, rounded petals. It makes a lovely ground cover for dappled shade, particularly near a pond or stream – it loves moist conditions – and requires a very protected position in frosty gardens. Use the mauve impatiens in planter boxes on the south side of the house (in warm, moist gardens), along the edge of a shady pathway, or at the base of a dripping tap. Plant it in light, well-drained, compost-enriched soil and water regularly. Propagate from cuttings planted in riversand.

Natural distribution: It grows in the southern and eastern Cape, eastern Natal, Lesotho and Swaziland.

Lampranthus coralliflorus

MESEMBRYANTHEMACEAE

Mauve vygie

30 cm × 45 cm

Flowering time:
Spring

This is a moderately fast-growing trailing plant with small, cylindrical, succulent leaves and cyclamen-pink 'vygie' flowers, which only open fully on bright, sunny days. Mass plant it to form a ground cover in a rockery or on a steep bank, or interplant with other colourful vygies for a spectacular show of colour in spring. Plant the mauve vygie in well-drained, compost-enriched soil and water moderately from autumn to spring, especially in the summer rainfall area. Propagate from seed or from cuttings taken in summer.

Natural distribution: It grows in the south-western Cape.

LEFT AND RIGHT *Lampranthus* sp., which is similar to *L. coralliflorus*.

Osteospermum jucundum ASTERACEAE
Trailing mauve daisy

20 cm × 60 cm   to

Flowering time:
Autumn to spring

Large daisy flowers, varying in colour from pink to purple, are borne by this easily grown plant, which spreads and covers the ground rapidly. It requires a position in full sun for the flowers to open completely and should be used as a ground cover on sloping banks, or in a large rockery, or as an edging plant along the front of an informal border, or be allowed to cascade over a terraced wall. Plant the trailing mauve daisy in good, light, well-drained soil, adding plenty of compost, and water regularly throughout the year. Propagate from seed – which is a slow process – or by lifting rooted runners.

Natural distribution: It grows in grassland and mountainous areas, in the north-eastern Cape, Lesotho, Natal, Swaziland, the north-eastern Orange Free State and the northern and eastern Transvaal.

Pelargonium cucullatum GERANIACEAE
Wildemalva

1 m × 1 m

Flowering time:
Spring and summer

This is a fast-growing, sprawling perennial, with large, rounded, hairy leaves and mauve flowers marked with purple. It can be used in an informal shrub border, in containers on a sunny patio or in a large rockery. The plant is easily grown, tolerant of coastal conditions and requires little attention with the exception of regular watering. Plant it in light, sandy, well-drained soil, adding plenty of compost. Propagate from seed, or from cuttings planted in riversand.

Natural distribution: It grows in the south-western Cape.

LEFT *Pelargonium* sp., which is similar to *P. cucullatum.*

Pelargonium reniforme GERANIACEAE
Kidney-leaved pelargonium

15 cm × 30 cm

Flowering time:
Summer to autumn

The kidney-leaved pelargonium, which is a fast-growing, drought-resistant ground cover with small, rounded grey leaves, is a mass of bright magenta blooms in the flowering season. With its very attractive foliage, it could be used as a ground cover in large, well-drained planter boxes in full sun or planted about 30 cm apart in a rockery or along the edge of a border. Situate this pelargonium in a well-drained position, in light, sandy soil, adding plenty of compost. It requires little moisture as its tuberous roots store water. Propagate the plant from seed, cuttings or by dividing the tuberous roots.

Natural distribution: It grows in dry rocky places in the eastern Cape.

Scabiosa africana   DIPSACACEAE
Pincushion

30 cm × 30 cm

Flowering time:
Spring and autumn

This plant is a fast-growing perennial with finely divided grey-green foliage and mauve flower heads which are carried on long stalks and which resemble pincushions. The flowers last well in a vase. Mass plant it to form a ground cover, or use it in smaller groups in a rockery. It could also be used as an edging plant along the front of an informal border. Plant the pincushion in any well-drained soil, adding plenty of compost, and water regularly. Prune the plant back after flowering to keep it neat. Propagate from seed or from cuttings, or by lifting rooted sections.

Natural distribution: It grows in the mountains of the Cape Peninsula.

Sutera grandiflora   SCROPHULARIACEAE
Wild phlox

1 m × 0,5 m

Flowering time:
Almost throughout the year
(especially good in autumn)

The wild phlox is a fast-growing perennial with aromatic grey-green leaves and large heads of phlox-like flowers which are light purple in colour. It is suitable for a large rockery or an informal shrub border. As this plant tends to be a bit sparse and to sprawl, it should be planted fairly close together – about 30 cm apart – in large groups of at least five. Plant it in ordinary, light, well-drained garden soil, adding plenty of compost. Water well in summer and less in winter. Cut the wild phlox back almost to ground level at the end of winter. Propagate from seed.

Natural distribution: It grows in the mountains of the eastern Transvaal and Swaziland.

Tulbaghia violacea   ALLIACEAE
Wild garlic

40 cm × 25 cm   to

Flowering time:
Summer

Clumps of strap-shaped grey leaves are formed by this fast-growing, drought-resistant plant. It bears round heads of small mauve flowers which are carried on long stalks. While this species smells of garlic, *Tulbaghia simmleri* does not, and bears sweetly scented flowers in spring. Plant the wild garlic in small groups in a rockery, use it as an edging plant along the front of an informal border or along a pathway, or mass plant it to form a ground cover, in sunny or partially shaded positions. The soil should be a good, well-drained loam containing plenty of compost. Although this plant will tolerate poor soils, it will not grow as well. Water regularly in spring and summer but less in winter. Propagate the wild garlic from seed or by dividing larger clumps.

Natural distribution: It grows in the south-eastern and eastern Cape and southern Natal.

LEFT AND RIGHT *Tulbaghia simmleri.*

Adiantum capillus-veneris ADIANTACEAE

Maidenhair fern

30 cm × 30 cm  to

Foliage plant

This fast-growing, delicate fern has flat, heart-shaped leaflets carried on wiry black stems. Plant it in a protected position near a stream or pond or use it in window boxes or large containers on the shaded, southern side of the house. It grows well indoors in a container placed near a north window but out of direct sunlight. Stand the container on a layer of pebbles to keep it above the level of the water that drains into the saucer. This will help to prevent root rot and will provide the extra humidity necessary for good growth. Plant the maidenhair fern in good, light, well-drained soil, adding plenty of compost and leaf mould. This type of potting mix is essential if ferns are to succeed. Water well – the soil must be moist at all times – in summer and winter. This fern spreads by means of slender rhizomes. Propagate it from spores, which is a slow and difficult process, or by dividing the rhizomes.

Natural distribution: This fern grows near moisture on shaded banks and cliff faces and is widespread in South Africa.

Blechnum punctulatum BLECHNACEAE

Pink-leaved blechnum

75 cm × 50 cm to

Foliage plant

Of moderate growth rate, this fern has glossy, sword-shaped fronds which are pinkish in colour when young and dark green when mature. Plant this blechnum near a stream or pond as it prefers shady, damp places. It also makes an excellent container plant, either for the patio or indoors. The soil must be good, light and well drained and contain plenty of compost and leaf mould. Keep moist throughout summer and winter. This fern can be propagated from spores, which is a slow and difficult process, or by dividing the rhizomes. It is, however, much easier to buy ferns from a nursery.

Blechnum australe is a species very similar to *B. punctulatum*.

Natural distribution: It grows along damp forest margins, from the south-western, southern and eastern Cape through Transkei, Natal and Lesotho to Swaziland and the Transvaal.

Blechnum tabulare BLECHNACEAE

Mountain blechnum

1 m × 1 m  to

Foliage plant

This attractive fern has a moderate to slow growth rate and resembles a cycad, producing whorls of stiff, leathery fronds from a central stem which may eventually reach a height of 1 m. Suitable for a container, it may also be planted outside in a moist, shaded position protected from frost. Use good, light and well-drained soil containing plenty of compost and leaf mould. Keep moist throughout the year. This fern can be propagated from spores, which is a slow and difficult process. It is preferable to buy plants from a reputable nursery.

Natural distribution: This fern grows on the margins of evergreen mountain forests, or in very damp places in mountain grassland, from the south-western Cape through the eastern Cape, Transkei and Natal to the eastern and northern Transvaal.

Cheilanthes hirta   ADIANTACEAE
Lip fern

30 cm × 30 cm

Foliage plant

Of moderate growth rate, the lip fern has narrow, hairy, finely divided fronds. Situate it in a very lightly shaded position in a rockery, as it will not grow indoors. Plant it in any soil, adding plenty of compost, and water moderately. Cut back dead fronds after winter. Propagate from spores.

Natural distribution: This is one of the most widespread ferns in South Africa, growing in rocky places in extremes of habitat from wet, cool mountains to hot, dry desert throughout the country, except for the western and northern Cape, north-western Botswana and Namibia.

CENTRE *Cheilanthes viridis*, which is more robust than *C. hirta* and will grow well in a rockery or hanging basket. **RIGHT** Ripe spores on the underside of a leaf of *C. viridis*.

Chlorophytum comosum 'Vittatum' ASPHODELACEAE
Variegated hen-and-chickens

30 cm × 30 cm   to

Foliage plant

This is a good, fast-spreading ground cover, which forms clumps of strap-shaped green-and-white leaves. The insignificant white flowers are borne on long, arching flower spikes which have new leaves at their tips – when these touch the ground they take root and form a new plant. The variegated hen-and-chickens thrives in shade under trees, is an excellent edging plant for dappled shade and grows very well in hanging baskets and also in containers indoors. It will revive if damaged by frost. Plant it in good, well-drained soil, adding plenty of compost, and water regularly throughout the year. Propagate by dividing large clumps or by removing 'chickens' and replanting these separately.
    Chlorophytum comosum (hen-and-chickens) is very similar to *C. comosum* 'Vittatum', but has strap-shaped plain green leaves.

Natural distribution: It grows in warmer areas from the southern and eastern Cape to Natal, Swaziland and the Transvaal.

Cyathea dregei   CYATHEACEAE
Tree fern

3 m × 2 m

Foliage plant

This is a slow-growing plant which has a fibrous, dark brown stem, topped with arching fronds which are a lush green. As it thrives when planted near water and likes a moist atmosphere, it makes an excellent accent plant for a water garden. Plant it in good, light, well-drained soil, adding plenty of compost and/or peat. It must be watered every day in dry weather – remember to water its stem as well as the roots. The tree fern can be propagated from spores, but this is a difficult and slow process. Rather purchase plants from a nursery that has a permit to sell them.

Natural distribution: The tree fern grows in grassland along the edges of streams, and sometimes in forest, from the southern and eastern Cape northwards through Transkei, Natal, Lesotho and Swaziland to the northern and eastern Transvaal, Zimbabwe and Mozambique. It is a protected plant and a permit is necessary to remove it from the wild.

Cyperus textilis CYPERACEAE

Emezi grass, Basket grass

1,5 m × 1 m  **to**

Foliage plant

A fast-growing perennial, this plant forms a clump of bare stems, each topped by a rounded head of narrow, spiky leaves. An attractive accent plant for a dam or pond, it may also be planted alongside a stream, at the base of steps, or in any moist area which needs to be covered. Plant it in any soil, adding plenty of compost, and keep moist throughout the year. Emezi grass spreads fairly vigorously by means of rhizomes and may need to be thinned out from time to time. Cut back any brown, dry leaves. Propagate by dividing large clumps.

Natural distribution: It grows in the eastern Cape and eastern Natal.

LEFT The large form of *Cyperus textilis*. **RIGHT** The small form of *Cyperus textilis*.

Cyrtomium caryotideum var. *micropterum*

ASPIDIACEAE

(= *C. falcatum*)

Holly fern

75 cm × 75 cm   **to**

Foliage plant

This fern, which has a moderate growth rate, has glossy, dark green leaves which resemble holly. It is ideal for damp, shady places, near a water garden or under trees and may be planted in large containers on a shady patio, or in an indoor garden. The soil must be good, light and well drained and contain plenty of compost and leaf mould. Water regularly throughout the year. The holly fern can be propagated from spores but this is a slow and difficult process. It is easier to buy plants from a nursery.

Natural distribution: It grows in evergreen forests, along streams and in other moist places, from the eastern Cape through Transkei, Natal and Lesotho to the eastern Transvaal.

Gunnera perpensa HALORAGACEAE

River pumpkin

80 cm × 60 cm

Foliage plant

The river pumpkin is a robust, fast-growing perennial which has a rosette of large, pumpkin-like leaves carried on long reddish stalks. Masses of tiny green-red flowers are borne on a tall spike above the leaves. Use this plant next to a pond or stream as it prefers marshy conditions. Plant it in any good soil, adding plenty of compost or peat, and keep very wet in summer. The leaves die back in winter, although the plant may possibly be evergreen in some areas, and it may be kept fairly dry during this period. It spreads by means of rhizomes and should be propagated by dividing large clumps.

Natural distribution: It grows in the Cape, Lesotho, Natal, Swaziland, the Orange Free State and the Transvaal.

Hydrocotyle bonariensis APIACEAE
Water nasturtium

15 cm × 60 cm   to

This fast-growing perennial produces attractive, round, shiny leaves which resemble those of the nasturtium and which are carried on long stalks. It has tiny, insignificant white to cream flowers. It loves marshy conditions and should be planted at the edge of a pond or stream where some of the runners will extend into the water and the leaves will float on the surface. It grows quickly and easily in any soil. Add plenty of compost or peat and keep well watered. The plant produces runners which root when they touch the ground. Propagate by dividing large clumps or by removing the rooted runners.

Centella asiatica (pennywort or waterhearts) is very similar in appearance to the water nasturtium and has the same cultivation requirements. It prefers moist conditions and a partially shaded position and can be used as a ground cover or grown in a hanging basket or large container on a shady patio.

Natural distribution: The water nasturtium grows in the Cape and Natal, whereas the pennywort is more widespread and also occurs in Lesotho, Swaziland, the Orange Free State, the Transvaal, Botswana and Namibia.

RIGHT (BELOW) *Centella asiatica.*

Foliage plant

Myrsiphyllum asparagoides ASPARAGACEAE
Cape smilax

30 cm × 80 cm to   to

Attractive shiny foliage and insignificant white flowers distinguish this fast-growing perennial. Use it as a ground cover, plant it in a hanging basket, or allow it to cascade over the top of a wall. Train it up a small trellis or allow it to cover an old tree stump. Plant the Cape smilax in any soil, adding plenty of compost, and water regularly. Once established, it is fairly drought resistant. If burnt by frost, it will recover rapidly in spring. Cut the plant back to ground level when it becomes untidy. Propagate it from seed or by dividing the clumps.

Natural distribution: It grows in the north-western, south-western, southern and eastern Cape, southern Natal, Lesotho, Swaziland, the eastern Orange Free State, the southern, eastern and northern Transvaal and Namibia.

Foliage plant

Pellaea calomelanos ADIANTACEAE
Blue rock fern

25 cm × 25 cm

Of moderate growth rate, this fern has wiry black stems and beautiful blue-green fronds. It tolerates dry and moist climates and, as it prefers to grow amongst rocks, is best grown in light shade on a rockery. Plant the blue rock fern in any soil, adding plenty of compost, and water regularly. Cut back dead fronds after winter. Propagate from spores, which is a slow and difficult process.

Natural distribution: It grows amongst rocks in warm areas throughout South Africa, Lesotho, Swaziland, Namibia, Botswana, Zimbabwe and Mozambique.

CENTRE Underside of a young leaf. **RIGHT** Underside of a leaf showing ripe spores.

Foliage plant

Pteris vittata ADIANTACEAE
Banded fern

1 m × 0,75 m

Foliage plant

This fast-growing fern has fairly narrow, leathery fronds which are up to a metre long. Plant it in light shade under trees or in a container on a patio. It prefers partial or light shade rather than dense shade, and should always be placed where the sun can reach it for a short part of the day. It is an easily grown fern, given the right conditions – the soil must be good, light and well drained and contain plenty of compost and leaf mould, and the plant must be watered regularly every day, especially in hot, dry weather. Cut the fern back after winter, if damaged by frost. Propagate from spores, or by carefully dividing the larger clumps – replant immediately.

Natural distribution: It grows in warmer, drier areas, but always near water, from the northern and eastern Cape northwards through most of South Africa, Zimbabwe, Namibia and Mozambique.

Rumohra adiantiformis ASPIDIACEAE
Knysna fern, Seven week fern

1 m × 1 m

Foliage plant

The attractive glossy foliage of this fast-growing fern is often used in flower arrangements. The fronds are leathery, coarsely toothed, triangular and light green in colour. Plant the Knysna fern in dappled shade under trees, in a container on a patio, or near a water feature – the shade must not be too dense or the fern will not grow well. It requires good, rich, well-drained soil, containing plenty of compost and leaf mould. Water well, keeping the soil moist throughout the year. Propagate from spores, or by dividing the larger clumps and replanting them immediately.

Natural distribution: It grows on forest margins, on forest floors, and sometimes on rocky hillsides, from the south-western Cape through the eastern Cape to southern Natal, the northern and eastern Transvaal and Zimbabwe.

Thelypteris dentata THELYPTERIDACEAE
Toothed fern

75 cm × 75 cm

Foliage plant

This fern with its attractive foliage – long, pinnate fronds with toothed edges – and moderate growth rate, spreads by means of a short, creeping rhizome. Plant it in shade under trees, next to a water feature or in a container on a shady patio – it will grow fairly easily. The toothed fern requires good, rich, well-drained soil, containing plenty of compost and leaf mould. Water well, keeping the soil moist throughout the year. Cut the fern back if damaged by frost. Propagate it from spores or by carefully dividing the larger clumps and replanting them immediately.

Natural distribution: It grows along mountain streams in wetter, warmer areas, from the eastern Cape through Natal, Lesotho and Swaziland to the eastern and northern Transvaal and Zimbabwe.

RIGHT (ABOVE) Underside of a young leaf. **RIGHT (BELOW)** A leaf showing ripe spores.

4 ANNUALS

Annuals are short-lived plants which grow from seed and complete their life cycle within one season. As they flower so soon after planting, annuals are the quickest way of providing colour in the garden. Plants that originate in dry areas like the north-western Cape, where the rainy season is short, grow particularly quickly – as is witnessed by the breathtaking annual display of spring flowers in Namaqualand. Indigenous annuals come in a variety of bright colours and, as many of them have the same growth requirements, one can mix the seed and sow them together for cheerful splashes of colour.

Annuals can be used in flowerbeds, as edging plants, in rockeries and in containers. Although not permanent like perennial ground covers some of them can be used for the same purpose, i.e. to bind the soil, suppress weed growth and keep the root areas around large shrubs and trees cool and moist.

These plants are all propagated from seed which can either be sown directly into the flowerbeds or in trays. The soil in the bed should be well prepared before you sow (see p. 227). Rake the area to level it and break up any large clods, and water the day before sowing so that the soil under the surface is moist but the surface itself is dry when you sow. If the seed is very fine it should be mixed with fine sand in a shaker and sown in this way to get an even spread. Once the seed is sown you should rake the area lightly and then tamp down the soil using the flat end of a metal rake. This helps to lodge the seed in the soil. Water the area with a fine spray which will not wash the seed away or bury it too deeply.

As the seedlings grow those that are too close together will have to be transplanted into a less crowded part of the bed. This should be done during the cooler times of the day and transplanted seedlings might have to be protected from the midday sun for a few days.

Once the seedlings are established you should fertilise them, initially using slow-release 3:2:1 followed about three weeks later by 3:1:5, the high potassium content of which encourages the plants to flower. Annuals should be watered regularly and thoroughly so that the water penetrates the soil to a depth of at least 10 cm.

If you prefer to sow into seed trays a good germinating medium such as a light, well drained organic potting mix must be used. A 6 cm thick layer in each tray should suffice. This medium should be moistened before you sow and kept moist during germination. The sown seed should generally be covered to the same depth as its diameter. Fine seed, therefore, is covered more lightly than larger seed. Fine vermiculite or clean river sand are the best materials for this purpose. After watering the seed with a fine spray the tray can be covered with a pane of glass which must be removed as soon as the seed has germinated. Prick out the seedlings from the seed tray when they reach the 'true leaf' stage and plant them in a six- or twelve-pack tray where they can 'grow on' until ready to be planted into the garden.

Indigenous annuals are easier to grow than exotic plants. They require little care and are ideal for low-maintenance gardens. Many seed themselves but it is nevertheless worthwhile collecting the seed at the end of the season. Single flowers should be picked when the seed heads begin to ripen and then stored in a paper bag. If the plant produced several flowers on a stalk the whole stalk should be picked and hung upside down in a paper bag until the seed has dried and fallen into the bag. The seed of indigenous plants is available from a few specialist nurseries and can also be obtained by joining the Botanical Society of South Africa which produces a seed catalogue and provides this service for its members.

Anchusa capensis BORAGINACEAE

Cape forget-me-not

60 cm × 30 cm

The Cape forget-me-not is an erect, perennial herb, which is best treated as an annual in cultivation. It has long, narrow, hairy leaves and branched spikes carrying numerous small bright blue flowers. Mass plant it in a bed for a striking display, or use it in groups in a rockery, or as an edging plant along an informal border. Plant the Cape forget-me-not in ordinary garden soil, adding plenty of compost, and water regularly. Propagate it from seed, sowing this in December and January for an early spring display, in March for flowers in September and in August for flowers in autumn.

Natural distribution: It is very common in the Cape Province and also occurs in Lesotho, the Orange Free State, Swaziland, the southern Transvaal, Botswana and Namibia.

Flowering time:
Spring or autumn

Arctotis acaulis ASTERACEAE

Bushy arctotis

50 cm × 50 cm

This perennial is best treated as an annual in the garden. The leaves, which are dark green above and woolly white beneath, are very variable and may or may not be deeply lobed. Large golden yellow flowers – backed with red, and with a shiny black ring around the centre – are carried on long stalks. Many brightly coloured hybrids are also available. For a lovely display, plant the bushy arctotis about 30 cm apart in full sun, in well-drained soil, adding plenty of compost, and water well in winter. Propagate from seed, sowing this in mid-March for flowers in September and October. Protect young plants from frost.

Natural distribution: It grows mainly in the south-western Cape between Calvinia and Komgha.

Flowering time:
September and October

Arctotis fastuosa ASTERACEAE

Bittergousblom

60 cm × 60 cm

The bittergousblom is an annual herb with deeply lobed, slightly hairy grey-green leaves and orange daisy-like flowers, each petal of which has a dark brown blotch at its base. This plant forms a bushy clump and should be planted about 40 cm apart in groups in a rockery, or as a ground cover on a sunny bank. It tolerates coastal conditions and is easily grown. Plant it in any soil, adding plenty of compost, and water well in autumn and winter. Propagate from seed sown in March.

Natural distribution: It grows in Namaqualand and the south-western Cape.

Flowering time:
September

Arctotis hirsuta ASTERACEAE

Hairy arctotis

50 cm × 50 cm

Flowering time:
Spring to midsummer

The hairy arctotis is an annual herb with deeply lobed grey-green leaves and white, yellow or orange daisy-like flowers, which may or may not be marked with purple at the base. Plant this annual in groups in a sunny rockery or use it as an edging plant along an informal border. It grows in any well-drained soil, to which plenty of compost has been added. Water well in autumn and winter. Propagate this arctotis from seed sown in March.

Natural distribution: It grows on sandy soil, from Namaqualand southwards to the Cape Peninsula, and also in Namibia.

Arctotis venusta ASTERACEAE

Free State daisy

40 cm × 40 cm

Flowering time:
Summer or autumn

The Free State daisy is an annual herb and its grey-green leaves are long, narrow, irregularly lobed and softly hairy. The daisy flowers are either white, salmon or deep orange and have yellow centres. This plant has a bushy habit and makes a good choice for the edge of an informal border, for large tubs on a sunny patio or for a rockery. Plant this arctotis in groups in any well-drained soil, adding plenty of compost, and water well in the growing season. Propagate it from seed sown in spring for summer flowers and in autumn for a spring display.

Natural distribution: It grows in dry areas, in the eastern parts of Namaqualand, the northern and western Cape, the central Orange Free State, Lesotho, Transvaal, Botswana and Namibia.

RIGHT (ABOVE AND BELOW) *Arctotis acaulis*, which is similar to *A. venusta*.

Cenia turbinata ASTERACEAE

(= *Cotula turbinata*)

Bachelor's buttons

30 cm × 30 cm

Flowering time:
Spring

This annual, with its finely divided leaves and masses of yellow flowers which are round, flattish and button-like, is ideal for a rockery or a mixed border or for planting between paving stones. It likes sandy, well-drained soil, with the addition of sufficient compost, and plenty of water throughout the growing season. Propagate from seed sown in April, and when the plants are about 12 mm high, plant into the garden, about 10 cm apart.

Natural distribution: This plant grows in the south-western and south-eastern Cape.

Ceratotheca triloba   PEDALIACEAE
Wild foxglove

1 m × 0,3 m

Flowering time:
January to May

This erect annual, with its slightly hairy leaves and large, pale mauve or white foxglove-like flowers, is an attractive plant which grows very tall and has a sparse habit. Plant very close together – about 20 cm apart – for a good display, either in a large rockery or an informal border. The soil must be sandy and well drained, with plenty of compost added. Water throughout the season. Propagate this annual from seed sown in spring, and set the plants out in their permanent positions when they are about 5 cm tall.

Natural distribution: The wild foxglove grows on rocky koppies or disturbed areas, in Griqualand West, the eastern Cape, Transkei, Natal, Swaziland, the eastern and northern Transvaal and Botswana.

Dimorphotheca pluvialis   ASTERACEAE
White Namaqualand daisy

30 cm × 30 cm

Flowering time:
July to mid-September

The white Namaqualand daisy is an annual with narrow, bluntly toothed leaves and white daisy flowers which need full sun to open and which always face the sun, i.e. north. It requires sandy, well-drained soil, with the addition of plenty of compost, and good watering throughout the growing season. Propagate from seed sown in late March or early April. Sow on a calm day or the wind will blow the seed away. This must be thickly sown onto well-prepared soil, and then kept moist until it germinates four to ten days later. Young plants must also be kept moist until they reach a height of about 10 cm. The plant takes three months to flower.

Natural distribution: It grows in the south-western Cape, Namaqualand and Namibia.

Dimorphotheca sinuata   ASTERACEAE
Orange Namaqualand daisy

30 cm × 30 cm

Flowering time:
July to mid-September

A loosely branched annual with shallowly lobed leaves, this Namaqualand daisy bears large orange daisy flowers. The flowers need full sun to open and they always face the sun, i.e. north. The plant requires sandy, well-drained soil, with the addition of plenty of compost, and good watering throughout the growing season. Propagate from seed sown in late March or early April. Sow on a calm day or the wind will blow the seed away. This must be thickly sown onto well-prepared soil, and then kept moist until it germinates four to ten days later. Young plants must also be kept moist until they reach a height of about 10 cm. The plant takes three months to flower.

Natural distribution: It grows in sandy places in Namaqualand and Namibia.

Dorotheanthus bellidiformis

MESEMBRYANTHEMACEAE

Bokbaaivygie

10 cm × 25 cm

Flowering time: Spring

This small annual, with its tiny, flat, succulent leaves, bears large, shiny 'vygie' flowers in colours ranging from white through to pink, orange and yellow. Ideal for a rockery or steep embankment, the bokbaaivygie may also be mass planted between paving stones for a lovely show. The soil must be good, light and well drained, with plenty of compost added. Propagate from seed sown – in full sun – in March. This will yield flowers from about August to mid-October. The seed should be sown in seed trays or the open ground and kept moist throughout. Germination will take between one and three weeks. Young plants must also be watered well until the flowering season, after which watering can be reduced.

Natural distribution: It grows on the sandy plains near the sea in the Cape Peninsula, especially on the west coast.

Felicia australis   ASTERACEAE

Blue Karoo daisy

20 cm × 20 cm

Flowering time: Spring

This annual herb branches from the base, has narrow, linear leaves and daisy flowers that are deep blue and have yellow centres. Plant this felicia in groups in a rockery – it also makes an attractive edging plant along an informal border. Use good, light, well-drained soil, adding plenty of compost, and water well through-out the growing season. Propagate this plant from seed sown in full sun in March or April – choose a slightly protected position in very cold gardens. Germination takes about one week.

Natural distribution: This felicia grows from Namaqualand to Laingsburg in the Cape Province.

LEFT AND RIGHT *Felicia hirta*, which is similar to *F. australis*.

Felicia bergerana   ASTERACEAE

Kingfisher daisy

20 cm × 20 cm

Flowering time: August and September

The kingfisher daisy is an annual with very thin, smooth, grass-like leaves and masses of cobalt-blue daisy flowers with yellow centres. Incorporate it in a mixed border with, e.g. *Cenia turbinata*, or use as an edging plant – it will bloom for about two months. It requires good, light, well-drained soil, with the addition of plenty of compost, and a good supply of water throughout the growing season. Plant it in a slightly protected position in very cold gardens. Propagate the king-fisher daisy from seed sown in full sun in mid-March for flowers in August. Germination takes about one week.

Natural distribution: It grows from Namaqualand to Caledon in the Cape Province.

LEFT AND RIGHT *Felicia* sp., which is similar to *F. bergerana*.

Felicia dubia   ASTERACEAE

(= *F. adfinis*)

Dwarf felicia

15 cm × 15 cm

Flowering time:
September to October

Similar to the species described under *Felicia bergerana*, this annual has much smaller and daintier flowers and broader, slightly more hairy leaves. Plant the dwarf felicia in groups in a rockery – it also makes a good edging plant along an informal border. Use good, light, well-drained soil, adding plenty of compost, and water well throughout the growing season. Propagation is from seed sown in full sun in mid-March, in a slightly protected position. The seed must be fairly closely sown – these plants are very small. Germination takes about one week.

Natural distribution: It grows in Namaqualand and the south-western Cape.

Felicia heterophylla   ASTERACEAE

True-blue daisy

30 cm × 30 cm

Flowering time:
September to October

This bushy annual has azure blue daisy flowers with purplish centres. Plant it in groups in a rockery, use as an edging plant along an informal border or as a temporary filler for any bare, sunny area. It requires good, light, well-drained soil, with the addition of plenty of compost, and a good supply of water throughout the growing season. Propagation is from seed sown in the first week of March, in a protected position. Germination takes about one week.

Natural distribution: This felicia grows in the south-western Cape.

Gazania lichtensteinii   ASTERACEAE

Yellow gazania

20 cm × 20 cm

Flowering time:
Summer

This annual gazania has a clump of grey-green leaves and produces bright yellow daisy-like flowers on long stalks. Each petal has a black dot at its base. This very low-growing plant should be used in a rockery, on a sloping bank, between paving stones or in large containers on a sunny patio. Plant it in light, well-drained soil, adding plenty of compost. Propagate from seed sown in full sun in March or April and water moderately throughout the growing season.

Natural distribution: It grows in the dry areas of the north-western Cape, the Karoo and Namibia.

LEFT AND RIGHT (ABOVE) *Gazania krebsiana* subsp. *arctotoides*, which is similar to *G. lichtensteinii* except that the flower does not have a black dot at the base of each petal.
RIGHT (BELOW) *Gazania* sp., the flower of which is similar to that of *G. lichtensteinii*.

Grielum humifusum ROSACEAE
Yellow satin flower

10 cm × 20 cm

Flowering time:
Spring

This is a fairly prostrate, creeping annual with dark green leaves and cup-shaped lemon-yellow flowers. As it prefers well-drained, sandy soil it should be planted in a rockery, on a sloping bank or in a well-drained flowerbed. Water moderately throughout winter, the growing season. To propagate, sow seed in full sun in March or April for a beautiful display in spring. Set the young plants out about 20 cm apart.

Natural distribution: This plant grows in sandy soil in Namaqualand and the Clanwilliam area in the Cape Province, and in the Orange Free State and Namibia.

Heliophila coronopifolia BRASSICACEAE
Blue flax

60 cm × 30 cm

Flowering time:
Spring

The flower of this slender, erect-growing annual with its tiny leaves is composed of four bright blue petals, each with a white marking at its base. Plant the blue flax very close together – about 10 cm apart – in a large bed to create a good show, or use it in a sunny rockery. The seed can also be scattered amongst that of other annuals for an interesting and colourful display. Plant the blue flax in light, preferably sandy soil, adding plenty of compost, and water well in the growing season and slightly less while in bloom. Propagation is from seed sown in full sun in March or April. Germination takes about four to six days and the soil should be kept moist throughout.

Natural distribution: The blue flax grows in the south-western Cape.

LEFT AND CENTRE *Heliophila* sp., which is similar to *H. coronopifolia*.
RIGHT *Heliophila subulata*, which is similar to *H. coronopifolia*.

Lobelia erinus LOBELIACEAE
Wild lobelia

20 cm × 20 cm

Flowering time:
Almost throughout the year

This compact, bushy annual has masses of small violet flowers. It makes an excellent edging plant or may be planted in groups in a rockery. There are also some horticultural strains available which have a trailing habit and are ideal for window boxes and containers. Use good, well-drained soil, add plenty of compost and water well throughout. The wild lobelia prefers full sun but will flower in semi-shade, and is tolerant of coastal conditions. Propagation is from seed which may be sown in spring or autumn – in colder areas it is preferable to sow it in spring. It will take ten days to three weeks to germinate and is best sown in seed trays, which should be kept warm and shaded until the seedlings are ready to be planted out. Set the young plants out about 7-10 cm apart.

Natural distribution: It grows in the south-western and eastern Cape, Natal, the eastern Transvaal, Lesotho, Swaziland, the Orange Free State, Botswana and Namibia.

Nemesia ligulata　SCROPHULARIACEAE

Kappieblommetjie

20 cm × 20 cm　

This annual has yellow and white flowers, the three upper petals of which are white and pointed and the two lower ones rounded and yellow with orange markings. Mass plant in a rockery or in planter boxes on a sunny patio, in light, preferably sandy soil with plenty of compost added. Water well throughout the growing season. Propagate from seed sown in February or March, either in trays or out in the open, in a slightly protected position – choose a warm, sunny, protected place in colder gardens. Germination takes about one week. Set seedlings out about 15-20 cm apart.

Natural distribution: This plant grows in Namaqualand.

Flowering time:
Spring

Nemesia strumosa　SCROPHULARIACEAE

Nemesia, Cape jewels

30 cm × 30 cm　

This is an erect-growing annual which bears masses of bilabiate flowers in shades of cream, orange, red, mauve and yellow, and which looks good in a rockery or in planter boxes on a sunny patio. Plant this nemesia in light, preferably sandy soil with plenty of compost added, and water well throughout the growing season. Propagate from seed sown from February to March in a slightly protected position, either in trays or out in the open – the plant requires a warm, sunny, protected position in colder gardens. Germination takes about one week. Set seedlings out about 15-20 cm apart.

Natural distribution: It grows near Darling in the south-western Cape.

Flowering time:
Spring

Nemesia versicolor　SCROPHULARIACEAE

Weeskindertjies

50 cm × 50 cm　

This erect-growing annual bears bilabiate flowers which may be blue or yellow, or half white and half blue, or half yellow and half white. Plant it in a rockery or in planter boxes on a sunny patio. Use light, preferably sandy soil with plenty of compost added, and water well throughout the growing season. Propagate this plant from seed sown from February to March in a slightly protected position, either in trays or out in the open – the plant requires a warm, sunny, protected position in colder gardens. Germination takes about one week. Set seedlings out about 15-20 cm apart.

Natural distribution: It is common in the Cape Province, from Port Elizabeth to Namaqualand.

Flowering time:
July to November

LEFT AND CENTRE *Nemesia affinis,* which is similar to *N. versicolor.*
RIGHT *Nemesia versicolor.*

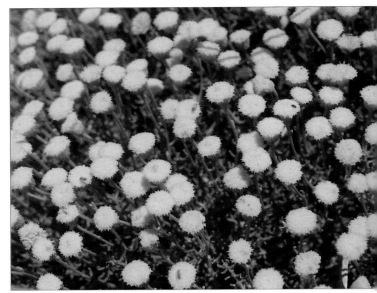

Oncosiphon suffruticosum   ASTERACEAE

Stinkkruid

30 cm × 30 cm

Flowering time:
Spring

This annual has finely divided, aromatic foliage and masses of small, round yellow flowers. Plant it in a rockery or along the edge of a flower border or scatter amongst other annuals for a colourful display. This plant will seed itself freely in the garden. Propagation is from seed sown in March – plant the seedlings 20-25 cm apart, in any soil, adding plenty of compost, and water well throughout winter.

Natural distribution: Stinkkruid grows in the Cape Province and Namibia.

LEFT *Oncosiphon piluliferum*, which is similar to *O. suffruticosum*.
RIGHT *Pentzia* sp., which is similar to *O. suffruticosum*.

Pentzia grandiflora   ASTERACEAE

Matricaria

40 cm × 40 cm

Flowering time:
Spring

Delicate, lacy, aromatic foliage and button-shaped yellow flowers distinguish this annual. Plant it in a rockery or along the edge of a flower border or scatter amongst other annuals for an interesting display. It will grow in any soil, provided plenty of compost has been added. Water well throughout winter. This plant seeds itself freely in the garden. It can also be propagated from seed sown in early autumn. Set seedlings out 20-25 cm apart.

Natural distribution: This plant grows in the south-western Cape, Namaqualand and Namibia.

RIGHT *Pentzia* sp., which is similar to *P. grandiflora*.

Senecio elegans   ASTERACEAE

Purple senecio

60 cm × 60 cm

Flowering time:
August to October

This bushy plant has soft foliage and masses of bright pink-mauve, daisy-like flowers, each with a yellow centre. It is suitable for use in a rockery or an informal border. Plant the purple senecio in good, light garden soil, adding plenty of compost, and water well in the growing season. Propagate from seed sown in March in a slightly protected position, either in seed trays or in the open ground. The seed may also be sown in spring for summer flowering, but plants do not grow as well. Set the seedlings out, 15 cm apart, for a mass display of colour. In areas that receive frost, provide protection from the early morning winter sun to prevent frost damage.

Natural distribution: The purple senecio grows in the coastal areas of the south-western and eastern Cape.

Steirodiscus tagetes   ASTERACEAE

Golden edging daisy

20 cm × 20 cm

The golden edging daisy, which forms a rounded bush with very attractive yellow daisy flowers is suitable for a rockery, or may be used as an edging plant in an informal border. Plant it in good, light soil, adding plenty of compost, and water well in winter. Propagate from seed sown at the beginning of March and set seedlings out close together – about 15 cm apart – for a mass display.

Flowering time:
September to October

Natural distribution: This daisy grows in the south-western Cape.

RIGHT *Steirodiscus* sp., which is similar to *S. tagetes*.

Ursinia anthemoides   ASTERACEAE

Ringed rock ursinia

30 cm × 30 cm

Ursinias are bright, cheery annuals for the spring garden and should be closely planted for a beautiful display. This species has finely divided leaves and large salmon to pale yellow flowers, each petal of which has a dark brown patch at its base. The flowers need full sun to open and, as they always face the sun, i.e. north, should be placed accordingly. Plant this ursinia in light, well-drained, sandy soil, adding plenty of compost. Propagate from seed sown in the open ground in March – choose a calm day so that the wind does not blow the seed away. Germination takes from five to seven days. The seedlings should be kept well watered, but not waterlogged. Inland they must be watered throughout winter, until they start flowering.

Flowering time:
Spring

Natural distribution: It grows in Namaqualand, the south-western Cape and also in the south-eastern Cape up to Port Elizabeth.

Ursinia cakilefolia   ASTERACEAE

Calvinia ursinia

30 cm × 30 cm

This ursinia is an annual with deeply lobed leaves. It bears masses of large, attractive, bright orange flowers, each with a purplish black centre, and should be closely planted for a striking display. The flowers need full sun to open and, as they always face the sun, i.e. north, the plant should be positioned accordingly. This ursinia requires light, well-drained, sandy soil, with the addition of plenty of compost. Propagate it from seed sown in the open ground in March – choose a calm day so that the wind does not blow the seed away. Germination takes from five to seven days. The seedlings should be kept well watered, but not waterlogged. Inland they must be watered throughout winter, until they start flowering.

Flowering time:
Spring

Natural distribution: It grows in the Namaqualand and Calvinia areas of the Cape Province.

Ursinia calenduliflora ASTERACEAE

Springbok rock ursinia

40 cm × 40 cm

Flowering time:
Spring

A bushy annual for the spring garden, this ursinia has bright orange-yellow flowers, each with an orange centre surrounded by a black ring, and should be closely planted for a beautiful display. The flowers need full sun to open and, as they always face the sun, i.e. north, the plant should be positioned accordingly. This ursinia requires light, well-drained, sandy soil, with the addition of plenty of compost. Propagate it from seed sown in the open ground in March – choose a calm day so that the wind does not blow the seed away. Germination takes from five to seven days. The seedlings should be kept well watered, but not waterlogged. Inland they must be watered throughout winter, until they start flowering.

Natural distribution: This ursinia grows in sandy places in Namaqualand.

Ursinia nana ASTERACEAE

Dwarf ursinia

15 cm × 15 cm

Flowering time:
Spring

This small, bright and dainty annual for the spring garden has yellow daisy-like flowers and should be closely planted for a beautiful display. The flowers need full sun to open and, as they always face the sun, i.e. north, the plant should be positioned accordingly. This ursinia requires light, well-drained, sandy soil, with plenty of compost added. Propagate it from seed sown in the open ground in March – choose a calm day so that the wind does not blow the seed away. Germination takes from five to seven days. The seedlings should be kept well watered, but not waterlogged. Inland they must be watered throughout winter, until they start flowering.

Natural distribution: It grows in sandy places in Namaqualand, the Little Karoo, the eastern Cape, Namibia, Lesotho, Natal, the Orange Free State and the Transvaal.

Ursinia speciosa ASTERACEAE

Namaqua ursinia

40 cm × 40 cm

Flowering time:
Spring

This brightly coloured and delicate annual for the spring garden has finely divided leaves and large orange, yellow or white daisy-like flowers. It should be closely planted for a striking display. The flowers need full sun to open and, as they always face the sun, i.e. north, the plant should be positioned accordingly. This ursinia requires light, well-drained, sandy soil, with plenty of compost added. Propagate it from seed sown in the open ground in March – choose a calm day so that the wind does not blow the seed away. Germination takes from five to seven days. The seedlings should be kept well watered throughout winter, until they start flowering.

Natural distribution: It grows in Namaqualand and southwards to the Malmesbury area of the Cape Province and also in Namibia.

5 CLIMBERS

Climbers are perennial plants which can equal the permanence and size of shrubs and trees, but which do not have the typical woody framework of these plants. In nature climbers are supported by surrounding shrubs and trees which enable the lax shoots to grow upwards towards the light. Most climbers are native to subtropical forests or cooler forested climatic zones. Very few climbers grow naturally in really hot and dry or very cold regions. In South Africa climbers constitute a relatively small part of the large variety of indigenous plants.

Despite their limited number we do have some extremely beautiful and versatile indigenous climbers which can be used for a variety of purposes. They can provide a shady ceiling over pergolas and carports or form an attractive curtain to disguise unsightly walls or any other vertical structure. Because of their rambling growth habit some climbers can be used successfully as ground covers or planted to cascade down embankments or retaining walls. Those that grow very vigorously and tend to become invasive can even be grown in large containers.

When planting climbers the soil is prepared in the same way as for shrubs (see p. 113). If climbers are grown in containers a very well-drained potting mix such as the following must be used to prevent root rot. Mix equal parts of coarse riversand, compost, organic potting soil and loam (or light garden soil). For a large container (with a height and diameter of about 75 cm) add 125 ml each of superphosphate, slow-release 3:2:1 fertililser and bonemeal. Place a 10 cm layer of pebbles in the bottom of the container to ensure good drainage. Climbers are fed and watered in the same way as shrubs (see p. 113). Those in containers which have to rely on a small volume of soil must be watered as soon as the top 10 cm of soil has dried out and must be fed monthly.

Climbers can be trained over a variety of support structures such as pergolas, freestanding screens, arches and posts. These structures must be constructed of suitable materials which blend with the design of the house and garden, are sturdy enough to support the weight of the climber and durable enough to withstand outdoor conditions. If a climber is trained against a wall that will require maintenance it must be provided with a trellis which can be attached to the wall by means of a hinge so that the plant-covered trellis can be bent back when maintenance becomes necessary.

Indigenous climbers all tend to have an informal intertwined growth habit and pruning is used mainly to train the plant into the desired shape. The manner in which a climber is trained depends on the type of structure it is meant to cover. If the plant is to provide a ceiling a leading shoot is selected, other shoots are pruned out at the base and all side shoots are removed. The main shoot should grow to the top of the structure in about two seasons after which it can be allowed to branch to develop a framework. Side shoots are then removed from this framework until the main framework of branches has developed. Thereafter side shoots are allowed to grow and fill in the gaps. If a climber is to cover a surface such as a wall, between five and seven shoots are encouraged and the others are pruned out. The shoots that remain are trained to spread out over the trellis. When they have reached the desired height the tips can be cut back to encourage the development of side shoots. Older plants are pruned mainly to thin out thick growth and remove dead material.

Aloe ciliaris ASPHODELACEAE

Climbing aloe

5 m × 1 m

Flowering time:
Throughout the year

This fast-growing aloe has narrow, succulent leaves and tubular red flowers, which are borne on long stalks. It belongs to a very small group of indigenous 'climbing' aloes, which do not actually climb, but rather scramble into the surrounding vegetation which they use as support. As the climbing aloe does not develop tendrils or suckers with which to attach itself it has to be secured against a supporting structure when grown in the garden. Plant it in full sun against a fence or trellis or allow it to scramble up amongst other shrubs. In gardens that receive frost it should be planted in a protected position, preferably against a north- or west-facing wall. It will also grow well in a large container. The climbing aloe requires good, light, well-drained soil, to which plenty of compost has been added and should be watered well in summer but kept dry in winter. If it is grown in a container a very well-drained potting mix must be used to prevent the roots from rotting. Prune the plant if necessary to keep it neat. Propagate from seed, or from cuttings planted in riversand and kept fairly dry to prevent rot. Protect young plants from frost.

Natural distribution: The climbing aloe grows in the drier areas of the eastern Cape.

Clematis brachiata RANUNCULACEAE

Traveller's joy

5 m × 2 m

Flowering time:
Summer

This attractive, delicate-looking but, in fact, very vigorous climber bears masses of fragrant creamy flowers, each with a conspicuous tuft of yellow stamens in the centre. These are followed by decorative feathery seedheads. The traveller's joy tends to spread rather fast by sending up 'suckers' from the roots and in a garden with limited space is probably best planted in a large container on a sunny patio. Provide a trellis for support, although it can be allowed to scramble into trees or be planted against a fence. Plant it in full sun or partial shade, in good garden soil, adding plenty of compost. Water well in summer and prune back in winter. Propagate this climber from seed or by lifting rooted runners.

Natural distribution: It grows in grassland and open woodland and is widespread in the Cape, Lesotho, Natal, Swaziland, the Orange Free State, the Transvaal, Botswana and Namibia.

Combretum bracteosum　COMBRETACEAE
Hiccup nut

3,5 m × 3,5 m

Flowering time:
October or November

A scrambling shrub, which may climb as high as five metres into surrounding trees, this plant has smooth leaves which are dull green above and paler below. It bears masses of bright orange-red flowers in rounded heads, followed by roundish, nut-like fruits. These marble-sized fruits are green at first, later ripening to brown. Unlike the fruits of other combretums, they are not winged but may have four or five vertical ridges. The common name of this plant is derived from the fact that the fruits are said to either cause or cure hiccups – which of the two is uncertain. This is a beautiful climber for a moist, warm garden but in areas that receive frost it should be planted in a well-protected position, e.g. a north- or west-facing wall. It can also be grown as a shrub by providing a strong stake for support and pruning away any unduly long stems – or winding them around the support – until it has developed a good shape. Plant the hiccup nut in good, rich, well-drained soil, adding plenty of compost, and water well in summer. Propagate from seed, or sideshoot cuttings taken with a heel.

Natural distribution: It grows in eastern Natal, Transkei and the eastern Cape.

National tree number 532.2

Combretum microphyllum　COMBRETACEAE
Flame combretum

4 m × 3 m

Flowering time:
Early spring

The flame combretum is a very vigorous climber or scrambling shrub with fairly large, slightly leathery, glossy, dark green leaves. Its arching branches become covered in showy crimson red flowers in early spring before the leaves appear, and in full bloom this is one of our most striking climbers. The small, decorative, four-winged fruits slowly change from a light yellowish green to pink-red and finally become light brown and somewhat papery when ripe. The flame combretum may be allowed to scramble into a large tree, up a fence or over a strong carport. Without support it will form a large, rambling and spreading bush. Sensitive to frost, it should be planted in a protected position, in light, well-drained soil, with the addition of plenty of compost. This plant occurs naturally along the banks of streams and requires a fair amount of moisture. It should therefore be watered particularly well in summer. Prune the flame combretum back hard, if necessary, to keep it in check. Propagate it from seed and possibly also from cuttings.

Natural distribution: It grows along the banks of rivers and streams, in the eastern and northern Transvaal, Swaziland, Zululand, Zimbabwe and Mozambique.

National tree number 540.1

Gloriosa superba   COLCHICACEAE

Flame lily

1,5 m × 0,3 m

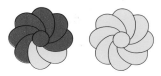

Flowering time:
December onwards

The flame lily is a tuberous climber with very attractive flowers, the wavy-edged yellow-and-red petals of which resemble flames. A yellow-flowered form, which tends to form a bush, is also available. Allow the flame lily to scramble up through trees or provide a trellis in semi-shade. Plant it in an equal mix of good garden soil and compost and/or leaf mould. In clay soils this climber should be planted in a raised bed, adding plenty of coarse riversand to the mix, as well as compost and leaf mould. In the winter rainfall area the flame lily must be planted in sandy soil in a very well-raised bed. It will start growing in October, rapidly reaching full size, and must be well watered until after the flowering season, when the foliage begins to turn yellow. This is the time to withhold water to prevent the tubers from rotting. Do not lift the tubers when the plant becomes dormant in winter – it remains in this state for about six months and must be kept dry during this period. Propagate from seed sown in September or October – this may take up to four months to germinate.

Natural distribution: It grows among bush on hillsides, along the Cape coast and in Natal, Swaziland, the northern Transvaal, Botswana and Namibia.

LEFT AND RIGHT (BELOW)   The yellow-flowered form of *Gloriosa superba*.

Grewia caffra   TILIACEAE

Climbing raisin

4 m × 2 m

Flowering time:
November to May

A shrub with a tendency to scramble, the climbing raisin produces starry yellow flowers and edible, spherical yellow-brown fruits, which have only a thin layer of flesh and are sweet, although slightly astringent. The climbing raisin could be planted in an informal shrub border and allowed to scramble into other bushes or pruned to keep it neat and shrub-like. Plant it in any good garden soil, adding plenty of compost, and water well in summer but less in winter. Propagate it from seed.

Natural distribution: It grows in deciduous woodland and wooded grassland, in the northern Cape, the western Orange Free State, the western Transvaal, Swaziland, southern Botswana and eastern Namibia.

LEFT AND RIGHT (ABOVE AND BELOW)   *Grewia flavescens*, which is similar to *G. caffra*.

Jasminum multipartitum   OLEACEAE

Starry wild jasmine

2 m × 2 m

Fast growing, this beautiful climber/scrambler has glossy, dark green foliage and bears masses of fragrant, white, jasmine-like flowers in spring. Plant a group under large trees to form a ground cover, train it over a trellis or carport or incorporate it in a shrub border. Without support it will form a large sprawling bush which is, nevertheless, still attractive. Plant in good, well-drained loam, adding plenty of compost, and water well. Prune the plant back after flowering to keep a neat shape and propagate from cuttings or seed.

Natural distribution: It grows in the eastern Cape, eastern Natal, Swaziland and the eastern Transvaal.

Flowering time:
Spring

Littonia modesta   COLCHICACEAE

Climbing bell, Yellow climbing bell

2 m × 0,3 m

This is a fairly fast-growing tuberous climber, which bears bell-shaped golden-yellow flowers, followed by large seed pods which split open to reveal spherical, shiny red seeds. Allow it to scramble up through trees or provide a trellis in sun or semi-shade. Plant it in an equal mix of good garden soil and compost and/or leaf mould. In clay soils this climber should be planted in a raised bed, adding plenty of coarse riversand as well as compost and leaf mould. In the winter rainfall area the climbing bell must be planted in sandy soil in a well-raised bed. It will start growing in October, rapidly reaching full size, and must be well watered until after the flowering season when the foliage begins to turn yellow. This is the time to withhold water to prevent the tubers from rotting. Do not lift the tubers when the plant becomes dormant in winter – it remains in this state for about six months and must be kept fairly dry during this period. Propagate it from seed sown at the end of August – this may take up to three months to germinate.

Natural distribution: It grows along the coast from East London into Natal, and in the eastern Orange Free State, Swaziland and the northern Transvaal.

Flowering time:
Summer

Plumbago auriculata   PLUMBAGINACEAE

Cape leadwort

3 m × 3 m

A shrub with a tendency to scramble, the Cape leadwort has small, delicate, pale green leaves and produces masses of powder blue or white flowers throughout summer. Allow it to scramble up amongst other shrubs or trees, or mass plant on a sloping bank, possibly interplanted with yellow tecomaria to provide a colourful combination. It may also be planted against a fence to form a screen or in an informal border where it can be kept neatly pruned. Use good, well-drained, compost-enriched soil and water in summer but keep fairly dry in winter. This attractive plant does particularly well in frost-free areas, but if damaged by frost it will recover rapidly in spring. Propagate from seed, cuttings or by removing rooted suckers from the root area.

Natural distribution: It grows in the eastern Cape, Natal, the Orange Free State and the Transvaal.

Flowering time:
Summer

Podranea ricasoliana   BIGNONIACEAE

Port St Johns creeper

6 m × 4 m

Flowering time:
Summer

The Port St Johns creeper is a very showy plant with compound, glossy, deep green leaves with scalloped margins. It bears bunches of large, trumpet-shaped pink flowers which are carried above the foliage and create a lovely display during the flowering season. Once established, the plant is drought resistant and tolerant of light frost. It must be provided with support and makes a beautiful creeper for a carport, or it can be planted along a fence to form a screen or against a strong trellis to provide shade for a sunny patio. It requires good, rich, well-drained soil, with the addition of plenty of compost. Water well in summer but less in winter. Prune the plant occasionally to keep it neat. If necessary, it can even be cut back hard to control its size. Propagate this creeper from cuttings.

Podranea brycei (Zimbabwe creeper) is very similar to *P. ricasoliana*. Its leaves, however, differ from those of the Port St Johns creeper in that they are a lighter green and do not have scalloped margins. The flowers are slightly smaller, are a deeper pink-mauve in colour and have more white hairs in the throat than those of the Port St Johns creeper. Both plants have the same cultivation requirements.

Natural distribution: Podranea ricasoliana grows in the eastern Cape and southern Natal, whereas *P. brycei* occurs in Zimbabwe.

RIGHT (BELOW) *Podranea brycei*.

Protasparagus plumosus   ASPARAGACEAE

(= *Asparagus plumosus*)

Asparagus fern

2 m × 1 m

Flowering time:
Summer

This vigorous climber has beautiful, fine, delicate foliage which is popular for flower arrangements. The flowers are white and fairly inconspicuous. If not controlled it tends to spread into surrounding shrubs by means of underground runners so it may be preferable to plant it in a large container. Always provide a trellis for support. The asparagus fern grows easily in any soil, and is fairly drought resistant, but for better results plant it in good, light, well-drained soil, adding plenty of compost, and water well in summer. Cut it back to ground level if damaged by frost or if it becomes untidy – it will quickly send up new shoots. Propagate this climber from seed or by dividing large clumps.

Natural distribution: It grows in the eastern Cape, eastern Natal, the eastern Transvaal and Mozambique.

Rhoicissus tomentosa   VITACEAE

Common forest grape

5 m × 3 m

This dense, fast-growing climber has attractive, dark green foliage, and bears large, decorative clusters of edible grape-like berries, which are purplish in colour, in autumn and winter. The yellow-green flowers are inconspicuous. Plant the common forest grape against a fence to form a screen – it serves this purpose particularly well – or allow it to cover a carport or a trellis, or a pergola, where it will provide shade for a sunny patio. It also grows well in hanging baskets. Once established, it is tolerant of drought and light frost. Plant the common forest grape in good, rich soil, adding plenty of compost, and water regularly. Propagate it from seed or from cuttings.

Rhoicissus digitata and *R. tridentata* are similar to *R. tomentosa*, and may be used as substitutes.

Natural distribution: The common forest grape grows in coastal and evergreen forest, in the Cape, Natal, the northern and eastern Transvaal and Swaziland.

National tree number 456.5

Flowering time:
October to December

LEFT AND RIGHT (ABOVE) *Rhoicissus tridentata*, which is similar to *R. tomentosa*.
RIGHT (BELOW) The berries of *Rhoicissus tomentosa* before they have ripened.

Senecio macroglossus   ASTERACEAE

Flowering ivy

3 m × 1,5 m

This fast-growing creeper has lemon yellow daisy-like flowers and attractive semisucculent, ivy-like foliage. It grows well in a large container on a sunny patio – provide a trellis for support – or allow it to climb into surrounding trees. The flowering ivy may also possibly succeed if mass planted as a ground cover on a sunny slope or bank. Plant it in good, light, well-drained soil, adding plenty of compost, and water regularly, especially in summer. Prune the plant back after winter to keep it neat. Propagate it from seed or from cuttings planted in riversand. The latter is the easier method.

Natural distribution: It grows in the eastern Cape, Lesotho, Natal and the eastern Transvaal (where it is fairly rare).

Flowering time:
Throughout summer

Senecio tamoides   ASTERACEAE

Canary creeper

5 m × 3 m

The canary creeper is a vigorous climber which has slightly succulent leaves and stems and bears masses of small, yellow daisy-like flowers in large, showy heads. It requires support in the form of a trellis, a fence or a nearby tree. Plant it in good, well-drained loam, adding plenty of compost. Water regularly, especially in summer. Prune the plant back if damaged by frost in winter. Propagate the canary creeper from seed, or from cuttings planted in riversand. The latter is the easier method.

Natural distribution: It grows in the forests of the eastern Cape, Natal, Swaziland and the northern and eastern Transvaal.

Flowering time:
Late summer or autumn

Thunbergia alata   ACANTHACEAE

Black-eyed Susan

3 m × 1,5 m

Small, slightly hairy leaves and masses of trumpet-shaped orange or yellow flowers, each with a black throat, distinguish this fast-growing creeper. Allow it to climb up into trees, mass plant it on a bank to form a ground cover, or plant it in large containers – provide a trellis for support – on a sunny patio. This creeper requires good, light, well-drained soil, with the addition of plenty of compost, and should be watered well in summer. Prune it back if damaged by frost – it will recover rapidly in spring. Propagate the plant from seed. It will also seed itself freely in the garden.

Natural distribution: It grows in the eastern Cape, Natal, Swaziland and the eastern Transvaal.

Flowering time:
Throughout summer

INDEX

Page numbers in *italics* indicate photographs.

PHOTOGRAPHIC CREDITS

All the photographs, with the exception of those indicated below, were taken by the author. The use of the following slides is gratefully acknowledged:

M. WELLS (NBI, PRETORIA)

Aponogeton distachyos (flower)
Conicosia pugioniformis (habit and flower)
Crassula perfoliata (flower)
Crinum campanulatum (habit)
Cussonia spicata (fruit)
Dombeya rotundifolia (habit)
Euphorbia caput-medusae (flower)
Gazania krebsiana (flower)
Gladiolus carneus (flower)
Grielum humifusum (flower)
Haemanthus coccineus (habit and flower)
Hemizygia transvaalensis (habit and flower)
Ixia sp. (habit and flower)
Kirkia wilmsii (habit)
Khaya nyasica (fruit)
Leucospermum reflexum (habit)
Limonium sp. (habit and flower)
Lobelia coronopifolia (flower)
Nemesia versicolor (flower)
Nuxia oppositifolia (flower)
Nylandtia spinosa (fruit)
Pentzia sp. (flowers)
P. grandiflora (habit and flower)
Phaenocoma prolifera (habit)
Protea grandiceps (flower)
P. magnifica (habit)
P. roupelliae (habit)
Rhamnus prinoides (berries)
Rothmannia globosa (flower)
Sesamothamnus lugardii (habit)
Schizostylis coccinea (flower)

L. HENDERSON (PPRI, PRETORIA)

Carissa bispinosa (habit)
Euphorbia confinalis (habit)
E. cooperi (habit)
E. evansii (habit)
Gardenia cornuta (fruit)
Oncoba spinosa (fruit)

N. KLAPWIJK (NBI, PRETORIA)

Brachylaena discolor (habit)
Diplorhynchus condylocarpon (habit)
Faurea saligna (habit)
Mimusops zeyheri (habit and fruit)
Rhus magalismontana (foliage)
Turraea obtusifolia (habit)

SIMA ELIOVSON PHOTOGRAPHIC COLLECTION OF FLOWERS

Agapanthus inapertus (habit)
Amaryllis belladonna (flower)
Anchusa capensis (habit)
Aristea major (flower)
Bulbinella floribunda (habit and flower)
Cenia turbinata (habit)
Coleonema pulchellum (habit)
Crocosmia paniculata (habit and flower)
Dissotis canescens (habit and flower)
Eucomis comosa (habit and flower)
Euphorbia ingens (habit)
Felicia heterophylla (habit and flower)
Gazania krebsiana (habit)
Gerbera jamesonii (mixed flowers)
Gloriosa superba (habit)
Greyia sutherlandii (flower)
Grielum humifusum (mass habit)
Heliophila coronopifolia (habit)
Ixia maculata (flower)
I. viridiflora (habit and flower)
Lampranthus sp. (habit and flower)
Lobelia erinus (habit and flower)
Maerua cafra (flower)
Nemesia ligulata (flower)
N. strumosa (habit and flower)
Nerine filifolia (habit)
N. sarniensis (flower)
Osteospermum jucundum (habit)
Scilla natalensis (habit and flower)
Sparaxis hybrids (flowers)
Ursinia anthemoides (flower)
Watsonia sp. (flowers)

PERCY SERGEANT MEMORIAL COLLECTION

Antholyza ringens (habit and flower)
Babiana disticha (habit)
Crassula coccinea (habit and flower)
Homoglossum priorii (flower)
Nerine sarniensis (habit)

P. VAN WYK (NATIONAL PARKS BOARD)

Bridelia mollis (habit)
Diplorhynchus condylocarpon (flower)
Nuxia oppositifolia (habit)
Xanthocercis zambesiaca (habit and fruit)

NATIONAL BOTANICAL INSTITUTE (CAPE TOWN)

Arctotis venusta (habit)
Babiana rubrocyanea (habit)

B. villosa (flower)
Dissotis princeps (habit)
Lobostemon fruticosus (habit)
Monopsis lutea (habit and flower)
Schefflera umbellifera (habit)
Steirodiscus tagetes (habit)
Ursinia anthemoides (habit)
U. sericea (flower)
U. speciosa (habit and flower)
Watsonia obrienii (habit)

NATIONAL BOTANICAL INSTITUTE (PRETORIA)

Aloe bainesii (flowers)
A. plicatilis (habit)
A. wickensii (habit and flower)
Aponogeton distachyos (habit)
Athanasia crithmifolia (flower)
Babiana stricta var. *regia* (flower)
Calodendrum capense (habit)
Crinum macowanii (habit)
Dimorphotheca sinuata (flower)
Diospyros austro-africana (habit and flower)
Dorotheanthus bellidiformis (habit and flower)
Euphorbia caput-medusae (habit)
E. cooperi (fruit)
E. ingens (fruit)
Faurea saligna (flower)
Ficus sycomorus (fruit)
Gerbera jamesonii (habit)
Gladiolus dolomiticus (flower)
Gloriosa superba (flower)
Greyia sutherlandii (habit)
Ilex mitis (flower)
Jasminum multipartitum (habit)
Leucadendron argenteum (cone)
Nemesia strumosa (flower)
Nymphoides indica (habit)
N. thunbergiana (flower)
Orphium frutescens (habit)
Osteospermum ecklonis (habit)
Protea compacta (habit and flower)
P. cynaroides (habit and flower)
P. grandiceps (habit)
P. neriifolia (white flower)
P. repens (white flower)
Rhus batophylla (habit)
R. leptodictya (fruit)
Schefflera umbellifera (flower)
Schizostylis coccinea (habit)
Trichilia emetica (fruit)
Tritonia crocata (habit and flower)
Turraea floribunda (habit)
Watsonia galpinii (flower)

SUSAN IMRIE ROSS (NBI, CAPE TOWN)

Spring flowers at Kirstenbosch, pp. 324-325

SHEILA BRANDT, CAPE TOWN

A *Senecio tamoides* in full bloom cascading down a terrace (pp. 346-347).

Amaryllis belladonna (habit)
Babiana villosa (flowers)
Bulbinella sp. (habit)
Clivia miniata (flower)
Crassula sp. (flower)
Crinum campanulatum (flower)
Crocosmia masonorum (habit)
Cyathea dregei (habit)
Euryops sp. (flower on cover)
Kalanchoe blossfeldiana (habit)
Lampranthus coccineus (habit and flowers)
Nerine bowdenii (habit)
N. sarniensis (flower)
Pelargonium sp. (flower on cover)
Scadoxus multiflorus (habit and flower)
Senecio tamoides (flower)

Sparaxis hybrid (habit)
Ursinia sp. (habit)
Watsonia sp. (flower)
Zantedeschia cultivar (habit)

MARIANNE ALEXANDER, CAPE TOWN

Photographs on the title page and pp. 8-9, 12-13, 112-113, 226-227.

Antholyza plicata (habit)
Aristea major (habit)
Babiana villosa (flower)
Clivia miniata (habit)
Dicoma zeyheri (habit)
Dierama pendulum (habit and flower)
Dissotis princeps (habit)
Dymondia margaretae (habit)
Eumorphia prostrata (habit and flower)
Freesia hybrid (habit)

Freylinia tropica (habit)
Gardenia thunbergia (habit, flower and fruit)
Geranium incanum (habit)
Halleria elliptica (habit and flower)
Heliophila sp. (flower)
Homoglossum huttonii (flower)
H. priorii (flower)
Lampranthus aureus (habit and flowers)
Leucospermum tottum (habit)
Nymphoides indica (flowers)
Phoenix reclinata (habit)
Phygelius capensis (habit)
Plectranthus fruticosus 'James'
    (mass habit)
P. fruticosus 'Ngoya' (flower)
Protea neriifolia (habit)
Sutherlandia frutescens (habit)
Steirodiscus sp. (flowers)
Thorncroftia succulenta (habit)
Thunbergia alata (flower)
Veltheimia bracteata (habit)

BIBLIOGRAPHY

Coates Palgrave, K. 1977. *Trees of southern Africa.* Cape Town: Struik.

De Winter, B., Vahrmeijer, J. and Von Breitenbach, F. 1987. *The national list of trees.* Pretoria: Van Schaik.

Eliovson, S. 1965. *South African wild flowers for the garden.* Cape Town: Timmins.

Gibbs Russell, G.E., Welman, W.G., Retief, E., Immelman, K.L., Germishuizen, G., Pienaar, B.J., Van Wyk, M. and Nicholas, A. 1987. *List of species of southern African plants.* Part 2: Memoirs of the Botanical Survey of South Africa No. 56. Second edition.

Le Roux, A. and Schelpe, E.A.C.L.E. 1981. *Namaqualand and Clanwilliam.* Claremont: Botanical Society of South Africa.

Palmer, E. and Pitman, N. 1971-1973. *Trees of southern Africa,* 3 volumes. Cape Town: Balkema.

Pienaar, K. 1984. *The South African What flower is that?* Cape Town: Struik.

Pienaar, K. 1985. *Grow South African plants.* Cape Town: Struik.

Poynton, R.J. 1984. *Characteristics and uses of selected trees and shrubs cultivated in South Africa.* Pretoria: Directorate of Forestry.

Sheat, W.G. 1983. *The A-Z of gardening in South Africa.* Cape Town: Struik.

Tree Society. 1964. *Trees and shrubs of the Witwatersrand.* Johannesburg: Witwatersrand University Press.

Van Wyk, B. and Malan, S. 1988. *Field guide to the wild flowers of the Witwatersrand & Pretoria region.* Cape Town: Struik.

Van Wyk, P. 1984. *Field guide to the trees of the Kruger National Park.* Cape Town: Struik.

NURSERY GUIDE

KEY

The following symbols appear below the address of each nursery to indicate in which type of plants it specialises:

R	= Retail	6	= Aquatics
W	= Wholesale	7	= Cycads
1	= Proteacaea	8	= Succulents
2	= Orchids	9	= Shrubs
3	= Trees	10	= Ericaceae
4	= Herbaceous	11	= Ferns
	plants	12	= Climbers
5	= Bulbs	13	= Seeds

Botanical Society of South Africa
Kirstenbosch
CLAREMONT 7735
(021) 797 2090/1/2/3

NATIONAL BOTANICAL GARDENS

Harold Porter NBG
P.O. Box 35
BETTY'S BAY 7141
(02823) 9711

Karoo NBG
P.O. Box 152
WORCESTER 6850
(0231) 7 0785

Kirstenbosch NBG
Private Bag X7
CLAREMONT 7738
(021) 762 1166

Lowveld NBG
P.O. Box 1024
NELSPRUIT 1200
(01311) 2 5531

Natal NBG
Pietermaritzburg
P.O. Box 11448
DORPSPRUIT 3206
(0331) 44 3858

Orange Free State NBG
Bloemfontein
P.O. Box 29036
DANHOF 9310
(051) 31 3530

Pretoria NBG
Private Bag X101
PRETORIA 0001
(012) 804 3200

Witwatersrand NBG
Roodepoort
P.O. Box 2194
WILROPARK 1731
(011) 662 1741

CAPE

Cabriére Concorde
P.O. Box 105
FRANSCHHOEK 7690
(02212) 2540
W/3/7/9/11/12

Cape Seeds & Bulbs
P.O. Box 4063
Idas Valley
STELLENBOSCH 7609
(02231) 7 9418
R/4/5/13

Cherrywood Nursery
P.O. Box 345
KENTON-ON-SEA 6191
(0464) 8 1732
R/3/7/9

Constantia Wholesale Nursery
P.O. Box 100
PHILLIPPI 7781
(021) 73 3054
W/1/3/4/5/6/8/9/10/11/12

Disa Garden Centre
Main Road
HOUT BAY 7800
(021) 790 3030
R/1/3/4/9/10

Feathers Wild Flower Seeds
P.O. Box 13
CONSTANTIA 7848
(021) 794 6432
R/13

Floraland Nursery
16 Walker Drive
Ben Kamma
PORT ELIZABETH 6015
(041) 30 7174
R/W/3/4/5/9/12

Groenland Protea Nurseries
22 Old Cape Road
GRABOUW 7160
(031) 75 2077
R/1

Kernkwekerye
P.O. Box 55
VANRHYNSDORP 8170
(02727) 9 1062
R/W/5/7/8/

Ketelfontein Kwekery
P.O. Box 169
COLESBERG 5980
(05852) 3340
R/W/3/4/9/12

Le Roux, John
`Haven'
Silvermine Road
NOORDHOEK 7985
(011) 789 1001
R/W/1

Loursford Estate Wholesale Nursery
P.O. Box 16
SOMERSET WEST 7130
(024) 51 6641
R/W/3/4/5/6/9/11

Nature's Garden/Gardenscapes
15 Constantia Road
WYNBERG 7800
(021) 797 8286
R/1/3/4/5/6/8/9/10/11/12

Newlands Nurseries, Parks & Forests
Union Avenue
NEWLANDS 7700
(021) 689 4184
W/3/9/

Rust-en-Vrede
P.O. Box 231
CONSTANTIA 7848
(021) 794 1085
W/5

Silverhill Seeds
18 Silverhill Crescent
KENILWORTH 7700
(021) 762 4245
R/13

Sonnestraal Nursery
P.O. Box 7123
Dalsig
STELLENBOSCH 7600
(024) 55 2110
R/W/1/3/4/5/6/8/9/10/11/12

Starke Ayres Nurseries
21 Liesbeek Road
ROSEBANK 7700
(021) 689 5847
R/W/1/3/7/9/11/12

Sunburst Flower Bulbs
P.O. Box 183
HOWARD PLACE 7450
(021) 54 4994
R/W/5

T. van den Berg Nursery
Wellington Road
Checkers Centre
DURBANVILLE 7500
(021) 96 4680
R/1/3/4/5/9/10

Turtle Rock Research
Osborne Lane
KOMMETJIE 7976
CAPE PENINSULA
(021) 83 1708
R/8

Voor Den Berg Farm Nursery
P.O. Box 293
ROBERTSON 6705
(02353) 623
R/W/1/2/3/5/9/10

Weltevrede Kwekery
P.O. Box 2335
STELLENBOSCH 7600
(02231) 7 6972
W/3/4/9/11/12

Weltevrede Vetplantkwekerye
P.O. Box 7183
NEWTON PARK
PORT ELIZABETH 6055
(041) 72 1180
R/W/8

NATAL

Burgess Nursery & Garden Centre
1 Langford Road
WESTVILLE 3630
(031) 86 4366
R/1/3/4/5/6/7/8/9/11/12

Celtiskloof Nurseries
P.O. Box 21
MERRIVALE 3291
(0332) 30 4647
R/W/1/3/4/5/7/9/10/11

Dunrobin Nurseries
P.O. Box 9
BOTHA'S HILL 3660
(031) 777 1855
R/W/3/4/5/7/8/9/11/12

Durban Municipality, Parks Department
P.O. Box 3740
DURBAN 4000
(031) 21 1303
R/W/3/4/5/7/9/

Giddy's Nursery
P.O. Box 45
UMLAAS ROAD 3730
(0332) 51 0478
R/W/7

Grabouw Nursery
P.O. Box 636
HILLCREST 3650
(031) 75 1077
R/1/3/4/5/6/8/9

Gro-on Nursery
34 Audley Road
COWIES HILL 3630
(031) 86 5678
1/3/4/8

Hilton Protea Nursery
31 Walters Road
HILTON 3245
(0331) 3 1567
R/W/1

Jesmond Dene Nursery
P.O. Box 511
PIETERMARITZBURG 3200
(0331) 7 1150
R/W/3/4/5/7/9/11/12

Karibu Nursery
P.O. Box 19
UMHLALI 4390
(0322) 7 1194/5/6
3/7/8/9/11/12

Lazydaze Nursery
P.O. Box 97
ROSETTA 3301
(0333) 3 7153
R/4/5/

Natal Parks, Game & Fish Preservation Board
Queen Elizabeth Park Nature Reserve
P.O. Box 662
PIETERMARITZBURG 3200
(0331) 51 2221
W/3/4/5/7/9/11/12

Petallyn Nursery
P.O. Box 1462
HILLCREST 3650
(031) 75 3400
R/W/3/4/9/12

Suregro Nursery
56 Caversham Road
PINETOWN 3610
(031) 701 2668
R/3/4/5/6/7/8/9/11/12

ORANGE FREE STATE

Bruwer Kwekery
P.O. Box 22180
EXTONWEG 9313
(015) 33 2072
R/W/3/9/

Fraaihuis Kwekery
P.O. Box 624
HEILBRON 9650
(01614) 2 2205
R/2/3/4/5/8/9/12

Platberg Kwekery
101 Biddulph Street
HARRISMITH 9880
(01436) 2 2420
R/3/4/5/6/9/11

Viljoenskroon Kwekery
P.O. Box 635
VILJOENSKROON 9520
(01413) 3 0741
R/7/8

TRANSVAAL

Aurora Veldblomme Kwekery
21 24th Street
MENLO PARK
PRETORIA 0081
(021) 46 7137
R/W/3/4/5/7/9/12

Belvedere Gardens
P.O. Box 592
MULDERSDRIF 1747
(011) 967 2051
R/W/3

Bergsig Nurseries
P.O. Box 539
CULLINAN 1000
(01213) 3 1341
W/3/4/9

Brits Municipal Nursery
P.O. Box 106
BRITS 0250
(01211) 4 1140
R/W/3/

Cordia Nurseries
P.O. Box 20085
ALKANTRANT 0005
(012) 87 1221
R/W/2/3/5/9/12

Coromandel Farm Nursery
Private Bag X1017
LYDENBURG 1120
(01323) 3983
W/3/5/9/11

Cycad Nursery
P.O. Box 15251
LYNN EAST 0039
(012) 548 0223
R/W/7/8/

Erica Nursery
P.O. Box 354
VANDERBIJLPARK 1900
(016) 87 3210
R/1/3/4/5/6/9/10

Ferndale Ridge Nurseries
P.O. Box 50135
RANDBURG 2125
(011) 789 2706
R/1/3/4/5/6/7/8/9/10/11/12

Franshoek Kwekery
P.O. Box 166
RUSTENBURG 0300
(01421) 9 2212
R/3/4/7/8/9/12

Hall, H.L. & Sons
P.O. MATAFFIN 1205
(01311) 5 2061
W/4/5/7/11

Klerksdorp Nursery
P.O. Box 3058
FREEMANVILLE 2573
(018) 9 2415
R/3/4/5/9/11/12

Kruger National Park Nursery
National Parks Board
SKUKUZA 1350
(1311) 6 5611
R/3/7/9

Letaba Nurseries
P.O. Box 425
TZANEEN 0850
(01523) 2 2939
W/3/

Malabar Farm Nurseries
P.O. Box 22
SKEERPOORT 0232
(01207) 725
W/4/9/12

Quality Plants Groothandel Kwekery
P.O. Box 912302
SILVERTON 0127
(012) 803 7135
W/3/4/9/12

Rosendal Farms
P.O. Box 141
TARLTON 1749
(011) 952 1027/2
R/W/3/4/9/12

Simpson's Nursery
P.O. Box 326
RIVONIA 2128
(011) 464 1005
W/4

Sunkloof Nursery
P.O. Box 15032
LYNN EAST 0039
(012) 808 0810
W/3/9/

Super Seedlings
P.O. Box 89180
LYNDHURST 2106
(011) 608 3453
R/W/3/4/9/

Tip Top Kwekery
P.O. Box 16689
PRETORIA NORTH 0116
(012) 542 2103
R/W/3/9

Twello Bosbou (Edms.) Bpk.
P.O. Box 69
BARBERTON 1300
(013142) 701
R/7

Witkoppen Wild Flower Nursery
P.O. Box 67036
BRYANSTON 2021
(011) 705 2703
R/W/1/3/4/5/6/7/8/9/10/11/12